D1329814

THE
AMERICAN GIRL'S
HANDY BOOK

LINA
BEARD

AND

ADELIA B.
BEARD

DOVER PUBLICATIONS, INC.
Mineola, New York

Bibliographical Note

This Dover edition, first published in 2008, is an unabridged republication of the work originally published as *The Girls Handy Book: How to Amuse Yourself and Others* by Charles Scribner's Sons, New York, in 1887.

Library of Congress Cataloging-in-Publication Data

Beard, Lina.
    [How to amuse yourself and others]
    The American girl's handy book / Lina Beard and Adelia B. Beard.
      p. cm.
    Reprint. Originally published: New York : Scribner, 1887: under title: How to amuse yourself and others : the American girl's handy book.
    A reprint of a gay nineties publication for young ladies instructing them in such hobbies as fancy needlework, handmade dolls, china painting, painting in oils, heraldic painting, preservation of wild flowers, and many others.
    ISBN-13: 978-0-486-46772-6
    ISBN-10: 0-486-46772-4
    1. Handicraft—Juvenile literature. 2. Amusements—Juvenile literature. I. Beard, Adelia B. (Adelia Belle), 1857–1920. II. Title.

TT171.B38 2008
745.5—dc22

2008028441

Manufactured in the United States of America
Dover Publications, Inc., 31 East 2nd Street, Mineola, N.Y. 11501

PREFACE.

"I DO wish some one would write a book like that for girls," is the remark we have frequently heard when a new book of sports for boys has made its appearance ; but it was not until the publication of the "American Boys Handy Book" that it occurred to us to write a book for the American boy's neglected sisters, which should be equally original and practical.

In the "Girl's Handy Book," which it has been our endeavor to make peculiarly American, we have sought to introduce original and novel ideas, and by their aid to open new avenues of enterprise and enjoyment.

One of our objects is to impress upon the minds of the girls the fact that they all possess talent and ability to achieve more than they suppose possible, and we would encourage a belief in the truth of the remark said to have been made by a famous Frenchman : "When you Americans undertake anything you never stop to ascertain if it be possible, you simply *do it*."

We desire also to help awaken the inventive faculty, usually uncultivated in girls, and, by giving detailed methods of new work and amusements, to put them on the road which they can travel and explore alone.

We know well the feeling of hopelessness which accompanies vague directions, and, to make our explanations plain and lucid, we have ourselves, with very few exceptions, made all of the articles, played the games, and solved the problems described.

The materials employed in the construction of the various articles are within easy reach of all, and the outlay, in most cases, little or nothing.

We scarcely deem it necessary to point out the fact that in supplying healthy, sensible work and amusement for leisure hours, employment is given whose whole tendency is to refine the tastes and ambitions of our American girls.

A few of our chapters are taken from articles which were written by us for, and published by, the *Youth's Companion*, *St. Nicholas*, *Harper's Young People*, *Golden Days*, and *Wide Awake*.

CONTENTS.

AUTUMN.

CHAPTER XVII.

CHAPTER XVIII.

CHAPTER XIX.

CHAPTER XX.

CHAPTER XXI.

CHAPTER XXII.

WINTER.

CHAPTER XXIX.

CHAPTER XXX.

CHAPTER XXXI.

CHAPTER XXXII.

CHAPTER XXXIII.

CHAPTER XXXIV.

CHAPTER XLI.

CHAPTER XLII.

THE
AMERICAN GIRL'S
HANDY BOOK

The American Girl's Handy Book.

CHAPTER I.

FIRST OF APRIL.

THIS is the children's own day, and no assumption of dignity on the part of their elders can deter them from exercising the privileges granted to them by acknowledged custom and precedent.

"April fool! April fool!" cries my little nephew, as he dances with delight to see his aunt walk out of the room with a piece of white paper dangling from a hooked pin, attached to her dress.

"April fool! April fool!" shout the children in the street, thus announcing the success of some practical joke.

"April fool!" laughs everyone at the table, when some unfortunate bites into a brown, wholesome-looking cruller, only to find it a delusion and a snare, the coat of a cruller, but the inside of cotton.

"April fool! April fool!" is what even the little sparrows seem to chirp, as with a "s-w-h-e-r-r" they sweep down from the tree and, frightening away the kitten, take forcible possession of her bone. What does all this mean ? Why is the first day of April called " All-Fools-Day," and when or where did the custom of the day originate ? Who can tell ? No one seems to know. Even the derivation of the word April does not appear to have been definitely settled, and this saucy month, with her mischievous tricks and pranks, her surprises and mysteries, fools and puzzles our wisest men.

Through many centuries the observance of All-Fools-Day has descended to us. In many climes and many countries this day is chosen as the proper time for playing tricks on the unsuspecting.

" Festum Fatuorum," or " Fools' Holiday," is what it was called in England at the time of the arrival of the early Christians in that country.

Easily caught like the mackerel, which are plentiful on the French coast in April and are said to be deficient in understanding, the April fool in France derives his name from that fish, and is called " Poisson d'Avril " or "April Fish," and again, " Silly Mackerel." From the cuckoo, a bird that does not know enough to build its own nest, the appellation of " gowk " is taken, and is given to the foolish one in Scotland who allows himself to be duped on this day.

In India at the festival called Huli Festival held on the last day of March, the natives make merry at the expense of their friends, just as we do, and their fool is called " Huli Fool."

So in the East and in the West, in the North and in the South, in the oldest nation as well as the youngest, is this ridiculous custom observed, and, as if to make it still more ridiculous, no one apparently knows why.

Now, girls, since this holiday has descended to us from so far back that its origin appears lost in the dim twilight of past ages, there surely must be some reason for its existence, and that reason may be, that "a little nonsense now and then is relished by the wisest men," and is therefore wholesome as an occasional diet. So why not help to perpetuate it ; not with rude, practical jokes, but with comical surprises, and absurd, but unembarrassing, situations. Much harmless fun can be derived from the privileges of this day, devoted as it is to nonsense, and we introduce the April Fool Party as an excellent means of concentrating the fun, and furnishing plenty of merriment to the young folks who are bent on having a good time.

First of April Party.

I remember, when quite a little girl, I was granted the privilege of celebrating my birthday, which came on the 1st of April, with a candy-pull, and a few days previous to the event I started joyfully off to invite my friends. The invitations were laughingly given and accepted, and it did not occur to me that I would be suspected of playing a joke, although the party was to be on April-Fools-Day. It seems, however, that my good intentions were doubted, and the children were undecided whether to come or not. I had begun to suspect that a joke was to be played on me by their all remaining away, before they finally arrived in a body, having taken the precaution of coming in that way, so that if the party were a hoax they would all be fooled together.

I relate this incident that warning may be taken from my experience, and that it may be understood how important it is to make the guests invited to your First of April party realize that the invitations are given in good faith, and that your friends are expected to be on hand at the appointed time.

It is well, in giving a party of this kind, to have the whole programme laid out beforehand, so that everything may go smoothly and nothing be forgotten.

The few methods of April fooling given here need not con-
stitute the whole entertainment ; the list may be added to by
the young hostess, who will, no doubt, have many ideas of her
own to carry out.   We will head our list with the

Mirror Tableau.

This novel tableau is made ready in the following manner :

In a door-way, or bay-window draped with full curtains,
place a large mirror.   Instead of having the curtains suspended
from the usual pole, it is best to stretch a wire across the space
and slip the curtain-rings upon that, as they will slide more
readily on the wire ; and when it is time to draw back the drapery it should be done quickly.   A table placed before the curtains will serve as a barricade, keeping the too curious from taking a peep at the hidden mysteries before they are ready to be
revealed.

At the time selected, remove the table, and request all those
desiring to see the tableau to arrange themselves in front of the
curtain, and to remain perfectly quiet, as any movement will dis-
turb those taking part.

If the front rows of the audience can be induced to kneel or
sit upon the floor, those in the rear can obtain a better view,
and it will, at the same time, make the group more effective.
When perfect quiet is obtained, give the signal to your assistant,
who must stand opposite to you at the side of the curtain, and
with her help quickly draw aside the draperies, thus disclosing
the tableau of a group of young people, motionless, gazing into
the mirror with eager and expectant eyes.   For an instant the
audience will be held spell-bound, scarcely realizing that they
themselves are forming the pretty tableau.

" We are April Fools," written with soap on the mirror near
the top, as shown in the illustration, tells what character the
actors are assuming, and gives a name to the tableau.

The Mirror Tableau.

During the interval which should be allowed to intervene before introducing the next thing on the programme, the guests will find amusement in the many harmless practical jokes which are awaiting the unwary in all manner of places.

For instance, some boy will print APRIL FOOL in large white letters on his own back, by simply resting for a moment in a convenient chair upon whose snowy tidy the dreaded words have previously been printed backwards with white chalk. On the dark woolly surface of the coat, the white letters will be perfectly transferred, and the boy, little knowing what he has done, or the cause of the merriment, will join in the general laughter his appearance creates.

A treacherous divan can be provided by removing the top of a low, flat packing-box, and putting in its place brown wrapping-paper, tacking it down around the edges of the box. With a piece of drapery thrown over it, entirely concealing the box, and sofa pillows placed upon it, leaning against the wall, the divan looks exceedingly comfortable and inviting. But woe unto the person who mistakes appearances for reality, for to attempt to sit upon this seeming substantial couch is but to break through and sit upon the floor instead.

The box used for the divan should not be more than twelve inches high, so that the fall will be only funny, not dangerous.

The next diversion may be a

Noah's Ark Peep-show.

Make the peep-show of a box about two and a half feet long and one foot and a half high. Remove the top and both of the end-pieces (Fig. 1). Cut from pasteboard a slide to exactly fit the box, and place it in the middle, thus cutting off the view from either end, as shown in Fig. 1. Make a curtain in two pieces, and tack them around the upper edge of the

Noah's Ark Peep-show.

box, letting them meet at each end. Stout pieces of twine, stretched across the openings at the ends of the box, will serve to attach the drapery at these points.

Almost any kind of material will answer for this purpose, provided it is not too thin and is of some bright hue, for the peep-show should be made to look as gay as possible. Place the box upon a high stand, and so arrange it that a strong light will shine down into it, making the interior, from end to end, perfectly light.

From a list, previously prepared, of the animals supposed to be on exhibition, read the first two, and invite two persons, a girl and a boy, for instance, to look into the peep-show. We will suppose that the first animals on the list are the raven and the dove. Inform your would-be audience that you have **two** of Noah's special pets to show them ; that from the girls' **point of** view will be seen a raven, and from the boys', a dove

When taking their places at the box, one at each end, the two spectators must part the curtain, and, putting their faces between, hold the drapery together under their chins. This is to keep the remainder of the company from obtaining a glimpse into the wonderful show before their turns arrive.

When all is ready, and the two wondering faces are hidden between the folds of the peep-show curtains, with the words, "Behold the pretty dove, and the mischievous raven," remove the slide, and expose to the astonished gaze of each spectator a companion's familiar face at the opposite end of the box. Of course, upon retiring from the show, its secret must be kept, otherwise the joke will be spoiled for those whose turns are yet to come.

Before the next two take their station at the box, replace the slide and pretend to rearrange the show, to divert the suspicion that the box is empty.

The Supper

can be made the means of perpetrating many practical jokes. The shams must be so intermingled with the real delicacies that one can never be sure what the consequences may be of partaking too rashly of even the most tempting-looking morsel.

Small blocks of wood covered with batter and browned in the oven are excellent imitations of cakes. Dainty confectionery, in crimped papers, can be made of small radishes covered with icing of different colors. Button-moulds coated with chocolate will readily be mistaken for candy.

If a small pasteboard pill-box is first filled with flour, and the top then covered with tissue-paper pasted down around the edges, it will look, when iced, like a delicate little cake, and will cause much merriment when anyone bites into it; for the moment the paper cover is broken the flour will fly in every direction. The fertile brain of girls, on mischief bent, will suggest many more frauds of this kind, and enough surprises may be prepared to make the supper as merry as anything else on the evening's programme.

Before leaving this subject, once more let the caution be given to keep the jokes entirely harmless. It is only poor fun that can be obtained at the expense of injuring others, or by running the slightest risk of hurting them in any way.

The spirit of mischief must be kept within bounds even on All-Fools-Day.

Gathering Wild Flowers.

CHAPTER II.

WILD FLOWERS AND THEIR PRESERVATION.

ONG before the first green leaves make their appearance, while the snows of winter still linger in the shaded nooks, and the branches are still bare, though blushing with the full, flowing sap that tinges their tips pink, yellow, and red—when the air is filled with a sweet freshness and delicate fragrance—it is charming in our rambles to find scattered here and there upon the hill-side, down among the roots of the great trees, or under the hedges delicate little wild flowers waving on their fragile stalks with the faintest passing breeze. They are so exquisitely beautiful with their tender hues and graceful shapes, that a longing comes to possess them.

And why not keep them fresh at home? Plants live in the earth and require light, air, and moisture. All of these requirements can be and are fulfilled in thousands of homes where plants are kept, all over the world. But these are *wild flowers*. True, and they may need something to be found only in the wild woods. What, then, is it? Let us see. Earth, light, and air abound everywhere. Still, upon inspection we discover that the soil around our timid wild flowers is somewhat different from that to be found in our door-yards. But what is simpler than to take the earth up with the plant?

Be careful in

Transplanting Wild Flowers

to dig well all around and under the roots, so that the earth surrounding and clinging to the plant may be taken up at the same time (Fig. 2). After covering the root and soil adhering to it with a layer of clay, mud, or damp earth (Fig. 3) set the root in a large leaf, and tie it up with string or a wisp of grass (Fig 4), in order to make sure the soil

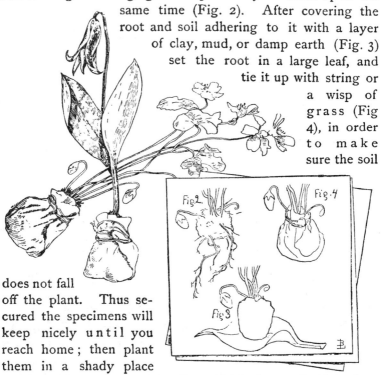

does not fall off the plant. Thus secured the specimens will keep nicely until you reach home; then plant them in a shady place and keep the ground moist. Beautiful little woodland gardens are made in this way, where within a few steps of the door a glimpse may be had of the fair forest flowers.

Sweet-scented white violets, delicate little anemones, odd yellow violets, and quaint jack-in-the-pulpits, with many others, not forgetting the graceful ferns, are now growing in the shaded corner of the writer's lawn, transplanted there from their home in the woods, where she found them one lovely spring morning, when out with a party of friends on a hunt for wild flowers.

The day was perfect, filled with sunshine and the song of birds. All nature appeared glad and joyous, and the trees seemed veiled in the softest greens and pinks of budding leaves.

It was a happy party that went wandering into the forest, straying here and there, and finding new treasures at nearly every step, stopping to gather a few of the violets that gave a purple tinge to the ground for yards around, then rambling on to the spot that was covered with the fragile anemone, each girl laden with the flowers she loved best. Some had taken them up roots and all, while others preferred the

Cut Wild Flowers.

For these it is best to use a tin box of convenient size and form shutting closely. The flowers must be fresh and not at all damp ; in such a box they can be kept for days bright and unfading. They may also safely be sent to friends at a distance, though it is better, when

Sending Flowers by Mail,

if you wish to send a quantity, to pack them in a strong pasteboard or wooden box. First lay down a piece of oiled paper of the proper size ; spread a thin layer of damp paper on this ; next a layer of flowers, then one of thin wet paper ; and so on until the box is full. Over the last layer place a dry paper, and cover this with oiled paper or tin-foil ; put the lid on the box and tie it down securely.

By this method a larger number of flowers can be sent in a given space than when simply inclosed in a tin box.

The writer has often sent daisies from New York to Cincinnati where they arrived as fresh as when first gathered.

For the benefit of those who wish directions for sending flowers by mail, we give the following on authority of the *American Agriculturist.*

"The law passed some years since by Congress, allowing packages of plants to be sent by mail, if not over four pounds in weight, was a capital arrangement for those who lived at a distance from railroad and express offices, but it is so hampered with the various constructions given by the Post Office Department, that it is difficult to know what is required by the officials. The law now is, we believe, as follows : A package, weighing four pounds or less, can be sent at the rate of two cents per four ounces, but the writing of the words "roots" or "plants" makes a letter of it, and is charged letter postage. Nothing should be written except the address, and the package must not be sealed, or contain any writing, and it must be so fastened that the postmaster can examine the contents if he wishes. The plants may, however, be numbered, and their names sent by letter."

Now let us think of some way in which these lovely blossoms can be preserved.

In Germany they excel in making decorations for rooms, dinner-tables, etc., of

Preserved Flowers.

Bright-colored flowers are best adapted to this method. White flowers are apt to turn yellow. Jack-in-the-pulpits, clover, roses, and daisies came out beautifully when the writer dried them, and why should not many other kinds do just as well? Try and see.

Procure three or four quarts of fine sand ; white scouring-sand is the best ; wash it perfectly clean. This can be tested by pouring the water off until it looks quite clear ; then dry the sand, by placing it in a clean tin in the oven. When it is dry—fully dry and cool—pour enough in a box to enable the flowers to stand by themselves, their stems embedded in the sand, which should be a mass of fine particles of uniform size.

If the flowers are cut so that they all measure nearly the same length from the tip of the blossom to the end of the stem, they can more readily be covered with sand.

Preserved Flowers.

The flowers must be fresh and entirely free from moisture. Place them stem downward in the sandy layer, and very gently and slowly pour in the sand a little at a time, until each leaf and petal is firmly held in place (Fig. 5); then fill the box with sand nearly two inches above the level of the flowers.

It is very essential that every particle of the flower rest in the sand, and that in filling up, the smallest petal has not been bent or crumpled.

Take care not to shake the box lest the flowers inside be injured. Set it in a warm, dry place, and let it stand at least two weeks.

This manner of preserving flowers retains the color, while the shape of the leaves and petals remains unaltered. The flowers will keep for years.

There are other ways also of preserving flowers.

Pressed Flowers and Leaves.

Although these are perfectly flat, they seldom fade and are very pretty and useful. Have ready a large book or a quantity of old newspapers and several weights. Use the newspapers for leaves and ferns—blotting-paper is best for the flowers. Both the flowers and leaves should be fresh and without moisture. Place them as nearly in their natural positions as possible in the book or papers, and press, allowing several thicknesses of paper between each layer. Remove the specimens to dry papers each day until perfectly dry.

Some flowers must be immersed—all but the flower head—in boiling water for a few minutes, before pressing, to prevent them from turning black. Orchids are of this nature.

If possible, it is well to obtain all parts of a plant, the roots as well as the seeds, for a more interesting collection can thus be made than from the flower and leaf alone.

It is advisable to be provided with a blank book or, what is still better, pieces of stiff white paper of uniform size on which to mount the flowers or leaves when dried ; also with a small bottle of mucilage and a brush for fastening them, and some narrow strips of court-plaster or gummed paper for the stems and thicker parts of the plants. The sooner they can be mounted the better. Place them carefully on the paper, writing beneath the locality and date of finding. Flowers and leaves thus prepared make beautiful herbariums. Should you desire

Leaves and Ferns for Decoration,

first press them nicely ; then give them a coat of wax, by ironing them on both sides with a hot iron over which a piece of beeswax has first been rubbed. Cover the specimens completely with wax, as this renders them quite pliable, and they are no longer brittle nor easily broken. Sprays of small leaves can be pressed entire.

To heighten the effect, use dry colors, rubbing them in, and selecting those corresponding with the color of the leaves when first gathered.

The colors must be put on before the coating of wax. Ferns should be gathered when nearly full grown, and, after they are pressed, painted light green with oil-colors ; in that case the beeswax is not used. The oil in the paint, like the wax, makes the specimens more substantial, and they look quite fresh and fair.

Sometimes the late autumn frosts will bleach the ferns perfectly white ; then are they even more delicate than before Nature changed their color. We have seen the

Color of Flowers Changed,

and it is a very pretty experiment, very simple, too. Immerse the flowers in ammonia, and you will be surprised to see white lilies change to a delicate yellow, pink roses turn a lovely light green, while dark-red sweet-peas assume blue and rich purple tints ; and the change is so rapid it is almost like magic. Another interesting experiment is making

Natural Wax Flowers

by dipping the fresh buds and blossoms in paraffine just sufficiently hot to liquefy it ; first the stems of the flowers ; when these have cooled and hardened, then the flowers or sprays, holding them by the stalks and moving them gently. When they are completely covered the flowers are removed and lightly shaken, in order to throw off the superfluous wax. The flowers are then suspended until perfectly dry, when they are found hermetically sealed in a film of paraffine, while they still keep their beautiful coloring and natural forms, and for a while even their perfume. Now let us find what can be done

To Freshen Cut Flowers.

When the heat has made them wilt, clip the stems and set the flowers in cold water ; in a few hours they will regain their freshness and beauty.

Some flowers, however, must be differently treated, such as heliotrope and mignonette ; these keep if placed *upon* damp moss or cotton and set in a cold place at night.

Rosebuds will retain their freshness for hours when not placed in water, if the ends of the stems are snipped off, and immediately tipped with melted sealing-wax ; this excludes the air, and so keeps the flowers from drooping.

If roses are wilted before they can be placed in water, cut off the ends of the stalks and immerse in very hot water for a minute or two, and they will regain their pristine freshness.

Another way to keep flowers fresh is to put a pinch of nitrate of soda into the glass each time you change the water.

Nitrate of potash or saltpetre in a powder has nearly the same effect, or a drop of hartshorn.

If plants are chilled by frost, shower them with cold water, and leave in a cool room ; or set the pot in cold water and keep in a moderately cool place. Now one word about

Crystallized Flowers,

that sparkle and look so beautiful. They must first be dried in sand, then crystallized in the same way as dried grasses—the rougher the surface the better will it crystallize. Dissolve as much alum in boiling water as it will hold ; when this is determined, pour it off and boil the solution down to one-half.

Suspend the flowers by a net-work of string tied across the top of a pail into which they must hang ; then pour into the pail the boiling alum water, which must completely cover the flowers, and leave it undisturbed twelve hours, or all night.

The flowers should not touch each other or the sides of the bucket. Be careful in removing them the next morning, as the crystals are easily broken off.

Flowers or sprays of grass may be beautifully frosted by dipping them in a solution of gum-arabic and sprinkling them with powdered isinglass.

Flowers are not only very beautiful, but many of them possess a fragrance so sweet that we would fain learn how to keep the

Perfume of Flowers.

Rose-leaves are the most simply prepared. Take a covered jar, fill it with sweet-scented rose-leaves, and scatter through them some salt. Keep the jar closed tight, and when the petals have dried the " scent of the roses will cling to them still," so that every time the jar is opened a delicious fragrance will fill the air. Or you can cover the rose-leaves with melted lard, and leave them for a day or two in some place at a temperature of about 140° F.; then cool it and knead the lard in alcohol. Pour off the alcohol in fancy glass bottles and use as handkerchief perfume.

For varieties we find this method:

"The delicate odor of pinks and other flowers may be obtained as follows: Get a glass funnel, with the narrow end drawn to a point; in this place lumps of ice with salt, by which a very low temperature is produced. The funnel should be supported on an ordinary retort-stand and placed near the flowering plants, when water and the ethereal odor of the blossom will be deposited on the exterior of the glass funnel, and will trickle down to the point, from which it drops at intervals into a glass vessel below. The scent thus obtained is very perfect, but is apt to become sour in a few days unless some pure alcohol is added. By this process many odors may be procured for comparison and study. To obtain the odor in perfection the blossom must be in its prime."

Dry some sweet clover, and the fragrance will be sweet and pleasant. Fill a fancy bag of some thin sheer material with the clover, and you will find that you have imprisoned the fresh breath of summer. Old-time lavender can be prepared in the same way.

Our thoughts so far have been for the flowers in their sea-son.   But did it ever occur to you that it is possible to have

Spring Flowers in Winter?

If you search in the woods during December you may find, tucked away in sheltered spots, little woodland plants which, when taken up and carefully transplanted in a flower-pot and set in a sunny window, will soon begin to grow, sending up tender stems, and in about three weeks will blossom.   The lit-tle fairy-like flowers seem even more beautiful coming in the cold wintry weather.

Fruit-tree twigs and sprays from flowering shrubs will blos-som when the ground is white with snow, if cut from trees about the first of February, placed in well-heated water in a warm room, and the water changed every day for some that is almost but not quite hot.

The twigs being kept warm will blossom in a few weeks.

It is quite a pretty idea to take up and plant in a little flower-pot

The Four-leaved Clover.

Very frequently you may find a tuft bearing only the mystic number, and should it happen to have a five- or six-leaved clover in with the others, they will add to the luck.

If you possess one of these charmed plants, it is said "good luck" will always be near at hand.

Besides the foregoing directions for the preservation of flowers, plants, etc., there are numerous other methods, which, although not experimentally verified by the writer, are no doubt as worthy of a place here as any of the former.

The following recipes have been culled from various old papers, books, etc.

Some Old-fashioned Methods of Preserving Flowers.

The first of these ways is more properly intended for bo-tanical collections, and is often resorted to by collectors of rare blossoms.   It consists in placing

Flowers in Alcohol,

and possesses the great advantage of preserving the flowers for years, and keeping their most delicate fibres uninjured.   They make invaluable specimens to sketch from, and though their beauty may be somewhat impaired by loss of color, their out-lines remain perfect.

Place the flowers in a wide-mouthed bottle, fill it to the top with alcohol, cork it tightly, and cover the cork with plaster-of-Paris or melted beeswax, thus hermetically sealing it.   Do not use sealing-wax, as experience has taught us that the fumes of the alcohol soften the wax, and not only spoil the neat appear-ance of the bottle, but allow the spirits to evaporate.

Another way is to

Bottle Flowers.

Carefully seal the ends of the stems with sealing-wax, place them in an empty bottle—both flowers and bottle must be per-fectly dry—cork the bottle, and hermetically seal it with either sealing-wax or beeswax.

The next method has greater possibilities of beauty, and consequently the reader will be more interested in learning

How to Preserve a Vaseful of Flowers for a Year.

Take home your basket of wild flowers, " nodding violets," cowslips, bright-eyed anemones, and all the lovely offerings of the woods, and before arranging them in the vase, carefully seal the stem of each flower.   Place a glass shade over the vase ; be careful that flowers, vase, and shade are perfectly

dry ; then fill up the groove in the wood, in which the shade
stands, with melted wax. By covering the wax with chenille
it can be perfectly hidden.

Flowers kept in this way will last for a twelvemonth.

The flowers preserved in an empty bottle may be taken
out, the wax cut from the stems, and, if arranged in a bouquet,
will last as long as perfectly fresh flowers.

Those in the alcohol lose their color after being immersed
for a time, and will not last when removed from the alcohol.

In following any of these directions be careful not to tie
the flowers. No string must be used. The flower stems must
be loose and separate from each other.

A florist of much experience in preserving bouquets for an
indefinite period gives this recipe for

Keeping Bouquets Fresh a Long Time.

When you receive a bouquet sprinkle it lightly with fresh
water, then put it into a vessel containing some soapsuds ; this
will take the place of the roots and keep the flowers bright as
new.   Take the bouquet out of the suds every morning, and lay
it sideways, the stems entering first, in clean water ; keep it
there a minute or two, then take it out, and sprinkle the flowers
lightly by the hand with water ; replace it in the soapsuds,
and it will bloom as fresh as when first gathered.

The soapsuds need changing every three or four days.   By
observing these rules a bouquet can be kept bright and beautiful for at least a month, and will last longer in a very passable
state.   From another source we learn how

To Keep Flowers or Fruit a whole Year perfectly Fresh.

Mix one pound of nitre with two pounds of sal ammoniac
and three pounds of clean common sand ; then in dry weather

take fruit of any sort which is not fully ripe, allowing the stalks to remain, and put them one by one into an open glass until it is quite full ; cover the glass with oiled cloth, closely tied down. Put the glass three or four inches down in the earth in a dry cellar, and surround it on all sides to the depth of three or four inches with the above mixture. The fruit will thus be preserved quite fresh all the year round.

In giving the following recipe for the manufacture of rose-water, it may be as well to state that the original verse is given, not for its merit as such, but simply because it is the form in which the recipe reached the writer.

Rose-water.

" When the bushes of roses are full,
    As most of them are about June,
'Tis high time to gather, or pull
    The leaves of the flowers. As soon
As you've picked all you need for the time,
    To each *quart of water* unite
A *peck of the leaves*, which, if prime—
    And they will be, if pulled off aright—
May be *placed in a still* near at hand,
    On a *very slow fire.* When done,
Bottle off, and permit it to *stand*
    For three days ere you cork down each one."

CHAPTER III.

THE WALKING CLUB.

SOUND of girlish voices is suddenly heard in the quiet village streets, as our Walking Club, issuing from the house of one of its members, starts off on the first tramp of the season. The gay chatter and bubbling laughter blend with the twittering and chirping of the birds fluttering among the budding trees, and all these merry sounds seem in perfect harmony with the youthful gladness of the bright morning.

There is a subtle power and exhilaration in the spring sunshine that stimulates the blood, and sends it tingling through our veins, as with light-springing steps we quickly leave the village behind us and penetrate into the outlying country, stopping now and then to secure a branch of the downy pussy-willow or brilliant red blossoms of the maple, and again to admire a distant view where the trees seem enveloped in a hazy mist of delicate color ; on we go, exploring sequestered spots or entering deep into the woods in search of early wild flowers.

Although possibly timid as individuals, as a club we are brave enough ; for a party of fourteen or sixteen girls, including

The Walking Club.

our merry little chaperon, may go, with impunity, where it would not be so pleasant for one to venture alone.

Once a week all through that delightful spring the club might have been seen, now upon a road leading in this direction, now in that. And, often as we stepped aside to allow a carriage to pass, its occupants would lean forward smiling, and waving their hands in greeting ; for the moment, perhaps, feeling in sympathy with the vigorous young life that preferred this mode of loco-motion to being carried about on the downiest cushions of the easiest of carriages. A ride which accorded with the unconven-tional mood of our club was not despised however, for, urged on by the girls, our little matron would make bold to accost some countryman driving a vehicle sufficiently large, and persuade him, in the terms of the country, to "give us a lift." Jolting about in a springless wagon or hay-cart was not in the least enervating, and we experienced no indolent wish to continue our journey on wheels when forced by diverging roads to leave our equipage. It was not until the ever-increasing heat of the sun, and our own languid disinclination to much exertion, warned us that the mildness of spring had passed, that we concluded to dis-band for the summer. In the fall we again fell into rank, and came home from our walks laden with the gorgeous trophies of autumn, as we had once carried in triumph the tasselled branches and dainty flowers of spring.

We continued our tramps into the early winter, when the frosty crispness of the air made it very bracing, and the brisk exercise of walking brought the healthy color to cheek and lip of the young pedestrians.

Such a club as this, which at the same time promotes health, good spirits, and sociability, is one that most girls will enjoy and derive benefit from.

A closer acquaintance with Nature, which these walks afford, is not the least of their benefits, and to her true lover, Nature has many delightful surprises and secrets to reveal ; and as has been said, even for for those who cannot read her deeper meanings she has a language which calls attention to her more outward forms of beauty, and which one may study until gradually, with slowly opening eyes, is seen more and more of the exquisite perfection of her work, that long ago might have been seen had one but chosen to look.

As a society, the Walking Club is one of the most informal.

No officers are needed, although a secretary may sometimes be found useful when any word is to be sent to absent members.

The membership of the club should be large enough to insure the attendance of at least twelve or fourteen on each walk ; for in this case, as I have said, safety lies in numbers. At a place of meeting previously appointed, the members should assemble, and, before starting on their walk, the route to be taken should be decided by vote ; a decision on this point will be more quickly arrived at if a chairman be appointed to keep order.

The first walk should not be too long. Three miles is a good walk to start with ; a mile and a half out and the same home again. Gradually the distance can be lengthened, and the club be able to take a ten-mile walk without feeling fatigue.

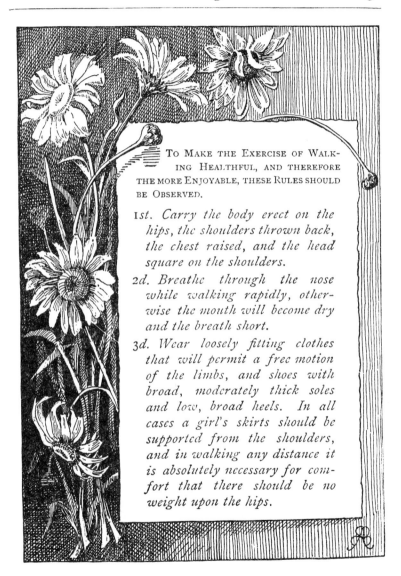

To Make the Exercise of Walking Healthful, and therefore
the more Enjoyable, these Rules should
be Observed.

1st. *Carry the body erect on the*
hips, the shoulders thrown back,
the chest raised, and the head
square on the shoulders.

2d. *Breathe through the nose*
while walking rapidly, other-
wise the mouth will become dry
and the breath short.

3d. *Wear loosely fitting clothes*
that will permit a free motion
of the limbs, and shoes with
broad, moderately thick soles
and low, broad heels. In all
cases a girl's skirts should be
supported from the shoulders,
and in walking any distance it
is absolutely necessary for com-
fort that there should be no
weight upon the hips.

EASTER

ANTHEMS

CHAPTER IV.

EASTER.

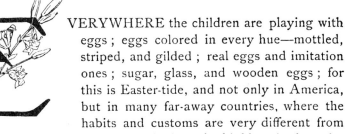

EVERYWHERE the children are playing with eggs ; eggs colored in every hue—mottled, striped, and gilded ; real eggs and imitation ones ; sugar, glass, and wooden eggs ; for this is Easter-tide, and not only in America, but in many far-away countries, where the habits and customs are very different from ours, does Easter bring to the children the highly prized, gayly-colored eggs.

How nice it would be if we could take a peep into these foreign countries, and discover what else Easter brings the little ones besides the pretty eggs, and also how the people of such widely differing nations keep this happy festival common to all.

If we could look into England now, we should find that the ceremonies there begin on Palm Sunday (the last Sunday before Easter), and on that day many people go a-palming, only they do not, of course, find palm, but gather instead branches of willow, which they stick into their hats and button-holes. On Good-Friday we might see, on almost every breakfast-table, those hot spicy cakes with a cross stamped on the face, known to many of us as well as to our English cousins, as "hot cross buns." We should feel very much at home looking into the churches on Easter Sunday, for we should find them beautifully decorated with flowers, and hear the Easter anthems chanted as we might in our own country. I do not think we can see in America, though, the ceremony which, on Easter Monday, is performed by the charity school-children in England. Were we among the spectators who, with shouts and merry laughter, crowd around to watch this performance, we should see the children take their places, with their backs against the outside of the church, and then join hands until a circle is formed around the building, thus completing what is called " clipping the church."

It would be great fun to see the Easter celebration in Russia, which includes many peculiar customs, and where the children receive presents as we do at Christmas, besides more eggs than any of us ever thought of possessing ; some of the eggs being beautifully made of glass or porcelain, and filled with sugar-plums or small presents. How amusing it would be to watch the people, following a custom always observed on Easter Monday in this queer land, as they go about kissing relations, friends, and acquaintances, wherever they happen to meet them.

If we were really in this great, cold, furry country, we might go with the children to make their Easter visits, and, on entering a house, hear the greeting, " Jesus Christ is risen," and the answer, " Yes, he is risen ; " then after kissing the inmates and exchanging eggs with them, go to visit elsewhere.

All this would seem very strange to American eyes ; and it would be a strange sight too, if we could look into the cities of Spain and see the people in the streets shooting at stuffed figures of Judas Iscariot.

A passing glance at Ireland on Easter morning would show us the people making haste to be out at sunrise to see the sun dance in a pool or pail of clear water.

It would be worth while to give more than a passing glance into Germany at this season, for in this country, where the children's happiness is so much thought of and so well provided for, Easter Monday is looked upon as a grand holiday, and all the young people appear in their gala costumes ready for any fun or frolic that may be going on. It is a pretty sight when the little peasant-girls, in their quaint gowns and odd little caps, dance on the green with the boys, whose costumes are equally as picturesque ; and it is also entertaining to watch them as they play various games with their many-colored eggs.

In Germany, too, we should find that the children believe as sincerely in the Easter hare as they do in Santa Claus in our country ; and the saying, that " the hares lay the Easter eggs," is never doubted by the little ones.

After visiting in imagination all these foreign countries to see their Easter celebrations, it may prove interesting to turn our eyes toward home, for, since our country is so large—as large almost as all Europe put together—perhaps some of our little citizens who have never been in Washington do not know how, in the capital of the United States, the children hold high carnival on Easter Monday, nor how the grounds of the White House and also of the Capitol are given up to them on this day that they may frolic on the lawns and roll their eggs down the hills. It would be as novel a sight to some of us as any found abroad, to see several thousand children rolling and tossing their eggs, while shells of every hue cover the grass in all directions.

The following newspaper item, cut from the *Evening Star*, Washington, D. C., April 27, 1886, shows how these rights of the little Americans are recognized and respected, and how unmolested they enjoy the privileges of Easter Monday.

"THE EASTER EGG-ROLLING.

"CHILDREN SHAKE HANDS WITH THE PRESIDENT.

" The crowd in the White House grounds greatly increased yesterday afternoon, so that the grounds were literally packed with children. The crowd was the largest and best appearing that has collected there in many years. The President and Colonel Lamont watched the children for some time from the library window.

At the President's reception at half-past one o'clock hundreds of children gave up their sport temporarily and thronged the East Room to shake hands with the President."

Easter Egg Games.

In the game they play at Washington, on the hills sloping from the White House, the child whose egg reaches the foot of the hill in an unbroken condition takes the one worsted in the journey down. Another game for two is played by knocking the eggs together ; each child holds an egg firmly in his hand so that only the small end is visible, and then the two eggs are struck against each other until one is cracked, when the victorious player adds it to his stock, or devours it on the spot. I would not like to state the number of eggs eaten on these occasions, but there is a boy (*not a girl*) who once consumed fourteen and lived to tell the tale.

Sometimes the egg which breaks another is called " the cock of one," and when it has broken two it is " cock of two," and so on. When an egg which is cock of one or more is broken, the number of trophies won by the victim is added to the score of the conquering egg and it becomes " cock of three " or more. Here is a game which comes from Germany, and although in that country it is played exclusively by boys, there is no reason why the girls should not participate in it as well. Two baskets are necessary for this game, one large and shallow filled with soft shavings, the other shallow also, but smaller, and filled with eggs. The plan of the game is that one player is to run a given distance, while another safely throws the eggs from one basket to the other, she who completes her task first being the winner. When the baskets are prepared, and the distance the eggs are to be thrown decided upon, the two contestants draw lots to determine who shall run and who shall throw. This settled, the player who throws takes the basket of eggs, and one after another quickly tosses them the length of the course and into the basket of shavings, which is placed on the ground at the end of the course opposite the thrower. In Germany this basket is held by an assistant, but anyone occupying that position might receive some severe blows from the hard eggs thrown by unpractised hands, and it answers the purpose just as well to place the basket on the ground. Meantime the other player runs the distance (decided beforehand) to an appointed goal, marks it as a proof of having touched it, and should she succeed in returning before all the eggs are thrown, the victory and prize are her reward ; otherwise they belong to the thrower.

The game finished, a prize is presented to the successful contestant. Should any of the eggs pitched by the thrower fail to light in the basket, they must be gathered up and thrown again before the runner returns, as the eggs must all be in the basket before the thrower wins the game.

" Bunching eggs " comes from Ireland, and is played in very much the same manner as the game played with a slate and pencil, and known to all children as " tit, tat, toe, three in a row." A pan or large dish filled with sand or sawdust is set upon a table, around which the children stand, each supplied with eggs ; the eggs of each player must be all of one color, and unlike those of any other player. The object of the game is for each player to so place her eggs, standing them upright in the sand, or sawdust, as to bring five in a row touching each other.

In turn each player puts down an egg, sometimes filling out a row for herself, at others cutting off the line of an opponent ; and the one who first succeeds in obtaining the desired row sings out—

> " The raven, chough, and crow,
> Say five in a row."

Another pretty game from Ireland called " Touch " is played in the following manner :

Six eggs of the different colors—green, red, black, blue, white, and gold are placed in a row in the sand used for the other game. One of the players is blindfolded and given a light wand or stick, with which she must touch one of the eggs, while at the same time she recites these lines :

> Peggy, Patrick, Mike, and Meg,
> See me touch my Easter egg ;
> Green, and red, and black, and blue,
> Count for six, five, four, and two.
> If I touch an egg of white,
> A forfeit then will be your right ;
> If I touch an egg of gold,
> It is mine to have and hold.

As is told in the rhyme, the eggs each have a different value. Green counts six ; red, five ; black, four ; and blue, two ; and the gold egg is worth more than all put together, for when a player touches that, she wins the game and a forfeit of an egg from each of the other players. The white egg is worth less than nothing, since it not only has no value but whoever touches it with the wand must pay a forfeit.

Each player is in turn blindfolded and makes her trial, keeping account of the value of the eggs she has touched. When the sum of twenty has been reached by anyone the game is ended, without the aid of the gold egg. The position of the eggs are changed after each trial, that the person about to touch them may not know where it is best to place her wand.

Easter Egg Dolls.

In some of the large confectionery stores in New York City may be found at Easter-tide quaint little Easter offerings, looking at first sight exactly like dolls' heads surmounted by pretty little head-dresses. As dolls are not peculiarly appropriate gifts for Easter, one naturally examines them closer, to ascertain if there is anything about them significant of the day, and in so doing quickly discovers that the heads are not made of wax or china, as was at first supposed, but are simply egg-shells from which the eggs have been blown, leaving the shell perfect. Little faces are painted upon these shells, and the cunning caps or bonnets are made of tissue-paper.

Now it is our purpose to teach the children who do not live in New York and have never seen these pretty toys, and also those who, having seen, cannot afford to purchase them, just how to make some of these little men and women, and how to fashion a variety of head-dresses not to be found in the stores.

To begin with, select several nice large eggs, those of a pinkish yellow are preferable, being something of a flesh-tint. These eggs should be blown, or the shells emptied of their contents; to blow them make a small hole in each end of the shell, and, taking it gently between the thumb and forefinger, put one hole to the lips; then blow, not too hard, but steadily, until the egg has all run out of the other end.

The face must be painted next, and to those who know nothing of drawing this will seem no easy task, until by carefully observing the following direction they will find that it is

Spring.

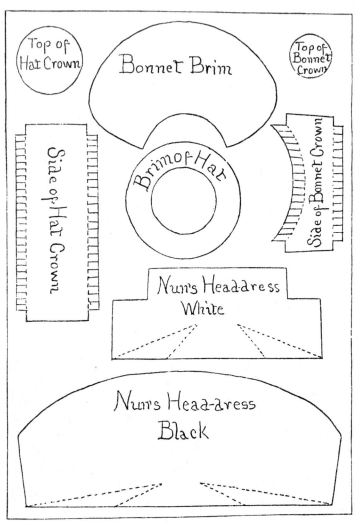

Patterns for Head-dresses.

in the power of anyone to produce as pretty a face as could be wished for.

Among picture-cards, or in almost any juvenile book, may be found many pretty faces of a suitable size which can be

The Nun.

transferred to the egg in this way. Lay a piece of tracing-paper over the head selected, and with a soft lead-pencil trace carefully all the lines indicating the features ; then place the paper on the shell so that the pencil-marks are next to it, and with a hard pencil, or ivory knitting-needle, go over the lines again, thus transferring the soft pencil-marks to the shell. Touch up and strengthen the features with a fine paint-brush and india-ink. Anyone understanding painting may color the face in natural tints, but it looks very nicely done merely in outline.

The simplest arrangement for holding the little head erect is a small pasteboard box turned upside down, and having a hole cut in the bottom just large enough to admit the small end of the shell ; this will support the head nicely, and also form the shoulders.

Make the hair of raw cotton blackened with ink, and fasten it on the head with mucilage. When all of the foregoing directions have been carried out it is time to attend to the head-dresses, and we will begin with the quaint and old-fashioned poke-bonnet. Cut this bonnet from ordi-

The Old-fashioned Girl.

nary brown wrapping-paper after the pattern shown in diagram ; sew together the ends of the " side of crown," then sew the curved side (which is cut in slits as shown in pattern, and folded back as indicated by dotted line) to the smallest part of brim ; fold in the strips marked on the straight " side of crown " and fasten on the " top of crown" with mucilage. The trimming for the bonnet consists of a fold and bow of colored tissue paper.

Make the man's hat of shiny black paper by the pattern in

diagram, and fasten together in the same manner as the bonnet, rolling the sides of the brim when finished. Black and white tissue-paper folded to fit the head, as shown by the dotted lines in the pattern, forms the head-dress of the nun.

By copying the head-dresses of different nations, an odd and curious assembly of these Easter-egg dolls can be formed ; but that must be worked out at some future time, for we have yet to tell how to construct some Easter toys that cannot be found in any store. The

The Dude.

Humpty Dumpty

who " sat on a wall," and the " Humpty Dumpty " who " had a great fall," must have been like the one I am about to describe, made of an egg ; for it is pretty certain that if he should fall, " all the king's horses and all the king's men couldn't put " this " Humpty Dumpty together again " any more than they could the other.

The diagram shows the frame of this little fellow and how it is joined together. A large egg should be chosen ; and when the contents have been blown from the shell, four holes must be pricked in it for the arms and legs to pass through, as shown in the diagram.   These limbs are made of rather fine bonnet-

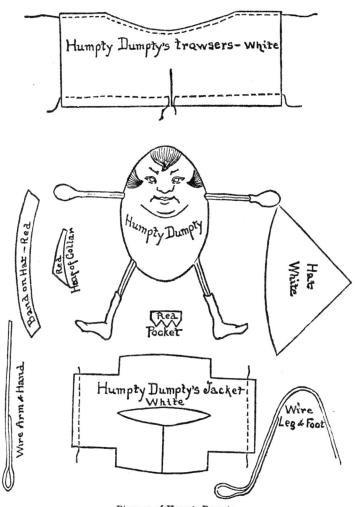

Diagram of Humpty Dumpty.

wire, the piece used for the arms being about eight inches long. The hand is made by bending up one end of the wire as in diagram, and with softened beeswax covering the loop thus formed. When one hand has been finished off in this way, the other end of the wire, still straight, should be passed through one of the holes near the small end of the shell and out through the one opposite, then bent up into a hand and arm in the same manner as described.

Humpty Dumpty.

The wire for the legs and feet must be ten inches long. The diagram shows how it is bent to form the feet. On this frame, wax can easily be modelled to look like a foot; a coating of red paint will add to the appearance, as red boots look well with the costume to be worn. The wire for the legs should be bent in a curve in the middle (see diagram) before it is passed through the shell. Again, as with the hands, one foot must be finished and the legs fastened on before the other foot can be made.

The figure of Humpty Dumpty being thus prepared, his face must be painted; water-colors are the best for this purpose. The jollier the expression of his face, the funnier the little man will look.

Patterns for trousers, jacket, and hat are shown in the diagrams. The trousers should be cut from white cotton cloth two and a half inches long and six inches wide. A slit an inch and a half long, cut in the middle, separates the legs of the trousers, which must, of course, be sewed up. Dotted lines at top and bottom show where a gathering thread should be run, the bottom gathers forming ruffles around the ankles. White should also be used for the jacket, cutting it three and a half inches long and five inches wide. The shape of the jacket may be seen in the diagram, dotted lines showing where the sleeves are to be gathered around the wrist. Collar and pockets of red— the patterns of which are given—finish the little garment. A white hat four inches around the brim and two inches high is decorated with a band of red, which should be sewed on the edge and turned up.

When dressing Humpty Dumpty, fasten his garments on to his body here and there with glue, which will hold them securely in place. The hat also should be glued to his head, as it is difficult otherwise to keep it on.

Miss Rolly-poly.

Little Miss Rolly-poly, who decidedly refuses to lie down, always regaining an upright posture, no matter in what position she is placed, is made in the following manner : After the contents have been blown from the shell, the hole of the small end is enlarged gradually until it is about a half-inch in diameter ; the shell is then placed in an upright position (a box with a hole cut in it just large enough to hold the egg firmly makes a good

Miss Rolly-poly.

stand) and melted sealing-wax is poured in ; on top of this melted lead is poured, all the while care being taken to keep the shell perfectly steady, that the weight may fall exactly in the centre and make a perfect balance. A small quantity of lead is sufficient for the purpose, as the shell is so very light.

Miss Rolly-poly requires no limbs ; when her babyish face is painted she is ready for her costume. The dress is simply made of a strip of colored cloth, and is two inches long and seven inches wide. The white apron is fastened to the dress as

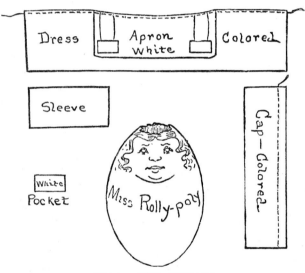

Diagram of Miss Rolly-poly.

shown in the diagram. Sleeves are made of pieces of the dress material about one inch long and one and a half inch wide. They are rolled up and fastened with needle and thread, then sewed on to the dress in the position shown in the diagram. Pockets are made for the apron, and the ends of the sleeves tucked in them, which makes it appear as though the hands were hidden in the pockets. The cap, made of the same material, or of a color harmonizing with the dress, is four inches round the brim and one inch high ; it is sewed together at the two ends, and gathered into a pompon on top, as is shown by the dotted lines in the diagram. A little glue should also be used to fasten this dolly's dress and cap on.

Mandolin.

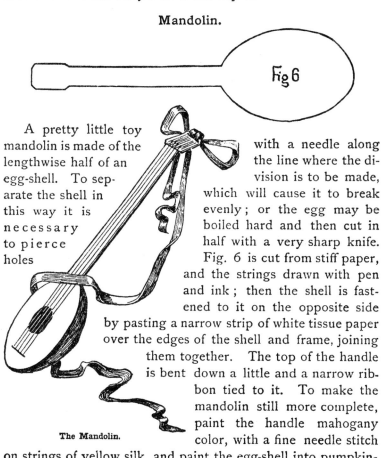

Fig 6

A pretty little toy mandolin is made of the lengthwise half of an egg-shell. To separate the shell in this way it is necessary to pierce holes with a needle along the line where the division is to be made, which will cause it to break evenly ; or the egg may be boiled hard and then cut in half with a very sharp knife. Fig. 6 is cut from stiff paper, and the strings drawn with pen and ink ; then the shell is fastened to it on the opposite side by pasting a narrow strip of white tissue paper over the edges of the shell and frame, joining them together. The top of the handle is bent down a little and a narrow ribbon tied to it. To make the mandolin still more complete, paint the handle mahogany color, with a fine needle stitch on strings of yellow silk, and paint the egg-shell into pumpkin-like divisions of yellow and mahogany.

The Mandolin.

The Owl.

To turn a hen's egg into an owl has not before, I imagine, been thought possible ; yet it is easy enough, and requires but a very

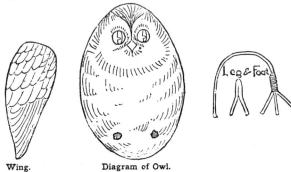

Wing.   Diagram of Owl.

short time to accomplish the transformation, when one knows just how to go to work.   No incubator is needed to hatch this bird, as only the shell is used, the contents having been disposed of in the manner before described. We commence the formation of the little owl by making two holes near the large end of the shell in the position shown in diagram.

Owl Complete.

By looking at the next diagram the manner of making the feet and legs may be seen.   A short piece of wire is bent in the shape given, and is wrapped on to a longer wire with strong thread, thus form-ing three toes, which are quite enough for a bird that will never walk.   One foot made, the wire is passed through the shell, having first been bent into a curve, as in the description of Humpty Dumpty. When the last foot has been fastened on, the wire should be pushed back into the shell, allowing but little of the legs to show. The wings are cut by the pattern given, and are painted to resemble feathers as much as possible. Brown is the best color to use. By the diagram may be seen how the head and body are painted.

Maple-wax Easter Eggs.

Empty the egg-shell of its contents and open a place at the small end the size of a silver dime. Stand it in an upright position with the largest opening on top, and leave it while you prepare the maple-wax, or candy. Mix enough water with some maple sugar to dissolve it, and set on the fire to cook ; when it will harden in cold water it is done. Carefully fill the egg-shell with the hot maple-wax, and keeping it in an upright position, set it on the ice to cool. When the wax is perfectly cold and hard, paste an artificial daisy over the opening in the shell. Maple-wax is the nicest kind of candy, and done up in this way will remain firm and hard for a long while ; and therefore these maple-wax eggs make excellent Easter gifts to send away to one's friend at a distance. The best way to pack them is to wrap them in cotton and then put them in a tin baking-powder box, filling up the interstices with cotton to keep them from knocking about.

The box, of course, must be wrapped in paper and tied securely with a string. Packed like this, they may travel safely all over the United States. The writer sent several the distance of over seven hundred miles, and they arrived at their destination in as perfect condition as when they left her hands.

Bonbon Box.

Select a box two or three inches high—a round one is best —which has a lid that covers the entire box. Cut some straw or hay in pieces long enough to reach from the top to the edge, and glue it on the sides of the lid, covering them completely. Prepare as many halves of egg-shells as will cover the top, allowing a space one inch wide around the edge. Glue the shells down, and fill up the spaces between with straw. Near the edge, on the opposite sides, glue a loop of narrow white ribbon ; these loops are to lift it with. Then glue straw on all the uncovered parts of the lid, making it a little thicker and higher at the edges. When the box is finished it resembles a nest of eggs, and makes an appropriate and acceptable Easter gift.

Easter Cards.

It is a very pretty custom, that of sending Easter cards, altogether too pretty to be allowed to lapse into disuse, as many

Stepping Through the White House

customs which are merely the expression of sentiment are apt to do in this busy, practical country of ours. One experiences a great deal of pleasure in selecting from the stock of beautiful cards found in the stores just before Easter those that seem suitable for one's friends, but more pleasure will be derived from home-made Easter cards, both to the sender and recipient; for it is true that into everything we make we put a part of ourselves, and into many a home-made article is woven loving thoughts which make the gift priceless, although the materials of which it is composed may have cost little or nothing.

Several years ago the writer was visiting a friend in the country twenty miles from the nearest town where Easter cards could be purchased, but when Easter approached we sent off our cards. just the same, and I am sure our friends were as pleased with them, and more pleased, than if they had been of the most expensive kind. This is how we made them :

It was an early spring, and the woods were filled with wild-flowers, anemones and violets mostly ; these we gathered, and arranging them in small bunches, stuck the stems through little slits cut in cards or pieces of heavy paper, as they are some-

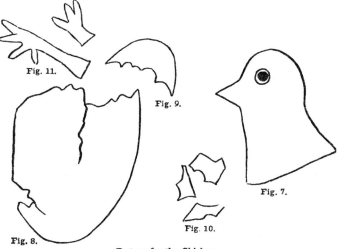

Fig. 11.

Fig. 9.

Fig. 7.

Fig. 10.

Fig. 8.

Pattern for the Chicken.

times fastened in books when pressed. Underneath the bouquet we wrote the name of the person for whom it was intended, with some friendly message appropriate to the season, and signed our own names ; then we carefully folded each in writing paper, taking pains not to crumple the flowers, and enclosing them in envelopes, sent them to their destination through the mail. Any kind of flowers can be used for these Easter cards, and instead of putting the stems through slits in the card, they may be tied to them with narrow ribbon. A card to be sent only a short distance should be put in a box just deep enough to leave room for the flowers, and fastened in some way to keep it from moving about; in this way it will reach its destination sweet and fresh.

To those who can paint their Easter cards we have no suggestions to offer, for they have an unlimited supply of designs at their command, and with their power of decoration, may turn almost anything into an Easter card, from a piece of satin ribbon, upon which they sketchily paint a spray of flowers, to an elaborate picture. A few suggestions are here given which our younger readers may like to carry out, as the cards we describe are easily made, and adapted to amuse the children.

" Stepping through the White House " the first card is called, and it represents a little chicken breaking through its shell. The pattern of the chicken is given in the diagrams. Fig. 7, the head and neck, is cut from yellow flannel; Figs. 8, 9, and 10, the main part and fragments of shell, are of white paper, and Fig. 11, the feet, of black paper. These are pasted to a tinted card, as shown in illustration. The eye and bill are made black with ink or paint.

The Little Quakeress.

Little Quakeress.

Half an egg-shell, with the face and hair painted on it, forms the head. The cap is made of white tissue paper cut in four strips ; one, for the crown, is six and a half inches long, and a little over one and a half wide; another, for the brim, is four and a half inches long and one inch wide ;

while the strings are each three and a half inches long, and one and a half wide. The crown is plaited in the centre, the brim folded lengthwise through the middle, and sewed to the crown. The strings are fastened on either side of the cap, and crossed in front; then the cap is pasted on the head, the surplus paper folded back, and the whole glued on a card. The ends of the strings are also fastened to the card, forming a Quaker kerchief.

Lawn-Tennis with Our Own Net.

CHAPTER V.

HOW TO MAKE A LAWN-TENNIS NET.

 ET us see ; it was that old medical gentleman, Galen the Greek, who first wrote upon tennis, speaking of the sport as healthy exercise, was it not ? Well, girls, it really does not matter much to us whether he was the first to write it up and the Greeks the first to play it, or whether the game originated in France in the fifteenth century, as some claim. What *we* want to know is, can we all learn to play tennis ? Does it cost much ? What kind of gowns and shoes must we wear ? And is it an enjoyable game ?

There is no doubt, we think, of its being a right royal pastime, as it has been called both the " king of games " and the " game of kings ; " the latter because it was enjoyed by princes and nobles—so much enjoyed, that in both England and France edicts were published forbidding the common people to play it.

Girls, do you wonder if they always had the choice of courts, and so never took part in the fun of spinning the racket in the air while the adversary called out " rough " or " smooth ; " or whether they played as we do, taking their defeats pleasantly and wearing their honors gracefully, while always doing their very best ?

They must have played well, for it is said that Louis XI., Henry II., and Charles IX., were experts, and that Henry VIII. of England was extremely fond of the sport.

We can easily learn to play this most popular and exhilarating of games. But we must be suitably clothed in order to thoroughly enjoy it and receive all the benefit the recreation brings to both mind and body.

Flannel seems to be the best material for a tennis suit—it is so soft and yielding, and so well adapted for a defence against either cold or heat. Then, make your tennis gown of flannel; the skirt in plaits, without drapery; the postilion basque of Jersey cloth, soft and elastic, matching the skirt in color.

An Old Game.

Sew the skirt of your gown on a sleeveless waist, made of lining or muslin. The Jersey will fit nicely over this, and you can play better and feel far more comfortable than when the weight is allowed to drag on the hips. For it is nonsense to attempt to take part in any athletic game unless you can have perfect freedom of action; in short, you should be so dressed as to be utterly unconscious of your clothing.

Either crochet a Tam O' Shanter hat or make one of the dress material, as these are not so apt to fall off while running as a straw hat. "Last, but not least," come the shoes. Of course, rubber-soled shoes are the best. But if these are not to be had, remove the heels from an old pair of ordinary shoes, and they will do very well ; heels roughen and cut the courts.

The actual cost of a lawn-tennis set need only be the price of the rackets and balls, and rope and cord necessary when you learn

How to Make a Lawn-Tennis Net,

which is not difficult.

First procure two pieces of cotton rope, three-sixteenths of an inch in size, each thirty-four feet long, costing about twenty-five cents apiece. Then one and a half pound of hammock

Stake.

Peg.

twine or macrimé cord, No. 24, which will not cost more than fifty cents. Next, two lengths of cotton rope for guy-ropes, each five feet, price, both included, ten cents ; making the total

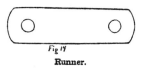

Runner.

amount $1.10 for a strong, firm, tennis net which will prove serviceable and last many a season.

The other materials necessary are all home-made. These consist

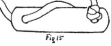

Runner and Guy-rope.

The Fid.

of two stakes, each five feet long (Fig. 12). Any kind of a strong pole, when sharpened at one end and a notch cut at the other, will answer the purpose. Four pegs, each one foot long (Fig. 13). These may be easily made of old broomsticks. Four runners (Fig. 14), each five inches long, one and a quarter wide, and about half an inch thick, with holes bored near each end large enough to allow the guy-rope (Fig. 15) to pass through. A fid or mesh-stick of any kind of wood (Fig. 16), about a foot or ten inches long, with circumference measuring three inches. A hammock-needle (Fig. 17), nine or ten inches long and one wide, which may be bought for ten cents, or whittled out of a piece of ash or hickory by some kind brother. Tassels are not necessary, though it is much better to have them, as they make the top line of the net more distinct and add to its appearance. Make about forty bright-colored tassels of worsted, or bits of flannel

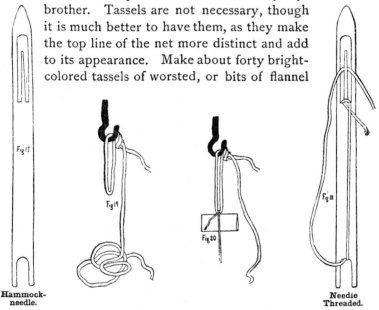

Hammock-
needle.

Needle
Threaded.

cut in very narrow strips, three inches long, allowing ten or twelve strips to each tassel. Commence your tennis net by first threading the needle ; take it in the left hand, and use the thumb to hold the end of the cord in place while looping it over the tongue (see Fig. 18); pass the cord down under the needle to the opposite side, and catch it over the tongue. Repeat this until the needle is full.

Next, take a piece of rope thirty-four feet long, and make a long loop in one end, tying the knot so that it can readily be untied again. Throw the loop over some convenient hook or door-knob (Fig. 19) with the knot at the knob or hook. Tie the cord on the needle to the loop, place the fid or mesh-stick under the cord close to the loop (Fig. 20), with the thumb on the cord to hold it in place (Fig. 25), while you pass the needle around the mesh-stick, and, with its point toward you, pass it through the loop from the top, bringing it over the mesh-stick. This will make the first half of the knot (Fig. 21). Pull this tight, holding it in place with the thumb while you throw the cord over your hand, which forms the loop as seen in Fig. 22. Then pass the needle from under

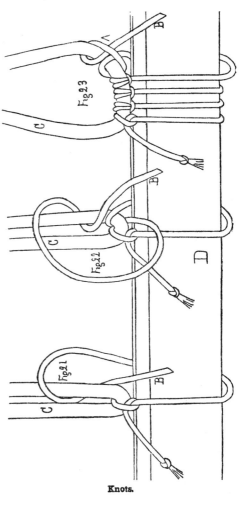

Knots.

through the loop, pulling it tight to fasten the knot. Hold it

in place with the thumb, and repeat these movements for the
next knot. Fig. 23 shows a number of these knots finished.
A in Fig. 23 is a knot before it is drawn tight; B in Figs. 21,
22, 23 is the string that runs to the needle, C is the rope, and
D is the mesh-stick. About two hundred and sixty-four of
these knots or meshes will make the
net the regular length, thirty-three
feet.

In knitting across, the meshes will
accumulate on the fid ; shove them
off to the left, a few at a time, to
make space for others. When the
desired number of meshes are finished
to form the first row, shove them all
off the fid, as shown in Fig. 24.

Begin the next row by again placing the fid under the cord (Fig. 24).
Take up the first mesh, drawing it
close to the mesh-stick, hold it in
place with the thumb while throwing
the cord over your hand, pass the needle on the left-hand side of the mesh
from under through the loop (Fig. 25);
pull this tight, and you will have tied the common knitting-knot.
Repeat this with all the loops until the row is finished.

When it becomes necessary to thread or fill the needle, tie
the ends of the cord with the knot shown in Fig. 26, which, when
properly tightened, cannot slip. Wrap each end of the cord
from the knot securely to the main cord with strong thread, to
give the net a neat appearance.

Continue netting until the net is three feet wide. Then untie the rope, and spread the net by sliding the knots apart, and
fasten the second rope to the bottom of the net by tying the rope

securely to the first mesh with the cord on the needle ; then carry the rope and cord to the next mesh, hold the rope, cord, and mesh firmly in place, and throw the cord over your hand, passing the needle down through the mesh under the rope and cord out through the loop (Fig. 27). Pull this tight, and continue in like manner, knitting each successive mesh to the rope until the net is all fastened on. Turn back the end of the rope and wrap it down neatly with strong string (Fig. 28). In the same way secure the other end, and also the ends of the first or top rope.

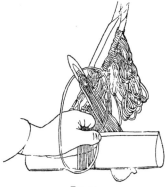

Fig. 25.

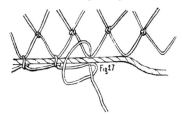

Fig. 26.

This completes the lawn-tennis net proper. The bright tassels can now be tied at intervals along the top of the net, and four pieces of twine fastened on each end of the net at equal distances apart. These are for tying the net to the poles (Fig. 29).

To erect the lawn-tennis net, plant the two poles firmly in the ground a little over thirty-three feet apart, tie the net to the poles, then drive in the pegs, two to each pole, about five feet from the pole (Fig. 30); slide a runner on each end of the

Fig. 27

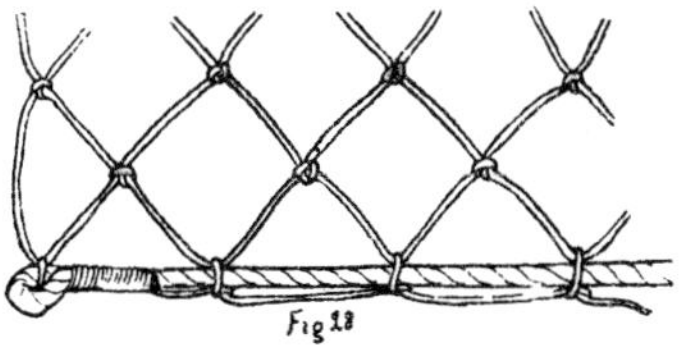

Fig. 28

two guy-ropes by first threading the rope through one of the holes in the runner, then pass the rope over the side down

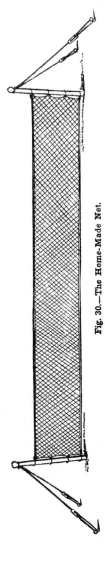

Fig. 30.—The Home-Made Net.

through the other hole and fasten it with a knot (Fig. 15). Next tie around the notch in the top of the poles the guy-ropes, with runners attached, and slip each loop made by the runner over each peg (Fig. 31), allowing the rope to fall in the groove A near the top of the peg; tighten the rope by pushing up the runners. The stakes are thus held in position by ropes running out to the pegs in the ground (Fig. 30).

Now we understand how to make and erect a lawn-tennis net; but what shall we do about the court? Of course, that must be all ready before we can set up the net. We must now learn how to lay out a

Lawn-Tennis Court.

The best ground for this is turf, though it may be of asphalt, or earth mixed with fine gravel; sometimes wood is used.

The diagram on page 64 (Fig. 32) shows the construction of a lawn-tennis court for two, three, or four-handed games.

Lay out the court with a hundred-foot measuring-tape, by marking the lines with whitewash, chalk, paint, or plaster-of-Paris.

First the side line, seventy-eight feet,

AB. This gives you one side of your court. Then the base line, thirty-six feet, AC, which, with their parallel lines CD and  DB, form the boundaries of a court for four-handed games. Now lay off the side lines of the single court, EG and FH, which are parallel to the others and four and a half feet inside of them. Divide the court across the centre by the net, fastened to the poles O and P. The lines EF and GH are called base lines. Twenty-one feet from the net, mark the service lines, MN and TV. Then make the central longitudinal line, IJ, and the court is complete.

Now everything is prepared for the game. Hold your racket firmly, and try to keep the ball flying over the net, back and forth, as often as possible.

For the guidance of those who have had no opportunity of learning to play lawn-tennis the following rules are given, as adopted by the United States National Lawn-Tennis Association.

First, however, we would say that it is not necessary always to have an umpire or a referee, as spoken of in the

Rules for Lawn-Tennis.

THE GAME.

1. The choice of sides, and the right to serve in the first game, shall be decided by toss ; provided that, if the winner of the toss choose the right to serve, the other player shall have choice of sides, and *vice versa*. If one player choose the court, the other may elect not to serve.

2. The players shall stand on opposite sides of the net ; the player who first delivers the ball shall be called the *server*, and the other the *striker-out*.

Fig. 32

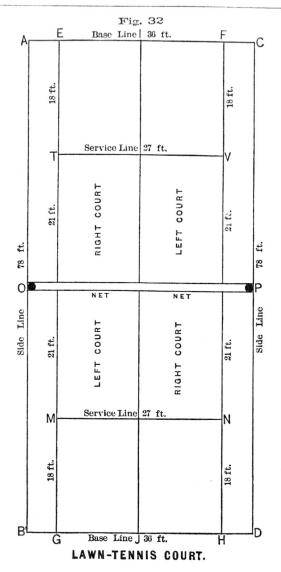

LAWN-TENNIS COURT.

3. At the end of the first game the striker-out shall become server, and the server shall become striker-out ; and so on, alternately, in all the subsequent games of the set, or series of sets.

4. The server shall serve with one foot on the base line, and with the other foot behind that line, but not necessarily upon the ground. He shall deliver the service from the right to the left courts alternately, beginning from the right.

5. The ball served must drop between the service line, half-court line, and side line of the court, diagonally opposite to that from which it was served.

6. It is a *fault* if the server fail to strike the ball, or if the ball served drop in the net, or beyond the service line, or out of court, or in the wrong court ; or if the server do not stand as directed by law 4.

7. A ball falling on a line is regarded as falling in the court bounded by that line.

8. A fault cannot be taken.

9. After a fault the server shall serve again from the same court from which he served that fault, unless it was a fault because he served from the wrong court.

10. A fault cannot be claimed after the next service is delivered.

11. The server shall not serve till the striker-out is ready. If the latter attempt to return the service he shall be deemed ready.

12. A service or fault, delivered when the striker-out is not ready counts for nothing.

13. The service shall not be *volleyed*, *i.e.*, taken, before it has touched the ground.

14. A ball is in play on leaving the server's racket, except as provided for in law 6.

15. It is a good return, although the ball touch the net ; but

a service, otherwise good, which touches the net, shall count for nothing.

16. The server wins a stroke if the striker-out volley the service, or if he fail to return the service or the ball in play ; or if he return the service or the ball in play so that it drops outside of his opponent's court ; or if he otherwise lose a stroke, as provided by law 18.

17. The striker-out wins a stroke if the server serve two consecutive faults ; or if he fail to return the ball in play ; or if he return the ball in play so that it drops outside of his opponent's court ; or if he otherwise lose a stroke as provided by law 18.

18. Either player loses a stroke if he return the service or the ball in play so that it touches a post of the net ; or if the ball touch him or anything that he wears or carries, except his racket in the act of striking ; or if he touch the ball with his racket more than once ; or if he touch the net or any of its supports while the ball is in play ; or if he volley the ball before it has passed the net.

19. In case any player is obstructed by any accident, the ball shall be considered a *let*.

20. On either player winning his first stroke, the score is called 15 for that player ; on either player winning his second stroke, the score is called 30 for that player ; on either player winning his third stroke, the score is called 40 for that player ; and the fourth stroke won by either player is scored game for that player, except as below : If both players have won three strokes, the score is called *deuce ;* and the next stroke won by either player is scored *advantage* for that player. If the same player wins the next stroke, he wins the game ; if he loses the next stroke the score returns to deuce ; and so on, until one player wins the two strokes immediately following the score of deuce, when game is scored for that player.

21. The player who first wins six games wins the set ; except as follows : If both players win five games, the score is called *games all ;* and the next game won by either player is scored *advantage game* for that player.   If the same player wins the next game, he wins the set ; if he loses the next game, the score returns to games all ; and so on, until either player wins the two games immediately following the score of games all, when he wins the set.   But individual clubs, at their own tournaments, may modify this rule at their discretion.

22. The players shall change sides at the end of every set ; but the umpire, on appeal from either player, before the toss for choice, may direct the players to change sides at the end of every game of each set, if, in his opinion, either side have a distinct advantage, owing to the sun, wind, or any other accidental cause ; but if the appeal be made after the toss for choice, the umpire can only direct the players to change sides at the end of every game of the odd or deciding set.

23. When a series of sets is played, the player who served in the last game of one set shall be striker-out in the first game of the next.

24. The referee shall call the game after an interval of five minutes between sets, if either player so order.

25. The above laws shall apply to the three-handed and four-handed games, except as below :

26. In the three-handed game, the single player shall serve in every alternate game.

27. In the four-handed game, the pair who have the right to serve in the first game shall decide which partner shall do so ; and the opposing pair shall decide in like manner for the second game.   The partner of the player who served in the first game shall serve in the third, and the partner of the player who served in the second game shall serve in the fourth ; and the same order shall be maintained in all the subsequent games of the set.

28. At the beginning of the next set, either partner of the pair which struck out in the last game of the last set may serve, and the same privilege is given to their opponents in the second game of the new set.

29. The players shall take the service alternately throughout the game ; a player cannot receive a service delivered to his partner ; and the order of service and striking out once established shall not be altered, nor shall the striker-out change courts to receive the service, till the end of the set.

30. It is a fault if the ball served does not drop between the service line, half-court line, and service side line of the court, diagonally opposite to that from which it was served.

31. In matches, the decision of the umpire shall be final. Should there be two umpires, they shall divide the court between them, and the decision of each shall be final in his share of the court.

ODDS.

A *bisque* is one point which can be taken by the receiver of the odds at any time in the set except as follows :

(*a*) A bisque cannot be taken after a service is delivered.

(*b*) The server may not take a bisque after a fault, but the srriker-out may do so.

One or more bisques may be given to increase or diminish other odds.

Half fifteen is one stroke given at the beginning of the second, fourth, and every subsequent alternate game of a set.

Fifteen is one stroke given at the beginning of every game of a set.

Half thirty is one stroke given at the beginning of the first game, two strokes given at the beginning of the second game ; and so on, alternately, in all the subsequent games of the set.

Thirty is two strokes given at the beginning of every game of a set.

Half forty is two strokes given at the beginning of the first game, three strokes given at the beginning of the second game ; and so on, alternately, in all the subsequent games of the set.

Forty is three strokes given at the beginning of every game of a set.

Half court : The players may agree into which half court, right or left, the giver of the odds shall play; and the latter loses a stroke if the ball returned by him drop outside any of the lines which bound that half court.

THE BALLS.

The balls shall measure not less than $2\frac{15}{32}$ inches, nor more than $2\frac{1}{2}$ inches in diameter ; and shall weigh not less than $1\frac{15}{16}$ oz., nor more than 2 oz.

The May-Pole Dance.

CHAPTER VI.

MAY-DAY.

Ho ! the merrie first of Maie
Bryngs the daunce and blossoms gaie,
To make of lyfe a holiday.

N the merry heart of youth the old song still finds an echo, and this day, with its relics of pagan customs, celebrating, in the advent of spring, nature's renewed fertility, is a festival full of fun for the children.

Some of the ceremonies of May-day, handed down from generation to generation, were brought to America in old colonial days by the English, but owing, perhaps, to the stern puritanical training of most of the early settlers, the customs did not thrive here as in the mother country, and many of them have died out altogether.

May-day is one of the many holidays still celebrated, that originated among the pagans ages ago, and it is said that the practice of choosing a May-queen and crowning her with flowers is a remnant of the ceremonies in honor of Flora, the goddess of flowers, which were held in Rome the last four days of April and the first of May.

There was, at one time, a very pretty custom observed in

Merrie England of fastening bunches of flowering shrubs and branches of sycamore and hawthorn upon the doors of those neighbors whose good lives and kindly habits were thus recognized by their friends.

The maids and matrons of England formerly had a way of their own of observing the day. On the first of May they would all go trooping out with the earliest rays of the morning sun, to bathe their faces in the magic dew, which glistened upon the grass once a year only, and was supposed to render the features moistened with it beautiful for the next twelve months.

When the writer was a wee little girl there lived next door to her home two old maiden ladies, who always kept a bottle of May-dew among their treasures. Although the ladies in question had long since passed that period when maidens are supposed to be lovely, superstitious persons might have found confirmation of a belief in the power of the dew, when they looked upon the sweet and kindly faces of these old maids. Faith in the fabled efficacy of May-dew will probably lose its last adherents when the two old ladies, very aged now, leave this world ; but other pretty customs, from which all the superstitious elements seem to have departed, should not be allowed to die out, and we intend this chapter on May-day sports as a reminder that May-day is a holiday and should be fittingly celebrated by the older girls as well as the little children, who, in these times, seem to be the only ones to remember the day.

May-day Sports.

A May-day custom, and a very pretty one, still survives among the children in our New England States. It is that of hanging upon the door-knobs of friends and neighbors pretty spring-offerings in the shape of small baskets filled with flowers, wild ones, if they can be obtained ; if not, the window-gardens at home are heavily taxed to supply the deficiency. When the dusky twilight approaches, it is time for the merry bands of young folks to start out on this lovely errand of going from house to house, leaving behind them the evidence of their flying visit in these sweetest of May-offerings. Silently approaching a door, they hang a May-basket upon the knob and, with a loud rap, or ring of the bell, scamper off, and flee as though for life.

These little Mayers are sometimes pursued, but few are ever caught, for the recipients of the baskets know that to capture a child, carry

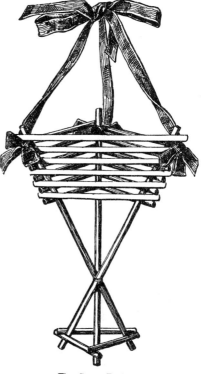

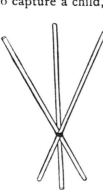

Fig. 33.   The Straw Basket.

her into the house and treat her to sweetmeats, usually dear to the youthful palate, will not compensate the little prisoner for being held captive and thereby missing the fun going on among the other children.

How to Make May-baskets.

The dainty little baskets which are used by the Mayers are generally of home manufacture. They are made of almost any material, and in a variety of shapes. Some, constructed of cardboard, are covered with crimped tissue-paper, or with gilt, silver, or colored paper. They are never large unless flowers are plentiful, and even in that case a small basket is prettier.

Our first illustration represents a May-basket made of straws. Fig. 33 shows the frame of this basket, for which three straws seven inches long are required; these are sewed together, two and one-half inches from the bottom, forming a tripod. For the sides eighteen straws are necessary, six on each side, of graduating lengths; the three top straws being five inches long and the lowest ones three and one-half inches. These are sewed to the frame, log-cabin fashion, one upon another.

The bottom of the basket is made of a three-cornered piece of card-board cut to fit; three straws, two and one-half inches long, hold the base of the frame in position. A handle formed of three ribbons finishes off this May-basket very prettily; a ribbon is tied to each corner of the basket; the other ends meeting form a bow, as shown in the illustration.

Birch-bark Baskets

are quite appropriate for wild flowers, and one in the shape of a canoe can be made from a strip of bark six and one-half inches long and four inches wide. Fig. 34 gives the pattern of this basket. The dotted lines show where the ends are to be sewed together; a ribbon sewed to each end of the canoe serves for a handle.

Card-board Baskets,

cut after the pattern Fig. 35, can be covered with gilt, silver, or crimped tissue-paper as desired; paper lace or fringe is sometimes placed around the edges of baskets of this kind, as a border to rest the flowers upon. The card-board basket shown in illustration is joined together by buttonhole stitching of colored-silk floss ; slits are cut in two sides and a ribbon slipped

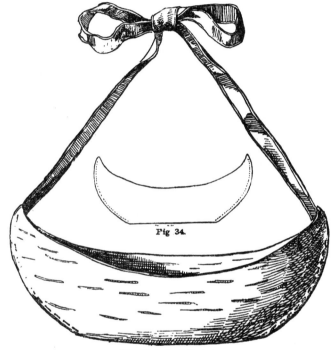

Fig 34.

The Birch-bark Basket.

through, the ends of which are tied in bow-knots to hold them in place.

May-day Combat.

This game, although suggested by the ceremonies which, according to Waldron, usher in the month of May in the Isle of

Man, is entirely new and bids fair to become popular, as it combines the elements of beauty, sentiment and mirth.

A number of young people separate into two parties, each having its queen ; one the Queen of May, the other Queen of Winter. The May-queen and her attendants should be decked with flowers, Winter and her retinue being without decoration.

Equipped with the appropriate implements of warfare between the two seasons, namely, a wreath of flowers for spring and a ball of raw cotton, or wool, representing snow, for winter, the contending forces draw up in opposing lines, the space between being about twelve feet. Each line is headed by its respective queen, who holds her missile in her hand.

The Card-board Basket.   Fig. 35.

The game is commenced by the two queens simultaneously tossing the wreath and ball to someone in the opposite line, whose name is called as the missile is thrown. Should the person to whom it is thrown fail to catch it, she is made prisoner and must do battle on the other side, being released only when she succeeds in catching the missile belonging to her own party.

When the wreath and ball are caught, they are instantly tossed back to the opposite rank, and so the game goes on. Hostilities must cease when prisoners are being taken or released, to be recommenced when both sides announce themselves ready.

If either queen is captured she is ransomed by the return of all the prisoners taken on her side ; should she have no prisoners to release, the game is ended.

If the May-queen and her forces are defeated, they must strip off their floral decorations and give them to the victors, who, decked in these trophies, become the representatives of Spring, and the Queen of Winter is made Queen of May and is crowned by her vanquished and dethroned opponent. The former May-queen and her retinue, after offering their congratulations, must serve as attendants on the triumphant queen and do her bidding.

When the May-queen proves victorious the programme is reversed, and Winter and her party become the subjects of May.

The May-pole.

An old writer, speaking of the May-games held in England, says, " Their cheefest jewell is their Maie-poole," and to leave the May-pole out of our list of May-sports would indeed deprive the day of one of its most important and prettiest features. The appropriate place for the May-pole is, of course, out of doors ; yet the climate in most of our Northern States is so changeable and uncertain it may be found necessary for comfort to hold the festivities in the house, and in that case the following directions for erecting the pole in a room of moderate dimensions will be found useful.

How to Erect a May-pole in the House.

A May-pole from ten to twelve feet high is as tall as the ceilings of most rooms will admit.

The pole should be round, smooth, and about five inches in diameter at the base, growing gradually smaller toward the top.

For its support a wooden box is necessary, the average size being three feet long, two feet wide, and one foot high. Re-

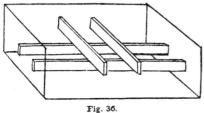

move the top of the box, and directly in the centre of it cut a hole large enough to admit the pole. Take two sticks, two inches wide, and long enough to fit lengthwise in the box, and two shorter ones fitting the

Fig. 36.

box crosswise, and nail them securely in the position shown in Fig. 36, driving the nails from the outside of the box. Slip the pole through the hole which has been cut in the top, and then stand it in an upright position between the four sticks in the centre of the box (Fig. 37). Be sure that the pole stands perfectly straight ; then, before nailing down the top, fill the box with sand, bricks, or stones, packing them tightly around the pole ; this will give sufficient weight to prevent its tipping. Nail the top on, and cover the box with moss or green cloth, and bank it up with flowers.

How to Dress a May-pole.

In olden times the May-poles were painted in alternate stripes of yellow and black, but a white pole is prettier and shows the decorations to better advantage. Tack the ends of eight or ten variously colored ribbons, one and one-half inch wide, around the pole near the top. For a pole ten feet high the ribbons should be four yards long. Around where the ribbons are fastened on, suspend a wreath of flowers, as shown in Fig. 38. Decorate the extreme tip of the pole with gaily colored streamers, or small flags.

May-pole Dance.

An even number of persons are required for this dance; half the number take the end of a ribbon in the right hand and half in the left; they then stand facing alternately right and left. When the dance commences, each dancer facing the right passes under the ribbon held by the one opposite facing the left; she then allows the next person going to the left to pass under her ribbon, and so, tripping in and out, under and over, the ribbons are woven around the pole.

After continuing for a while, according to the above directions, the dancers separate into two equal divisions, and each party, independent of the other, plaits a strip which hangs loosely from the pole.

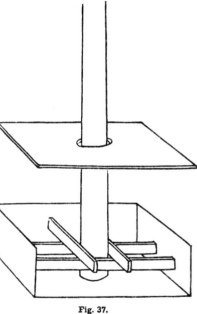

Fig. 37.

In performing this variation the two parties stand on either side of the pole, and all those facing the right pass on in that direction, going in and out as at first, until the last person going to the right has passed the last person going to the left in her division; then, transferring the ribbons to their other hands, they all turn and reverse the order. Thus they continue, going

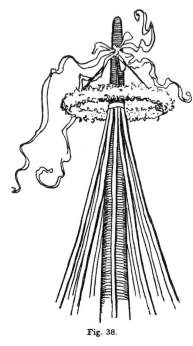

Fig. 38.

back and forth until the plait is about a foot in length, when another change is made by the two parties joining forces again ; this time, all those facing the left proceed in that direction, passing under the ribbons of all the others who are going to the right, thus forming two circles, one within the other. After going twice around the pole in this order, the dancers composing the inner circle take the outside and the others pass beneath their ribbons, again circling the pole twice ; then, after going through the first figure once more the dance may be ended, or the whole order may be reversed, and the ribbons, in that way, be unplaited again.

An appropriate song, with words set to a dancing air, should be sung by those taking part in the May-pole dance.

SUMMER

CHAPTER VII.

MIDSUMMER EVE.

N the minds of most of us, midsummer is associated with dry, dusty roads, parched vegetation, the shrill cry of the locust,* the shriller notes of the mosquitoes, and the hum of myriads of other insects; but, girls, midsummer does not come at this time: astronomy fixes the date at June 21st, the longest day of the year, when the leaves are still glossy green with the fresh sap circulating through their veins, giving them that healthy, juicy look so refreshing to the eye, and the heat of the sun has not yet dried to a white powder the firm country roads over which we delight to wander.

Ages ago the Pagans used to celebrate the day with rejoicing, because old Sol's bright face had broken loose from the clouds of winter, and the rain and mists of spring. They symbolized the revolution of the season by rolling great wooden wheels down the hill-sides; sometimes attaching straw to the outer circle and setting fire to it at night, making a miniature midnight sun as it dashed down the steep incline.

The people also believed that ill-luck rolled away from them with the fiery wheel, and to this day you will see Fortune or

---

* *Cicada*, commonly known among children as the locust.

"Ye vertue of a rare Cole that is to be found at Midsummer Eve under ye root of plantane and of mugwort ye effects whereof are wonderful. Whosoever weareth or beareth ye same about with them shall be freed from ye plague lightning & all ills"

Midsummer-eve Party.

Misfortune represented as travelling, like an acrobat at a circus, upon a wheel.

All the elves, brownies, and fays were supposed to be on hand at midsummer night, and it is this old superstition that Shakespeare has so beautifully illustrated in his " Midsummer Night's Dream."

It was on midsummer eve that the supposed invisible seeds of the fern could be gathered which rendered the fortunate possessor invisible whenever he chose to carry them about with him. Among other strange and some quite pretty superstitions, there is a tradition that a coal, found attached to the roots of the mugwort or plantain on midsummer eve, will keep away misfortune and insure good luck to the finder.

The girls of to-day who, although advanced enough to discard the superstitious element, can appreciate the poetic ideas symbolized by these ancient rites, may take hints for the entertainment of themselves and friends from the old belief in the mysteries and charms of midsummer eve.

Games can be invented, and pretty keepsakes and souvenirs exchanged upon this night, that will translate ancient paganism into modern good feeling and fellowship.

The New Fern-leaf Game.

Some one who has charge of the games shows to the assembled girls and boys a fern-leaf, and explains to them the legend connected with it, and the power of the seed to render the possessor invisible. Next she blindfolds them all ; then, choosing one from among them, she removes the bandage from the player's eyes without allowing the others to know who has been selected to be the bearer of the magic fern. After giving the fern-leaf into the keeping of the chosen one, she places the latter in the centre of a ring formed by the rest of the players, who take hold of hands and circle round ; then, still holding hands, they forward to the centre and return ; letting go hands, they forward again, this time the fern-bearer joins in the ranks. Once more the ring is formed and they circle round, singing these lines :

Round goes the wheel,	To the one who finds
Round goes the year,	The seeds of the fern,
For woe or for weal,	Misfortune and evil
Midsummer is here.	To good luck will turn.

At the word " turn," each player seizes another and cries out, " fern, fern ! " at the same time removing the handkerchief from the eyes.

To the one who really has captured the magic fern a pretty card or silk badge, bearing a pictured fern and some appropriate motto, is given, as a token that the entire company wish all possible good luck to the possessor.

The Plantain Test.

To test fortune in this way, fill a large pan or bowl with clean dry sand ; provide as many plantain-plants as there are players, and to the roots of all but one tie, with a narrow ribbon, a bonbon which contains within its wrapper a verse indicating that the wrong plant has been chosen. To the one reserved from the rest attach a small piece of coal, or charcoal, wrapped in a bonbon paper which also encloses a verse describing the magic powers of the coal. Place all of the plants in the sand, making them look as though growing there. All this should be prepared before the party assembles, that no one may know to which plant the coal is fastened.

When the appointed time arrives, explain to the company that to the root of one of the plants in the bowl is fastened a coal which, according to old superstition, will secure to the finder perfect health for life. Then let each person in turn pull from the sand one of the plants. The one who finds the coal should be heartily congratulated, as she is supposed to have gained the good will of fortune and to be exempt from all the ills that flesh is heir to. The plantain is not difficult to secure, as it grows in almost every grassplot, much to the annoyance of those who take pride in their l a w n s . Should the name be unfamiliar to some of our readers, the accompanying illustration will help them recognize the weed.

A pretty charm for the watch-chain can be made of the coal which is to bring the finder such good luck,* by having it cut to a proper size and shape, and a gold or silver band put around it. This will make it a souvenir, carrying out the old idea that the magic coal should be worn upon the person to bring the coveted good fortune.

Magic Plantain.

Rhymes to be enclosed in the paper with the magic coal:

Where my roots are intertwined
Lo, the magic coal you find.
Buried deep beneath the sand,
Waiting for your favored hand,

---

*Cannel coal is the best to use, for it is hard, will take a high polish like jet, and can be carved with a pen-knife.

I have held it free from harm ;
Take, and wear the mystic charm.
From the lightning's deadly stroke,
From the fire it may invoke,
From all illness, pain, and strife,
May it guard thee safe through life.

Rhymes to be enclosed in bonbons tied to the roots of plan-
tains which do not bring good luck :

Though ye seek, ye seek in vain
Fortune's favor thus to gain,
For I bring to you no coal
To write your name on Fortune's roll.

———

Pity 'tis you thought it best
To pick out me from all the rest,
For no root of mine comes near
The coal that brings good fortune here.

———

Chance capricious, captures choice ;
Fickle Fortune favors few ;
When deaf to love, or reason's voice,
What makes you think she'll favor you ?

———

I am no messenger of fate,
You find this out, alas ! too late ;
I bring no magic coal with me,
From pains and ills to set you free.

Any bright girl can scribble off little jingles of this sort that
will do very well for the plantain test, or appropriate quotations
may be selected for the purpose.

Fortune's Wheel.

Just where Fortune will fail each member of the company
present is discovered in the following game :

The entire party forms into a circle, standing about two feet apart; then a wheel or hoop is started around the inside of the ring, and kept going by each one giving it a gentle push with the hand, sending it to the person next in the circle. As the wheel goes around the players sing these lines, pronouncing a word as each player touches the wheel, as if counting out.

> Fortune's wheel we speed along
> The while we sing our mystic song.
> Bring happiness, fame, power, and wealth,
> True love, long life, good friends, and health,
> Success in music, poetry, art,
> And with it all a merry heart.

When the wheel drops at the feet of anyone as a gift of Fortune is being sung, or if they fail to strike it as it passes, or, striking, they send it into the centre of the ring instead of to their next neighbor, it denotes that Fortune will withhold that special gift from them, and they must leave the circle, for good luck has deserted them.

The game continues until only one player remains, and this person, who has succeeded in keeping the wheel moving, is Fortune's favorite, and will possess all the gifts the mythical Goddess can bestow.

Starfish Portière

CHAPTER VIII.

SEA-SIDE COTTAGE DECORATION.

IMPLY to enter a house is enough to start some people to planning how it can, might, or should be decorated. The love of beauty seems to be inherent in the feminine character, and it is the nature of most girls to make their surroundings as beautiful as circumstances will permit. Those who have taste and ability for decoration can see no barren or homely room without being seized with the desire to banish its uncomeliness, and substitute grace and beauty in its stead.

The ordinary cottage at the sea-shore is a boon to such natures, for it is peculiarly well adapted to amateur decoration. Its ceiled walls offer plain, even, flat tinted surfaces for any kind of ornamentation, and the absence of plaster makes it possible to drive nails wherever it is desirable to have them.

During a summer spent in one of these cottages on the coast of Maine, its many possibilities in the way of decoration were revealed, and personal experience has demonstrated that even the plainest of these temporary abiding-places is capable of being greatly beautified in a short time, and with materials usually close at hand, being obtainable from the fishermen and from the sea itself.

The windows first claim our attention in any house and our little cottage is no exception to the rule. With, or without, the regulation shades, windows should always be draped; the formality of their straight lines and angles can be subdued in no other way.

Fig. 39

Diagram of Ring.

Light, airy curtains are suitable for summer, and the prettiest, most graceful window-drapery imaginable can be made of ordinary fish-net. An oar for a pole; rings made of rope (Fig. 39); the looping formed of a rope tied in a sailor's knot; and a wooden hoop, such as is used to attach the sail to the mast on a sail-boat (Fig. 40) are all that are necessary for the completion of this nautical curtain. Small rings screwed into the oar, with corresponding hooks in the window-frame just above the window, will hold the oar securely in place. The looping should hang from a hook fastened in the wall near the window. The illustration given here will aid the imagination in picturing the effect of a window treated in this simple manner. Another pretty curtain may

Fig. 40

Looping for Curtains.

be made of unbleached cotton, with bands of blue at top and bottom covered with the ever- decorative fish-net.

Gray linen curtains, with strips of the net set in as insertion at top and bottom, will also be found extremely pretty and serviceable; or they may be composed of strips of linen and net, of equal width, running the length of the curtain.   Made up in either way the effect is excellent.

Sea-side Cottage Window.

From window-drapery we will turn to that suitable for the door-ways.   Portières, in a room where the prevailing tints are gray and light wood-color, should not present too violent a contrast to those subdued tones.   A curtain of wood-brown, neither

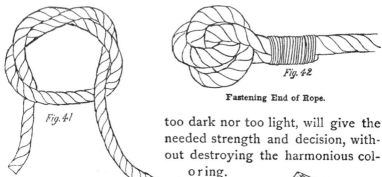

Fig. 41

Diagram of Tying Knot.

Fig. 42

Fastening End of Rope.

too dark nor too light, will give the needed strength and decision, without destroying the harmonious coloring.   One can be quickly and easily made of brown canton flannel and decorated with dried starfish, as shown in the illustration of the starfish portière.   The starfish are soft enough to admit of being sewed to the curtain, and they should be placed with the underside out, as that is much prettier than the back, showing as it does two shades of color.   A heavy rope with a knot at each end, stretched taut across the door-way and held in place with two hooks, will answer for a pole, and the drapery can be hung from it with iron rings.   If the rope is very heavy the ends will have to be parted into strands before the knots can be tied.   Figs. 41 and 42 show the manner of tying the knot and fastening the end of a moderately heavy rope.

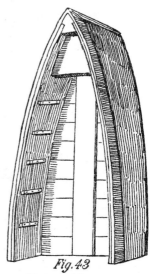

Fig. 43

Diagram of Book-shelves.

Book-shelves made of half of a flat-bottomed row-boat is not only an appropriate piece of furniture for a cottage by the sea, but also a very useful one. The fact of its shape allowing it to

Row-boat Book-shelves.

occupy a corner makes it a welcome addition to the furnishing, since there are so few things adapted to fill that angle.   Fig. 43

shows half of boat with cleats nailed on to hold the shelves, which must be made to fit the boat. The shelves, when resting on the cleats, are secure enough, and need not be fastened in any other way. If the book-shelves, when finished, are painted black, unvarnished, they will have the appearance of being ebonized.

The evidence of a womanly presence in the shape of a dainty

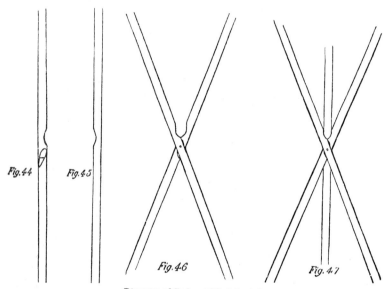

Diagram of Crab-net Work-basket.

work-basket always gives a home-like look to a room, and when this useful trifle happens to be prettily designed it contributes not a little to the decorations. The standing work-basket represented here is manufactured of a crab-net, with the handle removed, fastened to a tripod stand.

The tripod may be made of bamboo, or any kind of straight sticks about the length of a walking-cane. Upon one of the sticks two notches must be cut; one exactly in the centre, and the other at one side just below (see Fig. 44). The second stick needs but one notch, which should match the upper one on the first stick (Fig. 45). The third stick has no notches.

To fasten them together, Fig. 45 must be laid across Fig. 44 as in Fig. 46, and the two fastened together with screws. The third stick must then be placed across the others, fitting in the two upper notches; this must be secured with two screws, one passing through each of the other sticks (Fig. 47).

The stand when finished should be painted black, and the crab-net, which has previously been gilded, fastened in place by tying it on to each stick with a cord and tassel made of rope and gilded. Notches cut in the sticks, about three inches from the top, will afford a resting-place for the cord and keep it from slipping.

The hat-rack, which our drawing represents, makes an excellent and convenient hall-decoration. The materials used in its construction are a small mirror,

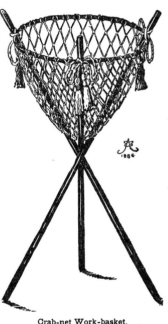

Crab-net Work-basket.

which can be procured at any country store; four boards, whose length and breadth depend upon the size of the mirror; two oars, with one-third of each handle sawed off; one dozen large-sized nails, or small spikes, and a piece of rope about twelve feet long. The frame is made by nailing the boards together as shown in illustration, placing the end-boards on top.

The opening left in the centre should be one inch smaller than the mirror. When eight of the spikes have been driven into the frame at regular distances the mirror must be fastened on the back with strips of leather or sail-cloth, as shown in diagram (Fig. 48). The diagram also shows how the oars are held in place and the rope attached. The knot

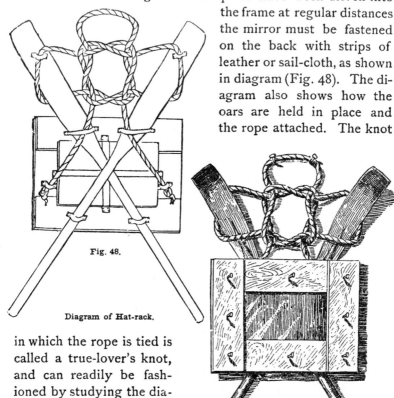

Fig. 48.

Diagram of Hat-rack.

Hat-rack.

in which the rope is tied is called a true-lover's knot, and can readily be fashioned by studying the diagram. Small nails driven through the rope where it crosses the back of the oar will keep the loops from slipping out of place. The remaining four spikes are to suspend the hat-rack from, and must be driven into the wall so that two will hold the top loop, and the others the extreme upper corners of the side loops.

The frame and oars may be painted black and the spikes and ropes gilded, or the whole will look well painted yellow or brown.

A handsome screen can be made in the following manner : Procure a nice, firm clothes-horse, saw off the legs close to the bottom cross-piece, then cover the whole neatly, on both sides, with dark green cambric. Next tack smoothly on one side of each fold light-brown wrapping-paper, which comes quite wide, and may be bought by the yard. For the border use dark-green canton flannel cut in strips eight inches wide. Tack this around each fold of the screen with gimp-tacks, and paste the inside edges smoothly over the paper.

The decorations of the screen shown in the illustration are composed entirely of products of the sea.

Two panels are shown. One is decorated with sea-weed, dried starfish, and shells. Sea-weed and shells also are used on the other, but a group of horseshoe crabs take the place of the starfish.

Sea-weed of various kinds suitable for this use can be found along the coast, and they may be gathered and dried in this way. Loosen the sea-weed from whatever it is attached to, and while still in the water slip a piece of stiff paper beneath it and lift it out. Quite a number can be carried on the same paper, but they should be taken home as soon as possible and placed in a tub of fresh water. The tub will give the larger kinds room to spread out, when a smaller vessel would cramp and rumple them. On sheets of paper, of the kind used for the screen, carefully lift each sea-weed out of the water, and with a small camel-hair brush straighten the parts that are too much folded, and separate those that lie too closely together. Should a plant be very much crumpled when taken out, quickly replace it in the water and try again.

Marine Screen.

When they have all been satisfactorily spread on the paper and have become partially dry, they must be pressed by laying the paper which holds the sea-weed on a piece of blotting-paper or folded newspaper, and over it a piece of linen or fine cotton cloth; then over that another piece of blotting-, or news-paper; then again the paper with sea-weed, and so on; when all are finished the entire heap should be placed between two boards with a moderately heavy weight on top. When the sea-weed is quite dry—which it will be in three or four days—it will be found that some varieties will cling closely to the paper on which they have been spread, while others can readily be removed. Do not try to separate the first-mentioned kind from the paper, but with sharp scissors neatly trim off the edges around the weed; the paper underneath being the same as that of the

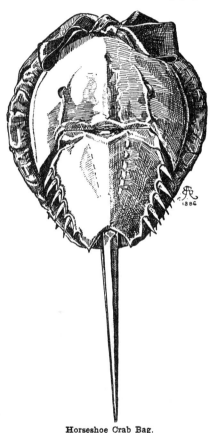

Horseshoe Crab Bag.

screen on which it is to be pasted, it will not show. The other sea-weed can be taken from the paper and fastened to the screen with mucilage.

Before commencing the decoration some idea of the design, or the effect to be produced, should be decided upon ; then with deft fingers the articles used can be glued in place. When the glue is dry the whole must be given a coat of white varnish. This will help to hold things in place, and will also keep the seaweed from chipping off.

Vase.

An odd little bag for holding fancy work is made of two large horseshoe crab shells, with a satin bag fastened between them and tied at the top with a bow of ribbon. The main part of the bag can be of cambric the color of the satin, cut to fit the shells, the puff showing at the sides being of the satin.

A pretty little vase can be made of the shells of three sea-urchins, of graduating sizes, placed one upon another, the smallest on top. The small hole in the bottom of the largest one should be filled up with damp plaster-of-Paris which will h a r d e n very quickly. The other two shells must have the small holes enlarged to the size of the one at the top ; they can then be joined together-

Candlestick.

er with the plaster, and the vase be used for flowers or vines.

A sea-urchin and good-sized starfish make the prettiest kind of a candlestick, and the addition of a brass-headed tack on every point but one of the starfish gives it a nice finish and furnishes feet for it to stand on ; the point left without a foot forms the handle by which it may be carried. The tacks should be stuck into the fish first, and then the sea-urchin fastened on with plaster-of-Paris. Not more than ten minutes are consumed in making a candlestick of this kind, and it will be found to be quite as useful as it is pretty and unique.

The walls of the cottage can be decorated in many ways with the beautiful ornaments the sea furnishes. Over one of the doors in the cottage alluded to at the beginning of this chapter there was an ornamentation that looked exactly like wood-carving, but was only a group of starfish arranged and tacked on the wall in a decorative form. The fish being nearly the exact color of the background, the deception was almost perfect.

If the walls of a room are divided off into panels, and each panel decorated in the manner described for the screen, the effect will be most exquisite.

On entering such a room one might almost imagine oneself to be a mermaid, and this a lovely chamber beneath the sea.

So much can be done by one's own hands it depends greatly, if not entirely, upon the taste or time one is willing to devote to it what this sea-side habitation shall be ; whether the little cottage shall be in harmony with its surroundings, seemingly a part of the place, or whether it shall be only a cheap frame-structure, looking as though it belonged in a country town and had been carried to the coast in a capricious gale of wind, with decorations, if it has any, inappropriate and unsuited to the sea-shore.

How to Dry Starfish.

Collect the most perfect specimens of all sizes, wash them in fresh water, and then spread on a board in a dry place (not in the sun) and leave them undisturbed for a few days, or until thoroughly dried.

How to Polish Shells.

Wash your shells in clean, fresh water; procure a small quantity of muriatic acid and have in readiness two-thirds as much water as acid. Place the shells in a basin, pour the water upon them, then the acid; let them remain a few minutes, then take them out and wash again in clear water. Rub each shell with a soft woollen cloth. A fine enamelled surface can be given by rubbing them with a little oil and finely powdered pumice-stone, and then with a chamois-skin.

To bleach fresh-water shells to a snowy whiteness, wash them perfectly clean and then put them in a jar containing a solution of chloride of lime, place the vessel in the sun, and, when the shells are sufficiently bleached, remove and wash them in clear water. Polish them in the manner before described.

CHAPTER IX.

A GIRL'S FOURTH OF JULY.

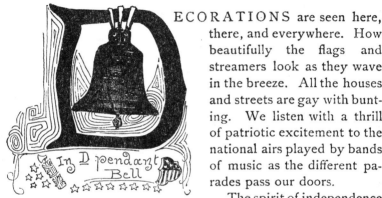

ECORATIONS are seen here, there, and everywhere. How beautifully the flags and streamers look as they wave in the breeze. All the houses and streets are gay with bunting. We listen with a thrill of patriotic excitement to the national airs played by bands of music as the different parades pass our doors.

The spirit of independence fills the very air we breathe. Whiz! zip! bang! go the firearms. The noise is enchanting and the smell of powder delightful.

This is our grand national holiday, the glorious Fourth, when all the United States grows enthusiastic, and in various appropriate ways manifests its patriotism.

The celebration, commencing in the early morn and lasting until late in the evening, gives ample time for fireworks, games, and illuminations. And the girls can take active part in, and enjoy these martial festivities, help to decorate the house and grounds, and in the evening do their part toward the illumination. Then there are the beautiful daylight fireworks to

The Fourth of July Party.

be sent off, and games to be played ; all adding to the enjoyment and making up their celebration of Independence Day.

Although

Interior Decoration

for the Fourth of July has not been considered as necessary as the decoration for the outside of the house, still it is appropriate and used to some extent, especially when the house is thrown open to guests. Then, with a little thought and care the home may be decked and adorned in the most attractive manner.

If you chance to be the happy possessor of the portrait of some revolutionary ancestor, let this form the centre of your decorations.

Bring forward any relics of the colonial times and make them hold a prominent place, for all such things are historical and of great interest, though of course they are not essential. Strips of bunting, cheese-cloth, or tissue-paper, in red and white and blue are necessary, and must do their part in adding to the gayety of the scene. These can be arranged in festoons, and made into wreaths, stars etc., to be used as ornaments on the wall.

There is nothing, perhaps, more appropriate for decoration than flags, though it requires some ingenuity to decorate with our American flag on account of the blue being in one corner. However we will try. Take two flags without staffs and baste them together as in Fig. 49, bringing the blues side by side ; pleat up the top of each to the centre and you will have Fig. 50 with the stripes at the bottom running from end to end.*

Now take two more flags reversed, the stripes being at the top the stars at the base, and pleat them in the centre, it gives the same idea in another form. For this style of adornment use the flags which may be had at any dry-goods store ; they come

---

* This flag represents the number of states as of the original publication of the book. The flag can be updated to represent the present-day American flag. [Editor]

by the bolt, cost but a few cents each, and are much softer and fold better than the more expensive glazed ones. Other modes of draping the stars-and-stripes will suggest themselves : place

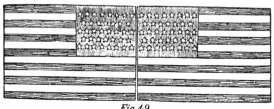

Fig. 49

the " colors " in different positions until some good design is found, and you will enjoy it all the more for having made the combination yourself.

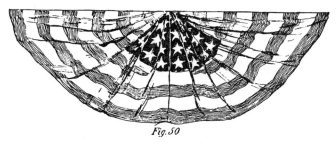

Fig. 50

Tiny flags fastened to the chandeliers, and pinned in groups on the curtains give to the room quite a holiday appearance. This is for the daylight. In the evening we will have

In-door Illumination,

which can be made very brilliant by simply using a number of lighted candles.

Should you desire to have it more elaborate, the words Liberty and Independence can be printed on the windows by cutting the letters forming the words from thick paper and gum·

ming them to the window-panes, so when the room is lighted they will show plainly from the outside.

You may also make of tissue-paper a Liberty-bell, Goddess of Liberty, American Eagle, and flags. Gum these on the edges and fasten them to the windows; place a bright light behind them and the tints of the paper will shine out in all their brilliancy. The Goddess of Liberty's face, the feathers on the eagle, and the lettering on the bell must all be drawn with a paint-brush and ink or black paint.

In making any or all of these, it will be of great assistance if you secure a picture of the object to copy from.

Having provided for the inside of the house it now behooves us to turn our attention to

Out-of-door Decoration

consisting principally of flags raised on poles, hung from windows, and disposed in numerous and various ways.

The many devices representative of our country may be used with good effect. Thus, a large United States shield can be made of colored paper or inexpensive cloth tacked on a piece of card-board, cut in the desired shape, and the shield suspended from the window flat against the house, as a picture is hung on the wall. Other emblems can be manufactured in the same way.

Small trees or tall bushes covered all over from top to bottom with flags and streamers look beautiful, and all the gayer, when the wind blows, causing them to wave and flutter.

Fasten the flags and streamers on the tree with string.

Some girls think that the

Illumination in the Open Air.

is best of all, for then they can give their fancy free play, and create all sorts of odd and novel designs.

The bright-colored Chinese lanterns are very decorative. Suppose we begin with these. Fasten securely here and there,

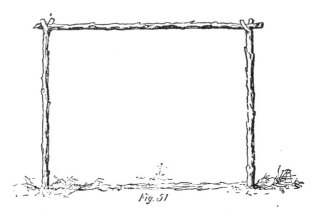

Fig. 51

on the lawn, large paper Japanese umbrellas in upright **positions.** This is accomplished by binding the handles of **the umbrellas**

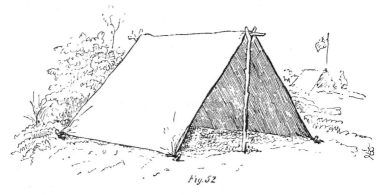

Fig. 52

securely to poles which have been sharpened at one end, and planting the pointed end of the poles firmly in the ground.

From every other rib of the umbrella suspend a lighted

Chinese lantern by a wire long enough to prevent any danger of setting the little canopy on fire. The effect produced is both novel and pretty.

A popular method of arranging the lanterns is stringing them on wires, stretched from house to house, or from tree to tree, so forming, as it were, a fringe of lights.

Again, they may be placed at intervals on the ground, fastened to trees or hung on the piazza, some in groups of twos or threes, others singly, these being of many odd shapes and sizes. Piazzas are very good sites for the display of colored umbrellas, which may hang, inverted, from the ceiling, with a tiny lighted Chinese lantern suspended from each rib. Let me repeat, be careful not to have the wires so short that the light is in dangerous proximity to the umbrella.

Another pleasing illumination is to make a large flag of colored-paper with strong pieces of tape pasted along both top and bottom, the ends of the tape extending beyond the flag. Tie the tape to two trees, poles, or pillars of the porch, and place a light back of the flag, to bring out the colors clearly and distinctly.

Illuminated tents are made by placing poles in the fashion of Fig. 51, and using large flags, low-priced colored cloth or strong paper as a covering, Fig. 52. The corners are tied down to pegs in the ground, and, when two or three candles are set in the tent, the effect is very pleasing.

All young people delight in the noise and excitement of

Fireworks,

and here are some pyrotechnics which any girl can easily make. They are daylight fireworks, and most of them may be sent off from a balcony or window, and all with no danger of fire or burns.

One of the simplest to try is the

Parachute.

Cut a piece of tissue-paper five inches square, twist each corner and tie with a piece of thread eight inches long, Fig. 53 ;

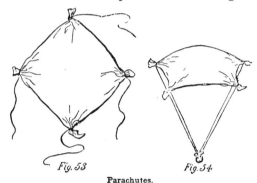

Fig. 53   Fig. 54

Parachutes.

wrap a small pebble in a piece of paper and tie the four pieces of thread securely to the pebble, Fig. 54. This makes a light airy little parachute, which, when sent out from the window, will, with a favorable wind, sail up and off over the house-tops. Make a number of parachutes in different colors and send them off one after another in succession. Next we will have what we call

Thunderbolts

fashioned of bright-colored tissue-paper. Cut the paper in pieces four inches wide and eight inches long. Then cut each piece into strips reaching about one-third of the length of the piece of paper (Fig. 55), pinch the uncut end of the paper together and twist it

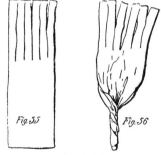

Fig. 55   Fig. 56

Thunderbolts.

tightly so that it will not become undone (Fig. 56). Open the window and throw these out a few at a time. They will

turn heavy end down and dart off with the fringed end fluttering. Now and then they will waver a moment in one spot, and
then dart off in another direction ; so they go whirling, zigzag-
ging and bowing as if they were alive.

Something different from these are the comical little

Whirls,

made by cutting circular pieces of writing- or common wrapping-paper into simple spiral forms (Fig. 57). The centre of the

spirals are weighted by small
pieces of wood, or other not too
heavy substance gummed on the
paper.

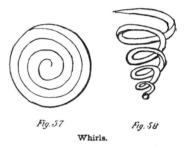

When a number of these are
freed in mid-air the weight will
draw the spirals out, and present
a curious sight, as with serpen-
tine motion they all come wrig-
gling and twisting toward the

Fig. 57   *Fig. 58*

Whirls.

ground (Fig. 58). In these paper fire-works, we know of nothing prettier than the

Winged Fancies,

consisting of birds and butterflies.

The birds may be cut out of wrapping-paper, measuring
seven and a half inches long and ten inches from tip to tip of
the wings (Fig 59), a burnt match stuck in and out of the neck,
will give the bird sufficient weight. When tossed from a height
these paper swallows fly and skim through the air in the most
delightful birdlike fashion.

Both birds and butterflies are folded through the centre
lengthwise, then unfolded and straightened out, this helps to
give them form and they fly better.

The patterns here given are possibly not as graceful in shape as could be made, but the writer drew the patterns from the

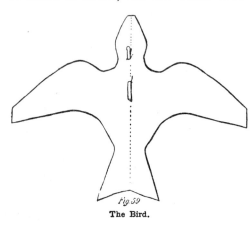

Fig 59
The Bird.

best fliers among an experimental lot of winged fancies, having found them better than others that could boast of more beauty.

Butterflies are made of bright colored tissue-paper cut from the pattern (Fig 60), and have short pieces of broom-straws as weights. These also should be lightly thrown from a height, when they will flutter and fly downward, sometimes settling on a tree or bush as if seeking the sweets of flowers, and appearing very bright and pretty as they float hither and thither on the air.

A ring of the ever-twirling

Pin-wheels

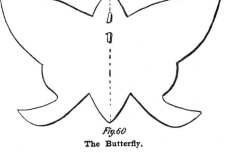

Fig.60
The Butterfly.

is gay and attractive, just the thing for the lawn on the Fourth of July. To manufacture one, select a nice firm barrel-hoop, and nail it securely on one end of a clothes-pole or broom-stick (Fig. 61), sharpen the other end of the pole to a point ; if the hoop seems inclined to split when nailing, first bore holes with a gimlet or burn them with a red-hot nail or wire for the nails to pass through.

Cover the barrel-hoop several inches deep with straw, lay the straw on and tie it down with string.

Prepare a number of pin-wheels by cutting squares of red and white and blue paper, fold them twice diagonally through the centre and cut the folds up within a short distance of the middle. Turn over every other point to meet the centre, pierce the four points and the centre with a pin, then fasten the pin firmly to the end of a stick. The pin must be left long enough to allow the paper to turn easily.

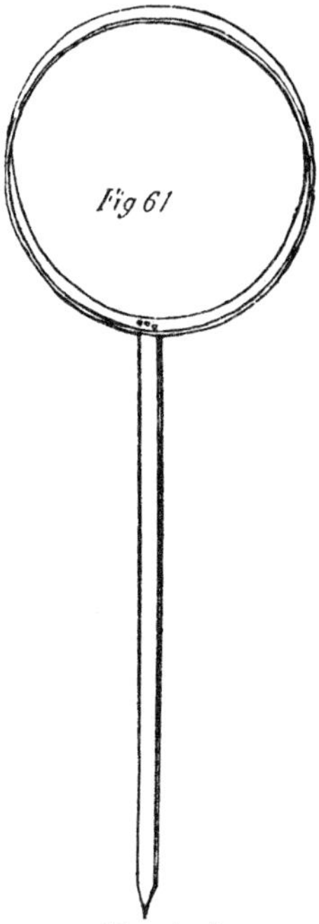

Stick the straw wreath full of pin-wheels, then plant the pole securely in the ground and you will have a ring of Fourth of July pin-wheels which will look pretty all day long.

Fig 61

Pin-wheel.

Be sure to place the wreath facing the breeze, so the pin-wheels may be kept in constant motion. Reserve the

Bombs

until the last. They are simple in construction, but quite startling when they go off.

Fasten together two very stiff flat pieces of steel (Fig. 62), those sold for the back of dress-skirts work well, and use a strong string many yards long to tie them with. Bring up the four ends of the steels and tie them with a slip knot

(Fig. 63), in order that it may easily fly open. Place the cage thus formed in the centre of a square piece of tissue-paper.

Now cut strips of different colored tissue-paper, four inches long, and twist each piece at one end.

Put these in the centre of the cage and bring up the four corners of the square of paper, allowing the string to come out of the top. Twist the corners together and close up the small openings by folding over the edges of the paper. This

Fig 62

makes a bomb somewhat resembling a common torpedo enlarged to many times its original size.

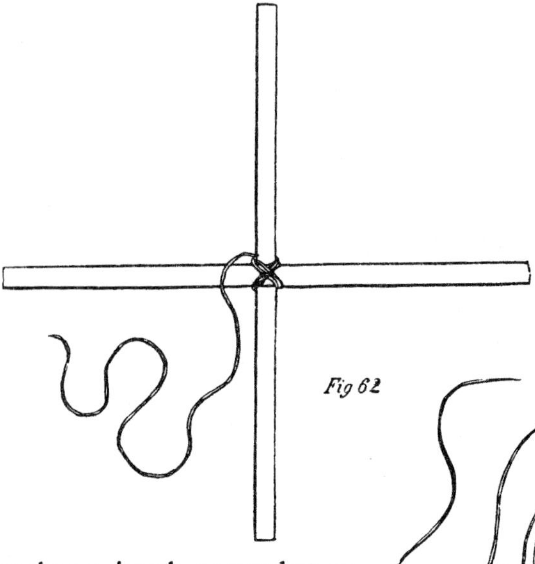

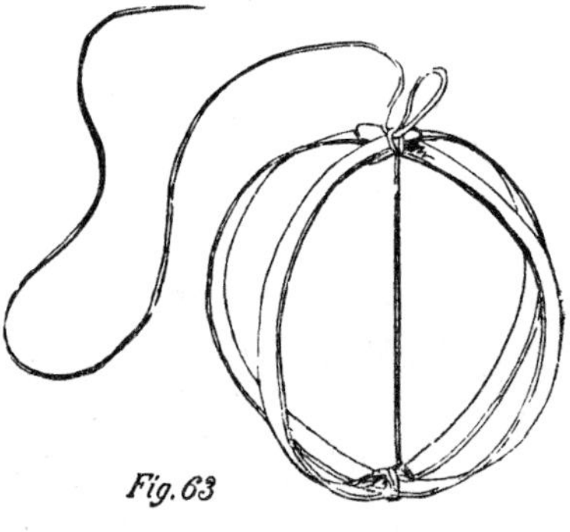

Pass the string through a

Fig. 63

screw-eye which has been screwed in the end of a flag-pole or broomstick, and place the pole out of the window. Then drop the end of the string down to the lawn below. Fasten one end of the pole in the window by binding it firmly to a strong, heavy chair, or secure it in any other way most convenient so there will not be the slightest danger of its falling.

Everything being ready, descend to the lawn, and pull the string so the bomb will rise slowly up to the pole.

When it is within a short distance of the screw-eye, give the twine a sudden sharp jerk which will cause the bomb to come in contact with the pole with sufficient force to untie the slip-knot, the elastic-metal ribs will fly back causing the bomb to burst and fill the air with bright shreds, flying, gliding, and darting everywhere in the most eccentric manner, making the air brilliant with floating colors.

Let your Fourth of July

Lawn Party

partake of the patriotic traditions, and as far as possible help to celebrate our Nation's birthday in an appropriate manner.

Paper fire-works may form part of the entertainment, it being optional with the hostess whether they come before or after the games, or are interspersed between them.

The party opens with the signing of the

Declaration of Independence.

To each guest is given a brown-paper bag, and when all have assembled on the lawn, the hostess steps forward facing the company, and asks all to kindly keep quiet and listen for a few moments while she reads or repeats their Declaration of Independence, she then reads :

We girls are, and of right should be, free and independent of all boys' sports, having resources and amusements befitting the celebration of the Fourth of July, independent of all those belonging exclusively to boys.

Then follows the signing of the same, by each in turn writing her name beneath the declaration. This accomplished, the hostess gives the signal and each guest fills her bag with air, by holding it close to her mouth, gathering it tightly around, and blowing into it, then grasping it firmly in the right hand, being careful not to let any air escape.

At another signal, all simultaneously bring their hands forcibly and quickly together, striking the paper bags with the left hand, which bursts the bags and causes a report almost equal to that of pistols.

All the bags exploding at one time, gives a salute worthy of the name and creates much merriment.

The salute may be varied by bursting the bags in quick succession, so that it will sound something like a volley of musketry.

This introduction is followed by games to be played on the lawn.

For the new game of

Toss,

make nine disks of card-board, painted or covered with paper, red and white and blue, three of each color.

Place in the centre of the lawn a fancy waste-basket, and let each player in turn stand at a distance of six feet from the basket. It is better to have the station marked by a stone or stick, at the place designated.

If played by sides, two stations, one on either side of the basket will be necessary.

The object of the game is to throw the disks into the basket, and they are valued according to color ; red counts one, white two, and blue three.

If played by sides, each side should play five rounds, ninety being the highest possible tally for any one player.

This is an easy and pleasant game, and may be played with or without sides. The hostess keeps account, and at the end of the game gives a knot of red, white, and blue ribbons as a prize to the one having the highest score.

We hardly recognize our old friends in the new and gigantic

Fourth of July Jackstraws.

These are all in holiday attire, and so much larger than any we have seen that they are even more attractive, and afford greater amusement than those which we have hitherto enjoyed.

It does not take long to make them. Cover a number of light slender sticks, three or four feet long, with paper or cloth, some red, some white, and others blue. The colors count respectively, red one, white two, and blue three. Provide another longer stick with a hook in one end to be used in taking the jackstraws from the pile.

Stand the sticks up so as to meet at the top, and spread out like a tent at the bottom. Each player then takes the hook in turn and tries to remove a jackstraw, without shaking or throwing down any of the others. The one scoring the highest, wins the game and is entitled to the prize.

Progressive games seem to be very popular, and deservedly so, as they possess an interest peculiarly their own.

Here is a new and novel one, called

Fig. 64

Progressive Mining.

It is played with flower-pots filled with sand or loose earth, called mines. A small flag on a slender staff is placed upright in the centre of each flower-pot (Fig. 64). The staff should be stuck down in the sand only just far enough to keep it steady in its position. Each player in turn removes a little sand from the mine with a stick called a wand, taking great care not to upset the flag ; for the one causing the flag to fall loses the game. The number of mines needed will depend upon the number of persons playing, as one flower-pot is required for every two players.

Fig. 65

Each one taking part in the game, is provided with a wand. Slender bamboo canes make excellent wands, and may be decorated with red, white and blue ribbons, tied on the handles. Should the canes be difficult to procure, then any kind of light slender stick will serve the purpose.

The hostess should prepare blank envelopes, each containing a ribbon badge, or score sheet, of different colors, two of each ; these are all numbered, the figures being painted or pasted on the ribbons to designate the place to be taken, thus two reds are marked 1, meaning that they are to occupy the first or prize mine. The blues are marked 2, showing that they take the second mine, and so on. The last or lowest place is called the booby mine. Each badge should have a small pocket attached (Fig. 65), for holding stamps ; these are cut in any desired form from gold and silver paper, which has previously been covered with mucilage on the under side, like a common postage-stamp.

The hostess passes around the envelopes, each guest takes one, and upon opening it discovers where and with whom she is to play.

The preliminaries being settled, and all having taken their places, the hostess starts the game by ringing a little bell.

When one of the players at the prize mine upsets the flag, the other calls out *prize*, and if the flags have not already fallen in the other mines, the couples play as quickly as possible until all the flags are down.

The winner at the prize mine fastens a gold stamp on her ribbon badge, while the loser at the booby mine, ornaments hers with silver seal.

The game is now rearranged, the winner at the prize mine remains at her station, and the loser goes down to the booby mine, while all those winning at the other mines move up, each one respectively to the next higher mine, for it is only at the prize mine where the loser moves her place and the victor remains stationary.

When these details are settled, the flag-staffs are again planted in the flower-pots and the signal given for a new game.

The player with the largest number of gold stamps on her score-sheet, receives the victor's prize, and the one having the most silver stamps is entitled to the booby prize.

The prizes are given when the game is ended. They should consist of some pretty little article made by the hostess herself, and, if practicable, appropriate to the day, such as a delicate satin sachet in the form of a Liberty bell, with the lettering painted on it.

A pretty pin-cushion, with a cover made of a miniature silken flag, or a dainty pen-wiper in the shape of Liberty's cap. Other more expensive gifts are not in good taste.

The booby prize should be something grotesque or comical.

As the mothers and sisters of 1776 took a full share in the

hardships and trials of the Revolution, and actively assisted in gaining our independence, it is eminently fit and proper that American girls should show their appreciation of such bravery and heroism by assisting in the annual celebration of our famous Independence Day.

Fourth of July seems heretofore to have been considered altogether too exclusively a boy's holiday, and it is with a hope of stimulating a renewed activity, and awakening in the heart of every girl in the United States a sense of proprietary interest in the day, that we suggest new methods of celebrating our national holiday.

CHAPTER X.

PRINTING FROM NATURE'S TYPES.

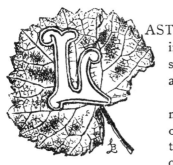

AST summer we made some lovely impressions of flowers, leaves, and sprays ; then we tried landscapes and all sorts of beautiful designs.

It is really delightful and fascinating work. You are led on and on, always with a fancy to try something else to see how it will come out, and seldom, if ever, is it a disappointment or failure, a new interest being felt with every fresh print made. Moreover, you are sure of having your picture original and the only one of its kind, for as no two flowers or leaves are precisely alike, so no print can be an exact copy of another. And then it takes only a few moments for the work which could not be accomplished in thrice the time should a drawing be made of the same design.

Let me tell you how to make an "Impression Album" a book of printed flowers and leaves. You who have house-plants will find it a delightful winter recreation, a novel pleasure, and you can enjoy the pretty work even more during your summer vacation, with wild flowers at your command.

The "prints" are taken from the natural flowers or leaves themselves. Girls who have no knowledge at all of drawing or of printing can with little trouble make these Impression Al-

Making Prints.

bums, and students of botany will find the work supplies valuable memoranda of leaves and plants, as the print preserves details of the form, fibre and veining of foliage and petal such as no drawing or photograph can. The printing can be made wholly accurate, giving all the minutiæ of construction.

Pink Oxalis.

The tools required to make these print-pictures

Smilax.

are simple, and consist of a piece of glass, a palette-knife or table-knife and some printers' ink which comes in small tin boxes and can be procured at any stationery store, and a pad made of a ball of cotton tied in a piece of soft silk or satin.

The printers' pad used by the writer for spreading the ink, was manufactured

Evergreen Moss.

of the satin lining taken from a gentleman's old hat, and answered the purpose admirably, being a good size, measuring nearly four inches in diameter. The album itself may be a common blank-book, with every other leaf cut out, in order to make room for the prints, which are on pieces of blank unruled paper of uniform size, and small enough to fit in the album and leave a margin all around the piece inserted, so that the book when opened may be neat and attractive. Having all your tools at hand, select the leaves you wish to print. These must be free from dust or dew and perfectly fresh.

First, with your knife, place a small quantity of printers' ink on the piece of glass and smooth it as evenly as possible over the surface. Then press the printers' pad down lightly, lifting, and again pressing, until the ink is evenly distributed on the pad ; next, select a leaf and place it face, or right side, downward on a piece of folded newspaper; press the inked pad down on the under side of the leaf, which is now, of course, lying upward, repeating the operation until the leaf is sufficiently covered with ink. Carefully place the leaf, inked side down, on the centre of the piece of paper you have previously cut for the album ; over this lay a piece of common yellow wrapping-paper,

Skeleton Geranium Leaves.

or any paper that is not too thick or stiff, and rub the finger gently all over the covered leaf. Remove the outside paper and very *carefully* take up the leaf. You will find an exact impress of the natural green leaf showing every one of the delicate fibres.

The picture is now ready to be pasted in the album, with a thin, delicate paste, touching only the corners. It is a good plan to write under each leaf the name of the plant or tree from which it was taken, with the date, and such facts as you would

like to recall. Very valuable botanical collections can thus be
made. Flowers are more difficult to print than leaves, owing
to less "relief" in the films;
still they make charming pictures when successfully
treated, sometimes

A Winter Landscape.
Printed from Nature's Type.

having the appearance of photographs of flowers with all the
lights and shadows.

When printing flowers, proceed in the same manner as with the leaves. Sweet peas, roses, daisies, wild carrot, clover, and verbenas, all make beautiful impressions which look like photographs. Grasses of various kinds also print well.

In making a spray, it is best to have a definite idea of the form you desire it to take. If possible secure as a copy a natural spray of the kind you wish to print. Then first print all the leaves in the positions they are to occupy, and connect them by drawing in the branch with pen and India-ink.

Maple Leaves.
Printed from Nature's Type.

The Winter Landscape is printed from dried twigs, grasses, and little leafless plants, so arranged as to resemble trees and shrubbery.

Only have a little confidence and you can make etchings from nature. Should you not understand drawing or composition, do not be discouraged; obtain a picture to copy, and then hunt up little plants and soft twigs as nearly as possible corresponding in shape and character to the trees in the copy; in this way you can produce very creditable landscapes.

Botanical impressions may be used for "fancy work" by being printed on satin, and the decorated satin made up as though it were painted or embroidered ; patches for silk quilts have been prettily decorated by this process. The printings also make beautiful patterns for outline work, much truer to nature than those made in any other manner and afford infinite variety for "borders" and "corners." Even satin dresses can be beautifully ornamented with impressions of leaves instead of the "hand painting" so long in use. You can, of course, see that should several colors of printers' ink be used, beautiful combinations and pleasing variety would be obtained, and that probably some unique and novel decorations would be secured.

Letter-paper ornamented with a delicate design printed from nature's types is very dainty and pretty, and in many other forms can these simple and beautiful decorations be used.

Then bring leaves and blossoms from the woods or dooryard, and half an hour may be delightfully spent in printing "impressions" which will teach a lesson in botany, while the great variety of leaf forms, difference in texture, fibre, veining and finish cannot fail to attract your attention and call forth your admiration.

Corn Roast.

CHAPTER XI.

PICNICS, BURGOOS AND CORN-ROASTS.

RACES of foreign ancestors are apparent occasionally in most of us, true Americans though we be. It is perhaps a spice of gypsy blood in our veins that sets our pulses throbbing with pleasant excitement when, seated in an old hay-wagon, we go bumping and thumping down the road prepared for a delightful holiday.

With camp-kettle swinging beneath, and coffee-pot stowed safely away within the wagon, do we not feel able to provide as savory dishes for our picnic dinner as any concocted by the gypsies themselves ? Surely no coffee is ever so delicious as that cooked over the camp-fire, albeit it tastes somewhat smoky when prepared by hands inexperienced in the art of out-door cooking ; but if the fish we broil is a little burned, and the baked potatoes rather hard in the middle, who cares ? Hearty, healthy appetites, which the early morning drive through the fresh, exhilarating air has developed, laugh at such trifles and dinner is voted a success in spite of sundry mistakes and mishaps in its preparation.

There are *picnics* and *picnics.* When one drives out in a fine carriage to meet a fine company, and partake of a fine lunch prepared by fine servants, is one kind.

When one goes with a large party, on a boat, and takes a lunch of sandwiches, cake, pickles, hard-boiled eggs, etc., which is spread on the grass at the landing and eaten as quickly as possible, is another kind; but the picnic most enjoyed by young people who are not afraid of a little work, which is only play to them, is the one where the raw materials for the dinner are taken and the cooking, or most of it, is done, gypsy fashion, by the picnickers themselves.

A pleasant innovation in the ordinary routine of a picnic is

A Burgoo.

Thirty or forty years ago the men of Kentucky, in celebration of a holiday, would get up what they called a burgoo. In character it was very much like the clam-bake of to-day, but instead of chowder, or baked clams, the company prepared and partook of a soup or stew made of almost everything edible. Early in the morning the party would meet at the appointed place and decide what each should contribute toward the making of this most delectable stew.

Those who were fond of hunting would go forth in search of birds, squirrels, rabbits, and game of all kinds, with which the woods were filled. Some caught fish, and others provided fowl, pork, vegetables, and condiments.

As the ingredients were brought in, those who had charge of the cooking prepared and dropped them into an immense pot which, half full of water, was suspended over a roaring fire.

When everything of which the stew was composed was

cooked to shreds, the burgoo was pronounced done, and was served in tin cups, and eaten with shell spoons, made by splitting a stick and wedging a mussel-shell in the opening.

That this was a most appetizing feast I know from an old gentleman who has frequently attended the burgoos and partaken of the stew. Of course at a picnic composed of girls and boys, it would not do to depend upon the game which might be shot and the fish which might be caught, for the dinner, but the burgoo should be adapted to the ways and means of the party, and each member should provide something for the stew. The following recipe will make enough for fifteen or twenty persons.

Burgoo Stew.

Two pounds of salt pork, the same of lean beef; two good-sized chickens, or fowls of any kind; two quarts of oysters, the same of clams; twelve potatoes, four turnips, one onion, two quarts of tomatoes, and any other vegetables which may be obtainable. Make a bouquet of parsley, celery, and a very little bay-leaf, thyme and hyssop, tied together with thread.

Fig. 66

Put the beef, fowl, pork, oysters, clams and a handful of salt in a large iron kettle, three-quarters full of water; skim it before it begins to boil hard, and add the other ingredients; keep the kettle covered and boil until the bones fall from the meat. Serve hot with crackers. Wild game and fish may also be added to the recipe. When a burgoo is decided upon, it is best to prepare a light lunch to be eaten about eleven o'clock, and have the heartier meal at four or five in the afternoon, as it requires some time for the stew to cook.

Our illustration shows four ways of suspending the kettle over the fire. While the girls are preparing the ingredients for the stew, the boys will build a fire in some such fashion as is shown upon page 135, and put the kettle on. The best way to boil coffee is to make or build a kind of little stove of stones and mud, and set the coffee-pot on top, as shown in Fig. 66; this will prevent the smoky taste it is apt to have when placed directly on the fire.

A Corn-roast.

During the season when green corn is plentiful, there is no better way of having a real jolly time than by getting up a corn-roast. It is not as elaborate an affair as the burgoo. Some green corn, a long pole sharpened at one end, for each member of the party and a large fire built in some open space where there will be no danger of causing conflagration makes us ready for the corn-roast.

Several summers ago a gay party of friends from New York and vicinity took possession of and occupied for a few months a little cottage at a place on the coast of Maine called Ocean Point.

Toward the end of August, when all places of interest had been explored, when the stock of shells, star-fish, and such like treasures had grown beyond the accommodation of an ordinary trunk, and the minds of the sojourners were beginning to be filled with thoughts of a speedy return home, green corn, for the first time that summer, made its appearance. This was hailed with delight, and a farewell lark, in the form of a corn-

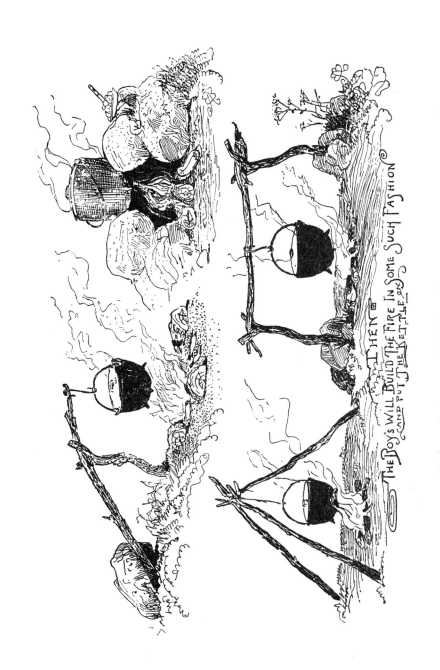

THEN
THE BOY'S WILL BUILD THE FIRE IN SOME SUCH FASHION
AND PUT THE KETTLE ON

roast, was promptly proposed and almost as promptly carried into execution.

The place selected on which to build the fire was a large rock jutting out into a little cove called "Grimes Cove." Here the party met about three o'clock in the afternoon, each member bringing only such dishes as were considered necessary for his or her own use. It is needless to say that the supply was not very plentiful, many limiting themselves to a cup and spoon; still as the supper was to consist merely of roasted corn, bread and coffee, these answered every purpose.

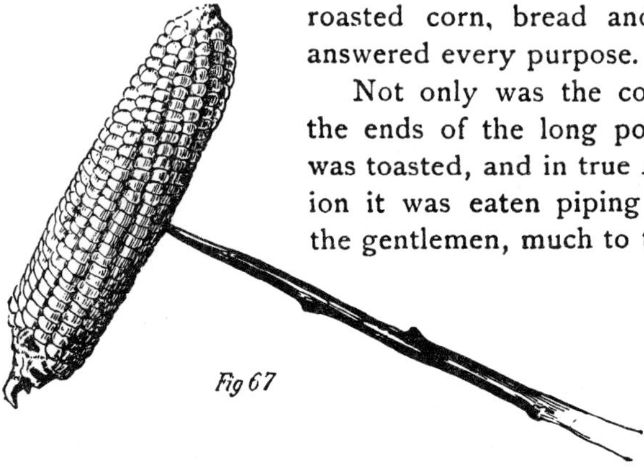

Not only was the corn roasted on the ends of the long poles, but bread was toasted, and in true American fashion it was eaten piping hot. One of the gentlemen, much to the amusement of the rest of the party, produced a piece of breakfast bacon, which he fastened on to the end of his pole and toasted over the glowing embers, declaring that it was better cooked in that way than in any other.

Fig 67

Yes, corn-roasts are great fun, and they can be held almost any place where a large fire can be safely built. It is best to allow the fire to burn down until it is a glowing pile of coals; then sticking the sharp end of a pole into an ear of corn (Fig. 67), and standing as far from the fire as the length of the pole will permit, it can be held close to the hot embers until thoroughly cooked; then with butter and salt this roasted corn is excellent eating.

Enough corn should be provided to allow several ears to

each member of the party, as mishaps are liable to occur, and the tempting ear of corn may be devoured by the flames, instead of the person for whom it was intended.

The poles, about six feet in length, should be as light as possible, for if too heavy they will tire the hands and arms of those holding them.

White Clover Design.

CHAPTER XII.

BOTANY AS APPLIED TO ART.

 HERE is a book of most lovely designs open to everyone whose eyes are open to see.

Grasses, leaves, blossoms, and even buds and seed-vessels supply material for beautiful patterns.

We need not look far for suggestions. Truly "that is best which lieth nearest; shape from that thy work of art."

At your very doorway the wonders of botany may be studied. Carefully inspect the tree blossoms in the early spring; the maple, willow, birch, any in fact which happen to be convenient, and you will find suggestions of rare designs.

Clover, plantain, pepper-grass, dandelions, vines and twigs, offer ideas which can be adapted to ornamental art.

A love of nature will quicken and stimulate the faculties; take the flowers and plants for instructors, and they will teach and guide you.

Though there cannot be found an exact duplicate of any blossom or leaf, still these may be conventionalized by arranging them in all sorts of symmetrical designs.

There is no mystery about the matter, for all the designs

are conceived upon the most simple of geometric laws. We
are now following in the steps of the old masters, and an unlimited field of new combinations opens before us.

When making designs for this chapter, the writer did not
select the objects she thought would be most decorative, but
anything which chanced to fall in the way ; and what she has
done you can do, provided, of course, that you have ordinary
skill with the pencil.

The Peony Leaf.

Suppose you do not know how to draw at all !   Even then
you can design.   Take the first thing you see, which in this

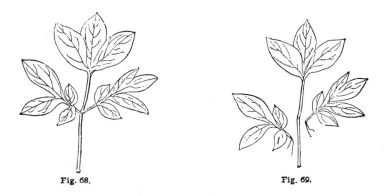

Fig. 68.   Fig. 69.

case happens to be a peony leaf (Fig. 68).   That is, assuming
that you are seated by the side of the writer.

Now watch ! We will pull it apart thus (Fig. 69).   Next
with a pair of scissors, a knife, or fingers snip off the stems,
and group the leaves in any way we chose.   We will try this
combination (Fig. 70).   If you do not understand drawing,
we must fasten the leaves down upon a piece of paper as they
are arranged, and trace around them, following their edges

with a pencil until the outline is complete (Fig. 70). By simply repeating this figure at regular intervals we have a very
pretty border design and
one that is truly original,
for the writer had no more
idea than you, what was
to be the result of this experiment. In order to
make the pattern exact,
draw lines as in Fig. 71,
for a guide ; then draw
the figure according to the
foundation lines (Fig. 72).
When finished, erase the
lines and the design stands
a conventionalized peony
leaf, Fig. 73. By making
a tracing of the first pattern, you can repeat it any

Fig. 70.

number of times. It requires no great or peculiar genius to
design well, and it is a mistaken, old-fashioned idea to suppose

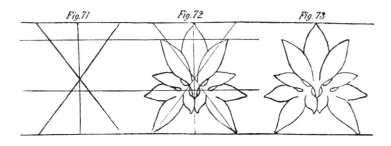

Fig. 71.   Fig. 72.   Fig. 73.

because you never have done any original work in art that you
never can. Do not slavishly follow other people, but believe

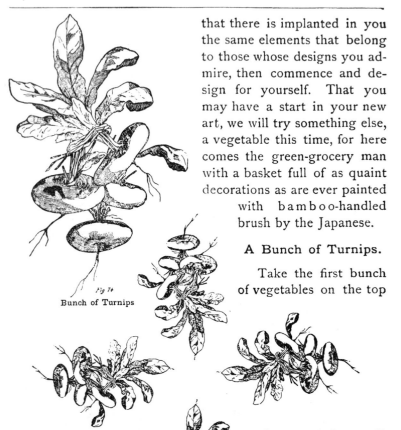

Fig 74
Bunch of Turnips

Fig. 75.

that there is implanted in you the same elements that belong to those whose designs you admire, then commence and design for yourself. That you may have a start in your new art, we will try something else, a vegetable this time, for here comes the green-grocery man with a basket full of as quaint decorations as are ever painted with bamboo-handled brush by the Japanese.

A Bunch of Turnips.

Take the first bunch of vegetables on the top of the basket. What are they? turnips? Well that requires a little skill as a draughtsman, but we will sketch this one and you can copy it (Fig. 74). Now repeat it (Fig. 75), or place the bunches in a row and you will have another border design. After a few experiments you will see that anything will make a decoration even the humble kitchen vegetables.

Decorative Lines.

Figs. 76 and 77 are simply graceful curves, such as anyone can make with a pen or pencil, and may be used in many

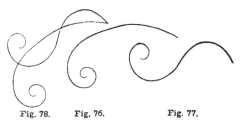

Fig. 78.   Fig. 76.   Fig. 77.

ways : cross them and they form Fig. 78, use this as half the design, duplicating it for the other half and it gives Fig. 79.

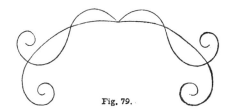

Fig. 79.

We now have graceful and beautiful foundation lines on which any vine or flower may be placed as ornamentation.   We will

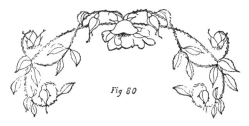

Fig 80

select the rose, allowing the lines to form the stems and using as ornament the bud, flower and seed-vessels, remembering that one side must be an exact duplicate of the other (see Fig. 80).

With these curves invent new designs by placing them together in different ways, and choose for decoration anything which may strike your fancy.

Plant Cross-section Designs.

Have you ever noticed how curiously some leaves are curled before opening ? Watch them as they commence to expand and grow, and you will be delighted with the great variety and unique designs formed by the folding and rolling of these leaf-buds.

Cut a bud square across in the centre with a sharp knife, and this will show the nicety of arrangment of the young

Fig. 81

Fig. 82

Fig. 83

Fig. 84

leaves. The leaf-bud of the sage (Fig. 81), rosemary (Fig. 82), apricot (Fig. 83), and still another variety of pattern (Fig. 84), are all singular natural designs.

The petals of flower-buds are also folded in many ways, affording odd designs ; if cut in like manner as the leaves, the cross-sections will be as beautiful. Fig. 85, the lilac bud, and the oleander (Fig. 86), give some idea of these odd designs.

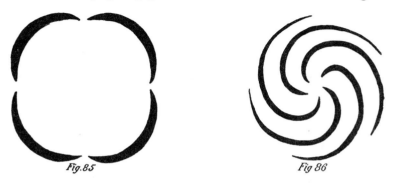

Fig.85   Fig 86

Submit all kinds of buds to the test by cutting them in halves, and carefully examining the two parts, observe how nicely and

Fig. 87

orderly the leaves are folded together. In this way you will find many natural ornamental patterns.

Nor must we neglect the seed-vessels ; when these in their

turn are cut open, they present excellent designs.   Fig. 87 is a
cross-section of the seed-vessel of the harebell.   Other seeds
will furnish queer forms and figures to be obtained in no other
way.

Flower Sprays.

The common white clover with its trefoil leaf is very pretty,
and if a few sprays are placed together in a graceful manner it

Fig.88

is surprising how readily they
lend themselves to decoration.
Experiment with these, gather
a few blossoms and leaves,
group them on the centre of a
piece of paper, and make an
outline of the group ; then
trace it off in order to repeat
the copy at equal intervals
from the central figure (see illustration, page 138) ; this
makes a very simple and yet
beautiful design for embroidery, needle-work, or wall-paper
pattern.   In the same manner try grasses and different kinds
of flowers.

Conventional designs can also be formed by simply inclosing
a natural spray in a geometrical figure.   Fig. 88 is a circle, but
a square, triangle, diamond, oval, or any geometrical figure
may take the place of the circle.

Changing the Color

of a natural object gives still another style of ornamental art.
A spray of flowers and leaves in one color on a background of
different tint is an example.   The spray may be brown on a

yellow background, or a dull blue on white background, either way it will be conventionalized. So you see that by merely making natural objects all in one tint, you can have a great variety of designs suitable for china, embroid-

Fig.89

ery, wall paper, and many other decorations. It is instructive to examine the panels, screens, or painted china of the Japanese. There is a freedom and crispness about their ornamental art, which is very attractive.

The method the Japanese frequently employ is to diminish the size of the fruit or flowers while increasing the size of the leaves, and vice-versa ; in this way they invent designs without losing the character of the object they copy, and it is really a very simple, yet effective method.

Suppose you try and see what you can make with it. The next time you have an opportunity, notice how the Oriental artists carry out this idea in their decorations, and it will help you in making your designs.

Fig. 90.

Fig.91

Burs.

The tenacious little burs found clinging to your dress after a country walk, when grouped together are not without beauty. Fig. 89 is formed of four of these burs placed at right angles making an ornament, and when the ornament is repeated at regular intervals as in Fig. 90, it forms a border design.

Seeds with downy or feathery tails are well adapted for decorations ; three grouped together (Fig. 91), is a design of itself,

which may also be re-duplicated (Fig. 92). The horse-chest-
nut or buckeye is decorative, and makes an odd design (Fig.
93). Also the seed-vessel of the
Velvet-leaf or Abutilon avicennæ
(Figs. 94 and 95).

The Water-Lily.

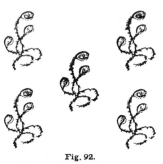

In the illustration of the water-
lily, the writer has conventionalized
it by curving the stem around the
flower and duplicating the same, always making the stem meet the next

Fig. 92.

lily, then inclosing the flowers in two straight lines, so forming

Fig. 93.

a water-lily border. Now, girls, you can realize how very simple it is to apply botany to art, and make for
yourselves new and original designs.

The knowledge of plants is not only interesting but useful in connection with art,
in selecting and determining appropriate designs for wood-carving, hammered brass, or

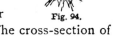

Fig. 94.

any kind of ornamentation or decoration. The cross-section of

Fig. 95.

some trees will furnish very good designs and the differently formed roots of plants and flowers will aid you in ornamental art.

So we find that Nature offers us exquisite designs, in many

Fig. 96.

shapes and forms, and we have only to stretch out our hand and take what we want.

"Beauty doth truly inhabit everywhere," for "it is mind alone that is beautiful, and in perceiving beauty, we only contemplate the shadow of our own affections."

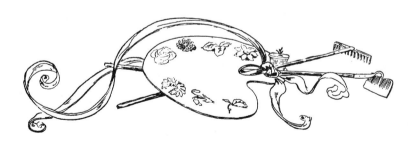

A Doorstep Party.

Quiet Games for Hot Weather

CHAPTER XIII.

DOOR-STEP PARTY AND QUIET GAMES FOR HOT WEATHER.

IN the State of Kentucky, in one of whose towns the writer's early childhood was spent, the summers are long, and frequently very hot spells occur when even in the early morning hours there is no refreshing coolness in the air. As the sun rises higher and higher in the heavens, its rays grow fiercer and fiercer, until by afternoon, the heat is so intense that few persons care to venture out of doors, unless compelled by business or necessity to do so.

At dusk, however, after the heat of the day is spent, and the air, although not cool, is a degree or two less hot, the population of the town makes itself visible. Ladies and children clad in the thinnest of white and light colored muslin gowns, emerge from the houses to sit upon piazza and door-step, and there welcome the husband, father, and brothers of the family upon their return from business; that business which is never neglected no matter what the thermometer may register. After tea the door-steps are once more taken possession of, and to enter the house again until ready to retire for the night, is not to be thought of. Friends and neighbors making social calls are received and entertained informally upon the door-steps, and sometimes when the party becomes too large for the steps to accommodate, chairs are placed upon the pavement immediately in front of the door, and no one feels, while occupying one of these seats, that the position is at all public or conspicuous.

Hatless and bonnetless as all of the ladies and children are, the warmth of the evenings making all head coverings and extra wraps unnecessary and uncomfortable, the streets present a gay and fête-like appearance seldom seen in our eastern towns.

At least this is as it was when, as one of the band of merry children, I played " Oats-peas-beans " and " Come Philanders," upon the sidewalk, and I do not think these customs have changed much since then.

Later, when I and my young friends had outgrown the " ring-around-arosy " games, we used to gather upon the door-step, and there chatter away about the day's doings, or whatever interested us at the time. When tired of talking, we would amuse ourselves by playing quiet games or telling stories. Sometimes the thoughtful mother of our young hostess would add to our enjoyment by serving some light refreshment, such as ice-cream or fruit. The greatest treat, and the one most appreciated, was when we were invited to partake of a great crisp frozen water-melon, whose blood-red core, sweet as sugar and cold as ice, quickly melted away between the rosy lips of the little guests. We were not always thus favored, however ; the refreshments were ever a pleasant surprise, but the pleasure of our evening was not marred by their absence.

The remembrance of what very pleasant times we used to have at these impromptu little parties, urges me to devote some pages of this book to the description of a door-step party, that by acting upon the suggestion, others may enjoy them even as did that group of little Kentucky girls.

Now is just the time for a door-step party ; now when the beauty of the evening lures us from the lighted parlor to the shadowy piazza whose coolness is so attractive after the long, hot summer day.   Here soft breezes fan our cheeks, and here, perhaps, the moonlight filtering through vine and trellis, is carpeting the floor with lacy shadows, and with its soft mysterious light is casting a glamour over all familiar things.

It is a modest little fête, this door-step party, a simple way of entertaining one's friends of a summer evening when the heat will not permit of the exertion of active games.   The delightful out-door surroundings give it a novel charm and make it entirely different from the frolics usually indulged in during the winter season.

Because the entertainment is not noisy it need not be the less enjoyable, and a party of bright, merry girls will derive plenty of amusement and fun from the quiet games of a door-step party.   The following will give an idea of what games are suitable for an occasion of this kind.

Five Minutes' Conversation

is not exactly a game, although there are rules which must be obeyed in order to make it interesting.

A programme with small pencil attached, like the one shown in Fig. 97, should be given to each guest upon her arrival. The engagements for five minutes' conversation are made by putting your name down on your friend's card opposite the time chosen for your conversation with her,

Five minutes only are allowed for one conversation.

Two or more consecutive engagements with one person are not allowable.   When engagements are made and programmes filled, the hostess, or anyone willing to be time-keeper, must ring a bell giving notice that the conversation is to begin.

At the end of five minutes the bell is to be rung again, when all talking must instantly cease, the exchange of positions be quickly made, and a new conversation be commenced.

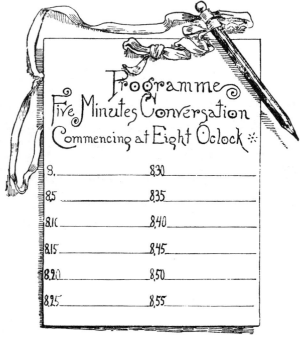

Programme
Five Minutes Conversation
Commencing at Eight O'clock

8.	8.30
8.5	8.35
8.10	8.40
8.15	8.45
8.20	8.50
8.25	8.55

Fig. 97

The time-keeper should be strictly attentive to her duties, for the bell must be rung regularly at the end of every five minutes.

The hour allotted to this new mode of conversation will pass very quickly, and cannot become in the least tiresome, as the time spent in talking to any one person is so very short.

Blind-man's Singing-school.

One of the party must be blindfolded to take the part of teacher. The class composed of the rest of the players should sit in a line facing her.

The teacher informs her scholars that they will begin the lesson by singing the scales. Then the head girl, or the one at the top of the line, sings ah! and the next, ah! a little higher or lower, and so it goes down the line ; each one in turn uttering ah! in any key or note she please ; in a high shrill voice, or the deepest tone a girlish throat is capable of. The teacher should listen attentively, and when she thinks she recognizes a voice she must command the class to stop while she makes some criticism on the manner in which the note is sung, at the same time calling the singer by name.

When one of the players is named correctly, she must be blindfolded and become teacher, while the former teacher takes her place in the class.

A general exchange of seats is made before the singing lesson recommences, that the voices may not be guessed by the direction from which they come. To give variety to this game the second teacher may direct the class to sing a song, selecting some well-known nursery rhyme ; then, beginning at the top of the line as before, each player must sing the word which comes to her to supply. It is the privilege of each teacher to direct the class to sing whatever she may choose, either song or exercise.

A Game of Noted Men,

is played in this way : The hostess begins the game by saying, I know a celebrated poet ; the first part of his name is very black, and the last is an elevation. Whoever gives the right name, which is Coleridge (coal, ridge), in her turn describes the name of some noted person. She may choose Shakespeare and say, I give the name of a noted author and poet ; the first part is something people are apt to do when they are cold, the last is a weapon of warfare.

There are quite a number of names which will do nicely for this game ; a few of them are—

Wordsworth—words, worth.   Shelley—shell, lea.
Cornwall—corn, wall.   Washington—washing, ton.
Howitt—how, it.   Fillmore—fill, more.
Milman—mill, man.   Longfellow—long, fellow.

When giving a name to be guessed, the profession of the man, whether poet, author, statesman, or soldier, must be given, but nothing else should be told about him.

What will You Take to the Picnic?

can be played very nicely while the party are enjoying some light refreshments.

The hostess alone should be in the secret, and these directions are addressed only to her.

Commence the game by announcing that you propose to give a picnic, that it depends upon what your guests will bring for lunch whether they will be allowed to attend, and that each one must furnish two articles of food. Then ask the person nearest you, What will you take to the picnic? If the name of neither of the articles she mentions commences with the initial letter of her Christian name or surname tell her she cannot go, and put the question to the next person, asking each in turn, What will you take to the picnic?

For example, we will suppose that the name of one of the party is Susan Davis, and she says she will take crackers and lemons, she cannot go, as neither of her names commence with

C or L ; but if she proproses to take salmon and doughnuts, she will be doubly welcome, since S and D are both her initials. Should she say sugar and cream, she could go for one of her names commences with S.

Continue to put the question to each player until all, or nearly all, have discovered why their proposed contribution to the lunch secures them a welcome, or debars them from attending the picnic.

Assumed Characters.

In this game some well-known novelist is selected—Dickens, for instance—and each player chooses one of his characters to personate, telling no one her choice. Then one of the players relates the life as though it were her own, and portrays with voice and gesture the character she has assumed. Of course no names must be mentioned.

The person who first guesses what character is being personated has the privilege of deciding who shall be the next to tell her story.

The game of Assumed Characters will prove to be very entertaining if each player does her part and makes her narrative as amusing and interesting as possible.

Shadow Verbs.

A white sheet is fastened tightly across a French window, or doorway opening upon the piazza, and a large lamp set behind it.

The company separates into two parties ; one enters the house, while the other remains seated upon the piazza facing the suspended sheet.

The outside party chooses a verb which the others are to guess and perform. When their decision is made they call the leader of the inside party and say, '' The verb we have chosen rhymes with rake," or whatever it may rhyme with. The leader then joins her followers and consults with them what the first guess shall be. It is best to take the verbs which rhyme with the noun given in alphabetical order. Bake would come first for rake, and if it is decided that they shall act this, several of the party step before the lamp, which casts their shadows on the sheet and, without speaking, go through the motions of making and baking bread. If the guess is right (that is if to bake was the verb chosen) the spectators clap their hands; if wrong, they cry, No, no.

When they hear the no, no, the actors retire and arrange what to do next. Make, quake, take, wake are all acted in turn, until the clap of approval announces that they have been successful in guessing the verb. Then the actors take the seats vacated by the spectators, who in their turn enter the house to become shadows and act the verbs chosen by the other party, and the game goes on as before. A little ingenuity on the part of the players in producing funny and absurd shadows makes the whole thing very laughable and causes great amusement.

There are an unlimited number of games that may be played, but the object of this chapter is not so much to describe the games as it is to illustrate those that are appropriate to the quiet and delightful entertainment known as a door-step party.

A Door-Step Party.

CHAPTER XIV.

HOW TO MAKE A HAMMOCK.

NDERNEATH the spreading branches of the cool, shady tree swings our hammock.

Through the intertwining boughs the golden sunlight is sifted in bright little dashes on the leafy foliage below. Lying ensconced in its lacy meshes idly listening to the hum of the busy bumble-bees at work among the red clover, or gazing up through the leafy canopy to the blue heavens where now and then fleecy white clouds float softly past, or watching a flight of birds skim o'er the distant horizon, who would not be lulled by the harmony of the summer day ! A delightful languor steals over us and we unconsciously drift into the land of dreams where perfect rest is found. We awaken refreshed, to again gently swing back and forth and vaguely wonder who could have first thought of this most delightful invention. It is said that we owe the luxury to the Athenian, General Alcibiades, who, in 415 B.C. first made the swinging bed. The word hammock is taken from hamacas or hamac, an Indian word which Columbus relates as being used by the Indians to signify a hanging bed composed of netting. What these uncivilized red men made with their rude implements, we ought to be able with our modern facilities to accomplish very easily and quickly.

Home-made Comforts.

It is not difficult to make a hammock ; anyone can soon knit one that is strong and comfortable, and it should not cost more

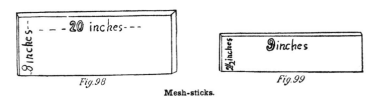

Fig.98   Fig.99

Mesh-sticks.

than fifty cents. The materials required will be one hammock-needle about nine inches long (this can be whittled out of hickory or ash, or purchased for ten cents) ; two iron rings two and one-half inches in diameter, which will cost about five cents each ; two mesh-sticks or fids, one twenty inches long and eight inches wide bevelled on both

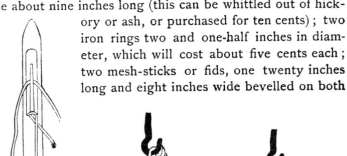

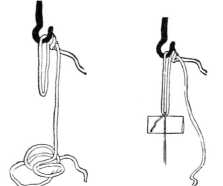

Fig. 100.—Hammock Needle.   Fig. 101.—The Loop.   Fig. 102.—Small Fid and Loop.

edges (Fig. 98) : the other nine inches long and two and one-half inches wide, bevelled on the long edge (Fig. 99); these you can easily make yourself from any kind of wood.

One pound of Macremé cord number twenty-four, or hammock twine of the same number, which can be had for less than

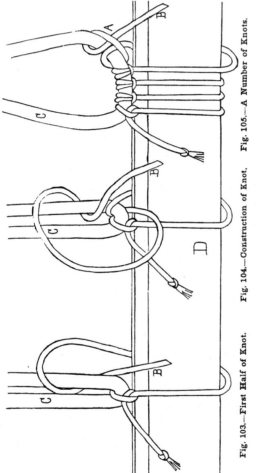

Fig. 105.—A Number of Knots.

Fig. 104.—Construction of Knot.

Fig. 103.—First Half of Knot.

thirty cents; colored cord comes five cents extra.

Wind the cord in balls, as it is then more convenient to handle, and begin making your hammock. First, thread the needle by taking it in the left hand and using the thumb to hold the end of the cord in place, while looping it over the tongue (Fig. 100); pass the cord down under the needle to the opposite side and catch it over the tongue; repeat this until the needle is full.

Next, make a loop of a piece of cord two yards long and fasten this to any suitable place (Fig. 101)—a door-knob will do very well; then tie the cord on your needle three inches from the end to this loop. Place the small fid under the cord, the bevelled edge close to the loop (Fig. 102). With your thumb on the cord to hold it in place while you pass the needle around the fid, and with its point toward you, pass it through the loop from the top, bringing it over the fid, so forming the first half of the knot (Fig. 103). Pull this taut, holding it in place with your thumb while throwing the cord over your hand, which forms the loop as in (Fig. 104). Then pass the needle from under through the loops, drawing it tight to fasten the knot. Hold it in place with your thumb, and repeat the operation for the next knot. Fig. 105 shows a number of these knots finished. A is a loosened knot, making plain its construction. B, in Figs. 103, 104, and 105, is the cord running to the needle, and D is the fid.

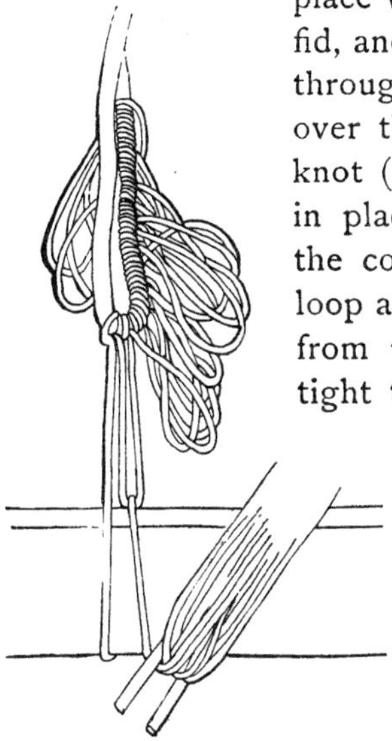

Fig. 106.—Meshes.

When thirty meshes are finished shove them off the fid (Fig. 106), as this number will make the hammock sufficiently wide.

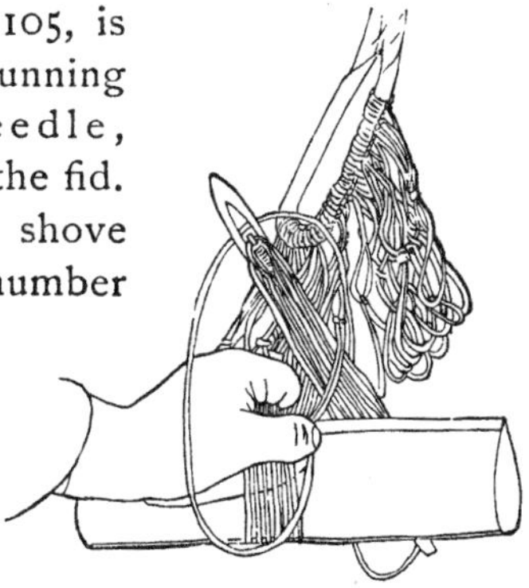

Commence the next row by again placing the fid under the cord, and take up the first mesh, drawing it close to the fid; hold it in place with your thumb while

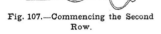

Fig. 107.—Commencing the Second Row.

throwing the cord over your hand; pass the needle on the left hand-side of the mesh from under through the loop thrown over your hand (Fig. 107); pull this tight and you will have

tied the common knitting-knot ; proceed in like manner with
all the loops in rotation until the row is finished.　When it is

Fig. 108.—Fisherman's Knot.

necessary to thread or fill your needle,
tie the ends of the cord with the fisherman's knot shown in Fig. 108, which
cannot slip when properly tightened.
Wrap each end of the cord from the knot
securely to the main cord with strong
thread to give a neat appearance
to the hammock.

Continue knitting until thirty
rows are finished.

Then use the large fid, knitting one row on the short side
first, next one on the long side.
This accomplished, knit the
meshes to the ring by passing
the needle through it from the
top, knitting them to the ring in
rotation as if they were on the
mesh-stick or fid (Fig. 109). When
finished tie the string securely to
the ring, and one end of your
hammock is finished.

Cut the loop on which the
first row was knitted, and
draw it through the knots.
Tie the end of the cord on
your needle to the same
piece used in fastening

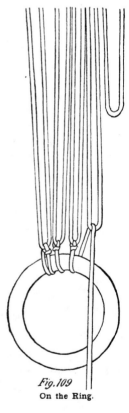

Fig.109
On the Ring.

Fig 110

the end of the first needleful to the loop (Fig. 110), and knit
the long meshes to the other ring as described.　This completed, the hammock is finished.

To swing it, secure two pieces of strong rope and fasten them firmly to the iron rings, the length of the rope depending upon the space between the two points from which you wish it to hang. These should be if possible twelve or fifteen feet apart and at least ten feet high, to give your hammock sufficient room to swing freely.

This suspended bed will furnish a welcome retreat when the weather is too warm to admit of games, walks, or other amusements. Then, with some favorite book, or if even reading is too much of an exertion, simply to lie indolently in the hammock is a comfort, so restful and quiet that the time quickly passes, and we are made better and brighter for our short, passive repose.

Very decorative nets, and useful ones of many kinds, including fish-nets and minnow-seines, are made with the same stitch as that used in the hammock. The size of the mesh is regulated by the circumference of the fid, and the twine used is fine or coarse, according to the style of net desired.

Barrel Hammock.

When in the Catskills last summer the writer saw for the first time a hammock made of a barrel. It was painted red and looked very cheery and inviting hanging under the green boughs; the two colors, being complementary, harmonized beautifully.

This hammock was made of a piece of strong rope twenty feet long threaded in and out of barrel staves, and was substantial and durable. The construction of such a hammock is very simple. Remove the top and bottom hoops and nails from a firm, clean barrel. Then before taking off the remaining hoops draw a pencil-line around both ends of the barrel, being careful to have the marking three inches from and parallel

THE WAY IT IS MADE.

to the edges ; this is for a guide when making the two holes in each end of all the staves. Bore the holes with a five-eighth of an inch augur or a red-hot poker, using the pencil-line as a centre ; leave an equal margin on both sides of the staves, and at the same time enough space in the centre to preclude all danger of breakage.

Fasten the staves to-gether by threading the rope through the hole from the out side of the first stave, then across the inside of the stave down through the other hole (see illustration). Continue threading until one side is finished, then in like manner thread the other side. Knock off the remaining hoops and the staves will appear as shown at bottom of illustration. Tie the two ends of the rope together and fasten loops of rope on both ends ; these should be of sufficient length to conveniently swing the hammock. When threading the staves let the rope be loose enough to leave a space of an inch or so between each stave when the barrel is spread out in the form of a hammock.

In this way you can have a serviceable hammock, the cost of which will be about twenty-five cents and a little labor.

Grandmamma's Dolls.

CHAPTER XV.

CORN-HUSK AND FLOWER DOLLS.

NO such beautiful dolls as delight the hearts of the children of to-day, ever peeped forth from the Christmas-stockings of our grandmothers or great-grandmothers when they were little girls. In those times there were not, as there are now, thousands of people doing nothing but making toys for the entertainment and pleasure of the little ones, and the motherly little hearts were fain to content themselves with lavishing unlimited affection and care upon a rag, wooden, or corn-husk baby, made and dressed at home. Since then almost every child tired of, and surfeited with handsome and expensive toys, has been glad at times to get grandma to make for her a real old-fashioned dollie which might be hugged in rapturous moments of affection without fear of dislocating some of its numerous joints, or putting out of order its speaking or crying apparatus;

and might in times of forgetfulness be dropped on the floor and suffer no injury thereby. Such a doll is just the kind to adopt for the summer. The fine French doll with its delicate wax or china face, silky hair, and dainty toilets, is more suited to the elegances of the parlor than to the wear and tear of out-door life, and everyone knows that summer holidays spent in the country are far too precious to be wasted taking care of anyone's complexion, let alone a doll's ; so it is best to leave the city doll in her city home, safe out of harm's way, and manufacture, from materials to be found in the country, one more suited to country surroundings.

Fig. 111
Head Commenced.

Corn - husks, corn - cobs, and ordinary garden flowers can be made into dolls which, although not quite so pretty nor so shapely as those produced from more costly material, yet possess a charm of their own which the children are not slow to perceive.

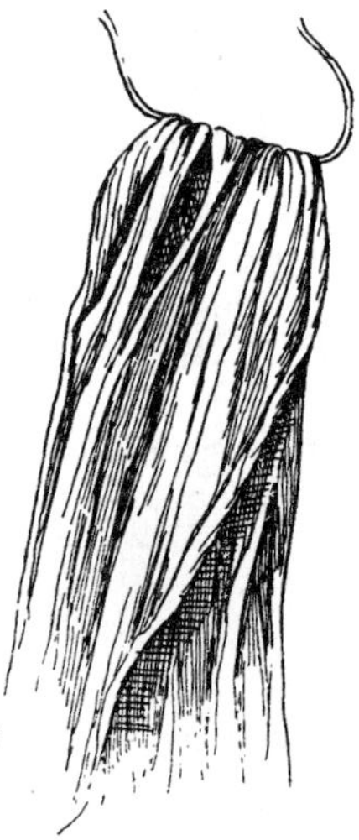

Little Indian girls, to whom store babies are unknown, make the most complete and durable corn-husk dolls, and the following directions tell just how to construct them :

Provide yourself with the husks of several large ears of corn, and from among them select the soft white ones which grow closest to the ear. Place the stiff ends of

Fig. 112
The Corn Husk.

two husks together, fold a long, soft husk in a lengthwise strip, and wind it around the ends so placed as in Fig. 111. Select the softest and widest husk you can find, fold it across the centre and place a piece of strong thread through it (as in Fig. 112), draw it in, tie it securely (Fig. 113), place it entirely over the husks you have wound, then bring it down smoothly and tie with thread underneath (Fig. 114); this will form the head and neck. To make the arms,

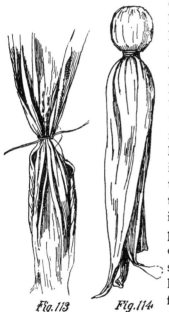

divide the husks below the neck in two equal parts, fold together two or more husks and insert them in the division (Fig. 115). Hold the arms in

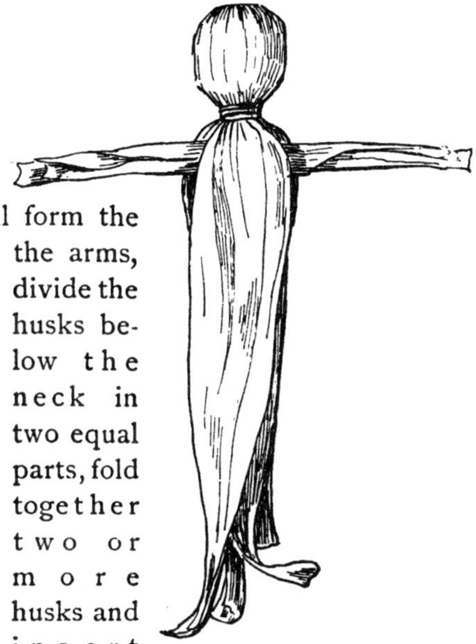

Fig. 115
Head and Arms.

Fig. 113
Corn-husk Tied.

Fig. 114
Head Finished.

place with one hand, while with the other you fold alternately over each shoulder several layers of husks, allowing them to extend down the front and back. When the little form seems plump enough, use your best husks for the topmost layers and wrap the waist with strong thread, tying it securely (Fig. 116). Next divide the husks below the waist and make

the legs by neatly wrapping each portion with thread, trimming them off evenly at the feet.   Finally, twist the arms
once or twice, tie, and trim them off at the hands.   The features
can be drawn on the face with pen and ink, or may be formed
of small thorns from the rose-bush.   Fig. 117 shows the doll
complete, minus its costume, which may be of almost any style
or material, from the pretty robe of a civilized lady to the more

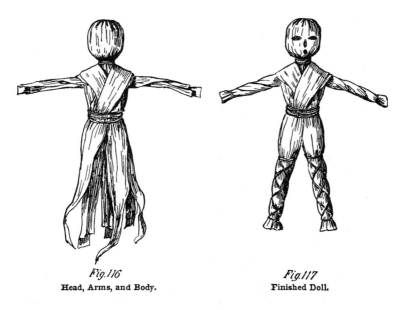

Fig. 116
Head, Arms, and Body.

Fig. 117
Finished Doll.

scanty garments of its originator, the Indian.   The doll is represented in full Indian costume in Fig. 118.   The war-paint and
tomahawk are not necessary here, as he is smoking a pipe of
peace.   His apparel is composed of one garment, which is cut
from a broad, soft corn-husk, after the pattern given in Fig. 119.
A narrow strip of husk tied about his waist forms the belt.

His head-dress is made of small chicken feathers stuck at

regular intervals into a strip of husk. The corn-silk hair is placed on his head, and on top of that one end of the head-dress is fastened with a thorn.

A small twig is used for the stem of his pipe, and two rose-bush thorns form the bowl. Instead of using a thorn for his

Fig.118
A Real Indian Doll.

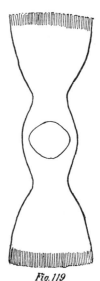

Fig.119
The Indian's Dress.

mouth, a round hole is punched in the face and the stem of the pipe inserted.

Mary Jane.

Here is another way of making a doll which is very easy and simple. First find a young ear of corn, one on which the silk has not turned brown ; then with a crab-apple for a head and a leaf of the corn to dress her with, you have your material.

Cut off squarely that end of the ear where the husks are puck-
ered, to join the stalk, and carefully take the silk from the other
end, disturbing as little as possible the closely wrapped husks.

Roll part of the leaf (as indicated in Fig. 120) for the arms,
then with a small twig fasten the head to the arms ; stick the

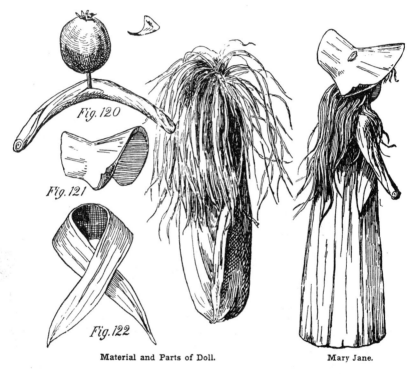

Fig. 120

Fig. 121

Fig. 122

Material and Parts of Doll.   Mary Jane.

other end of the twig into the small end of the corn-cob, and
the doll is ready for dressing.   Her bonnet is made of the leaf
just where it joins the stalk (Fig. 121), and is fastened to her
head with a thorn.   Before adjusting the bonnet, however, the
silk must be placed on the head to form the hair.

Make the scarf of part of the leaf (Fig. 122), fold it around the shoulders, and secure it with thorns.

The features also are made of thorns.

When her toilet is complete, you can but acknowledge that this rosy-cheeked little maid, peeping from beneath her poke-bonnet, is very cunning indeed.

Flower Dolls.

The flower lady with the baby is made of a yellow gourd flower; the small gourd attached, which has just begun to

form, serves for her head; a green gourd leaf is used for her shawl, and her bonnet is made of a smaller leaf folded to fit her head. The baby is a white gourd bud, with a cap made of a

leaf. A small twig stuck through part of the lady's shawl,
through the baby, and into the lady doll, holds the child in
place and makes it appear as though clasped in the mother's
arms.

The features of both dolls are scratched on with a pin and
then inked. To make the lady stand erect, a small twig is stuck
into the heart of the flower, and the other end into the top of a
small paste-board-box lid.

The other flower doll is made of the common garden flowers.
The underskirt is a petunia ; a Canterbury-bell forms the over-
skirt and waist; small twigs, or broom-straws stuck through
buds of the phlox, are the arms, and the head is a daisy with
the petals cut off to look like a bonnet.   The features are made
with pen and ink on the yellow centre. A reversed daisy forms
the parasol.

If the flowers named are not at hand, those of a similar
shape will answer just as well.

Gaily dressed little ladies can be made of the brilliantly
tinted hollyhocks, and many other flowers can also be transformed into these pretty though perishable dolls.

CHAPTER XVI.

HOW TO MAKE A FAN.

" That graceful toy whose
moving play
With gentle gales relieves
the sultry day."

FAN is only a pretty trifle,
yet it has been made rather
an important one. To man-
age a fan gracefully was some
time ago considered very essential by fair dames of society, and in the dainty hand
of many a famous beauty it
has played a conspicuous
part. Queen Elizabeth regarded it with so much favor that
she was called the " Patron of Fans," and she made a rule that
no present save a fan should be accepted by English queens
from their subjects.

Although held in such high esteem, it is only since the in-
flux of any and every thing Japanese that we have had fans in
such profusion, and have discovered how effective they are
when used for decorative purposes.

A brilliantly tinted fan is of equal value in giving just the
right touch of color to a costume or the decorations of a room,
and this chapter will show how the girls can make the fans

themselves, and have for use or for the adornment of their rooms those of various shapes, sizes, and colors. The first fan

Butterfly Fan.

represented here is made in the form of a butterfly. The principal articles necessary for its manufacture are a strip of smooth, brown wrapping-paper, stiff enough to keep its folds, and two sticks for handles. The ribbon which, in the illustration, ties the handles together looks pretty, but is not indispensable ; an elastic band, or one made of narrow ribbon, slipped over the sticks will do as well.

The paper must be twenty-eight inches long and five and one-half inches wide. In order to fold it evenly it should be ruled across with lines one-half inch apart, as shown in diagram of butterfly (page 179). When the paper is prepared the pattern can be copied from the diagram, which is half of the butterfly. By counting the lines and using them as guides for obtaining the proportions, an exact reproduction of

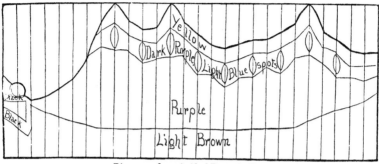

Diagram of one-half of Butterfly Fan.

this pattern can be made. The outlines being drawn, the paper must be plaited, one fold on top of another, until twenty-seven plaits have been laid. Smoothing out the paper again, the butterfly should be painted with water-colors in flat, even tints.

The lower part of diagram is the body of the insect and is of a light-brown color, also the space just below the head, which is surrounded by a strip of black.

The head and eyes are black, the eyes having a half-circle of white to separate them from the head. The main part of the wings

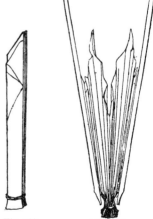

Fig. 123.   Fig. 125.
Folded Fans.

Fig 724
Handle.

are a brownish purple, next to which comes a border of very
dark purple with light-blue spots. The outer border is light
yellow. When the paint is quite dry the extra paper at the
top of the butterfly is to be cut away. Again the fan must be
plaited in the
folds already
formed, and
the plaits
fastened to-
gether at one
end with a
strong needle
and thread, as
shown in dia-
gram (Fig. 123).
Fig. 124 shows
the shape of the
handles, two of
which are re-
quired; they
should be about
nine inches
long, one-third
of an inch wide,

The Mikado Fan.

and one-eighth of an inch thick. A handle must
be glued to the last fold at each end of the fan (see
Fig. 125). The fan should be kept closed until the
glue is dry, when it may be opened and used at pleasure.

Our next sketch is that of the Mikado fan, and represents a
Japanese lady who, with her fan held aloft, is making a bowing salutation.

This fan is made of the same paper as that used for the butterfly, and is cut the same width; there are, however, twenty-

nine plaits instead of twenty-seven, as in the other. The diagram gives the pattern in two parts, and the colors it is to be painted ; the face and hands should be of a flesh-tint and the features done with black in outline. The directions for putting together the butterfly apply as well to the Mikado fan.

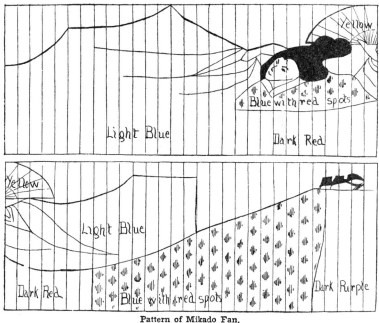

Pattern of Mikado Fan.

The third illustration shows a fan made in the shape of a daisy. Diagram on page 183 shows a section of the pattern.

White paper should be used, and it must be laid in thirty-four plaits, which will give the flower fifteen whole and two half petals, the half petals being at each end.

The tinted part of pattern indicates where it is painted yellow to form the centre of the daisy.

For a plain round fan no pattern is needed. It is made simply of a strip of paper, of the width used for the other fans, and has about thirty plaits. When fans of this kind are made of colored paper in solid tints they are very pretty. Pieces of bright, figured wall-paper left from papering a room can be utilized, and quite effective fans be made of them to use for decoration.

Daisy Fan.

Another style of fan is represented in our last illustration. It is made of twenty slats of cardboard cut after pattern Fig. 126. These slats are joined together at the top and centre with narrow ribbon passed through the slits cut for it, as shown in Fig. 127. Over the ribbon where it passes through the top slits, on the wrong side of the fan, square pieces of paper are pasted, which hold the ribbon down securely at these points. The paper is pasted only at each end of the ribbon in the middle row. It is best to leave one end of this ribbon loose until the fan is joined at the bottom; then opening the fan, and drawing the ribbon until it fits the fan smoothly, it can be cut the right length and the loose end fastened down. A ribbon is also used to hold the slats together at the bottom; a bow at each side keeps them in place (see Fig. 128). When a large fan for decoration is desired, the slats should be about eighteen inches

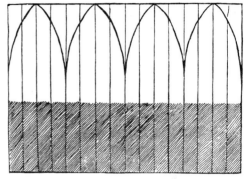

long, two and a half inches wide at the top, and one and a half inch wide at the bottom. The fan may be larger still, in which case it can be used as a screen to set before an empty fire-place. For this purpose the slats have to be two feet

Pattern for Daisy Fan.

long, four inches wide at the top, and two and a half inches wide at the bottom.

The proportions of the slats for a small hand-fan are eight

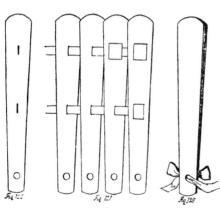

Construction of Cardboard Fan.

and a half inches long, one and a half inch wide at the top, and one inch wide at the bottom. The large fans should be made of heavier cardboard or pasteboard than that used for smaller ones.

Colored cardboard, which can be bought at almost any stationer's, is the best to use, but the slats of ordinary white cardboard may be covered with colored paper if more convenient.

These fans may be varied to suit the taste of the girls who make them. Instead of a solid color, one can be made with

alternate slats of red and white, blue and yellow, or any other colors that harmonize. Another may show all the tints of the rainbow, and for use on the Fourth of July one might display the red, white, and blue.

Some will look especially handsome if prettily painted. A dark-red fan with a branch of dogwood-blossoms painted across it makes a charming wall dec-

Cardboard Fan.

oration, as does also one of light blue with pine-branch and cone painted in brown or black.

A gilt fan lightens up a dusky corner beautifully; it can be curved around to fit the place, and catching and reflecting the light at all angles, as it does, it is quite effective.

CHAPTER XVII.

ALL-HALLOW-EVE.

R A D I A N T and beautiful October, whose changing color heralds the approach of winter, gives us our first autumn holiday, if Halloween can now be called a holiday.

Before the Christian era, in the days of the ancient Celts and their priests, the Druids, the eve of the first of November was the time for one of the three principal festivals of the year. The first of May was celebrated for the sowing; the solstice on the twenty-first of June for the ripening, and the eve of the first of November for the harvesting. At each of these festivals great fires were built on the hill-tops in honor of the sun, which the people worshipped. When Christianity took the place of the heathen religion, the Church, instead of forbidding the celebration of these days, gave them different meanings, and in this way the ancient harvest-festival of the Celts became All-Hallow-Eve, or the eve of All-Saints-Day, the first day of November having been dedicated to all of the saints.

For a long while most of the old customs of these holidays were retained; then, although new ceremonies were gradually introduced, Hallow-Eve remained the night of the year for wild, mysterious, and superstitious rites. Fairies and all supernatural beings were believed to be abroad at this time, and to exercise more than their usual power over earthly mortals. Because the fairy folk were believed to be so near us on Hallow-

Kaling.

een, it was considered the best evening of the season for the practice of magic, and the customs observed on this night became mostly those of divination, by the aid of which it was thought the future might be read.

Before proceeding further with this subject we desire our readers to appreciate and fully understand that we are far from wishing to inculcate any superstitious belief in the power of charms to forecast future events; that we regard all fortune-telling as nonsense, pure and simple, and only insert it here, as we would any other game, for the sake of the amusement it affords. Although, to make our descriptions more intelligible, we announce the results of charms as facts, we would not have it understood that they are to be taken as such.

Nowadays, so practical has the world become, no fairy, witch, or geni could we conjure up, were we to practice all the charms and spells ever known to soothsayer or seer. Our busy, common-sense age allows no fairies to interfere with its concerns, and these creatures, who existed only in the belief of the people, must needs vanish, to return no more, when that belief is gone.

A few fortune-telling games are all that now remain of the weird ceremonies that once constituted the rites of Halloween, and the spirit of this old heathen holiday is once more changed, for it is now considered only an occasion for fun and frolic.

It was the custom for quite a number of years of some friends of the writer to give a Halloween party on each recurring Halloween ; and merrier, jollier parties than those were, it would not be easy to devise. The home which opened wide its hospitable doors to the favored few on this night is a country-house, large and spacious ; there is a basement under the whole lower floor, which is divided into kitchen, laundry, and various store-rooms intersected with passages, and this basement, deserted by the servants, was given up to the use of the Halloween revellers. The rooms and passage-ways were decorated with and lighted by Chinese lanterns, which produced a subdued glow in their immediate vicinity, but left mysterious shadows in nooks and corners.

Putting aside conventionality and dignity as we laid aside our wraps, ready for any fun or mischief that might be on hand, we proceeded down-stairs and into the kitchen, where a large pot of candy was found bubbling over the fire. This candy, poured into plates half-full of nuts, was eaten at intervals during the evening, and served to keep up the spirits of those who were inclined to be cast down by the less pleasing of Fortune's decrees. With plenty of room and no fear of breaking or destroying anything, which is apt to put a check upon frolics in the parlor, the company could give full vent to their high spirits. Now in this room, now in that, again flitting through the dim passages and around dark corners, each person seemed to be everywhere at once, and although the party was limited to about twenty-five, there appeared to be at least twice that number present. Bursts of merry laughter and little screams of pretended terror would announce, now and then, that some charm was being gone through with and someone's fortune being told. All sorts of games were played, and the variety of our entertainment made the evening pass very quickly. All too soon the hands of the kitchen clock warned the guests that to reach home at a seasonable hour they must put an end to their Halloween festivities. A number of the following methods of telling fortunes were tried at these parties, one might say with success, for we certainly succeeded in accomplishing our main object, which was, to have a good time. By

Melted Lead

we used to ascertain what the occupation of one's future husband would be. The fortune is told in this way : Each girl, in

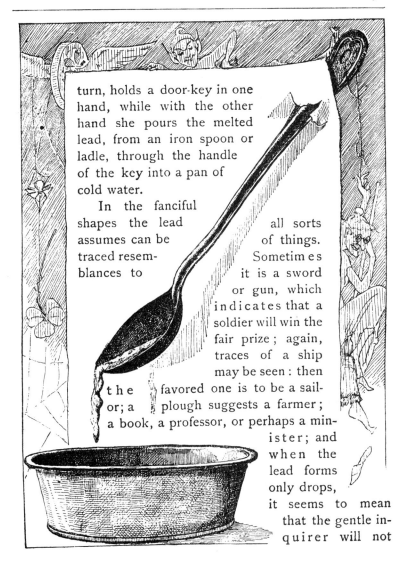

turn, holds a door-key in one hand, while with the other hand she pours the melted lead, from an iron spoon or ladle, through the handle of the key into a pan of cold water.

In the fanciful shapes the lead assumes can be traced resemblances to all sorts of things. Sometimes it is a sword or gun, which indicates that a soldier will win the fair prize; again, traces of a ship may be seen: then the favored one is to be a sailor; a plough suggests a farmer; a book, a professor, or perhaps a minister; and when the lead forms only drops, it seems to mean that the gentle inquirer will not marry, or if she does, her husband will be of no profession.

Nutshell Boats

foretell in a general way what their owner's future life will be. They should be prepared beforehand in this manner : Split an

English walnut directly in half, remove the kernel, and clear away any of the partitions which may remain in the shell; then place a short piece of heavy cotton string in the shell and pour around it melted beeswax. Mould the wax into a cone shape around the string,

Fig.130

as shown in Fig. 129, allowing the end to come out at the top. Fig. 130 shows what it is like when finished.

The tapers first being lighted, several of these little craft are launched at the same time, by their respective owners, upon the sea of life, or, in other words, in a tub of water.

When a light burns steadily until the wax is all melted, and the frail bark safely rides the waves (which are occasioned by stirring the water with a stick, or shaking the tub from side to side), a happy life is predicted, and a long one.

When two boats come in contact, it means that their owners will meet and have mutual interests some time during their lives.

If one boat crosses another's path, it denotes that their owners will do the same.

If two boats come together and continue to sail about side by side, their owners will in some way pass much of their lives together.

When a boat clings closely to the sides of the tub, refusing to sail out into the centre, it shows that its owner will be a stay at-home.

Touching often at the side of the tub is indicative of short voyages ; and extended travel is predicted when a boat seldom touches the tub.

It depends a good deal upon the fancy and imagination of those testing their fate how the antics of the little fleet are interpreted, and the meanings given to the movements of the boats create no end of fun.

"Three Luggies." *

" In order, on the clean hearth-stane,
The luggies three are ranged,
And ev'ry time great care is ta'en
To see them duly changed."

The three bowls, or dishes, one containing clear water, one milky, and the other nothing at all, are placed in a row on the hearth-stone or table, and the girl wishing to try her fortune is blindfolded and led up to where the dishes stand. She is then told to put her left hand into one of the bowls. If she dips her fingers in the clear water, she will marry a bachelor ; if in the milky water, a widower ; and if into the empty bowl, it is a sure sign that she will live in single blessedness all her days.

This ceremony must be gone through with three times, and the hand be dipped twice in the same bowl, in order to make the prediction of any value.

Roasting Nuts

is the charm by which the friendship of anyone may be tested. The applicant for knowledge on this point names two nuts, one for her friend and the other for herself, and then places them side by side upon the grate, or a shovel held over the fire. If they burn quietly, it is prophetic of a long and happy friend-

* Dishes.

ship kept up by both parties ; but if in roasting they burst with a loud report and fly apart, they are decidedly uncongenial, and should not seek much intercourse. The movements of the nuts while heating are closely watched, for the tempers of the persons for whom they are named is said to be thus revealed.

Kaling

is a mode of telling one's fortune not as well known, perhaps, as the foregoing methods. The ceremony is carried out in the following manner : Two girls are blindfolded and started off on the path to the kitchen-garden and cabbage-patch, where each pulls up the first stalk she finds. They then return at once to the house, where the bandages are removed and the mysterious stalks examined.

According to the state of the stalk, so will be the gatherer's fate. If it is straight or crooked, large or small, so will the future husband be ; if it has a pleasant taste, or the reverse, the character of the person will correspond, and the quantity of earth clinging to the roots denotes whether their riches will be little or great.

When there are no cabbages at hand, almost any other garden vegetable will answer ; and if there be objections to going out-of-doors, vegetables of various kinds, such as turnips, beets, and parsnips, may be placed on a table, and the persons blind-folded can choose from them. No doubt the charm will work as well with the plants upon a table as when they are pulled from a kitchen-garden.

The Magic Mirror,

which is simply a hand-glass on ordinary occasions, and gains its mysterious power only on Halloween, divulges, under certain conditions, the delightful secret of how many bits of good-fortune will fall to cne's share during the ensuing year. The conditions are that the person wishing to know how bright her prospects are shall go to an open window or door from which the moon is visible, and, standing with her face in-doors, hold her mirror so that the moon will be reflected in it. The number of moons she sees there betokens the number of times something pleasant will happen to her before the advent of another Halloween.

Three Tin Cups

partially filled with water are balanced on the small ends of three funnels, which are placed in a row on the floor, about two feet apart. Over these cups, one after another, each member of the party must leap in turn. Whoever succeeds in leaping over all three cups without knocking any of them off will make an early marriage. The person who knocks over one will marry when not so young. The marriage of the one who tips over two cups will be deferred until late in life, and she who leaps none of them safely will not be married at all.

To guard against wet feet very little water should be put in the cups—only enough to make the players careful about tipping them over.

The Ring Cake

is always an object of interest at Halloween parties. The cake itself is made like the ordinary kind, but before it is baked a plain gold ring is hidden in the dough, not to be taken out until the cake is cut and it falls to the share of the fortunate person in whose slice it happens to be found. The ring is sometimes put in a flour-cake, which is simply flour packed into a cake-mould so firmly that when it is turned out it retains the shape of the mould and can be sliced off with a knife. Each member of the party cuts her or his own section of flour, and whoever secures the ring, it is confidently stated, will be the first of the group to marry.

Some Halloween games apparently have no particular meaning attached to them, but seem to be devised for the purpose of creating as much fun as possible.

Bobbing for Apples

is, perhaps, familiar to most of our readers, but we give a description of it here for the benefit of the few who may not know the game so well.

In a large tub full of fresh, cold water several apples are placed, and it is the object of the participators to take them out of the water with their teeth.

As the rosy-cheeked, tempting fruit bobs about within easy reach, it looks simple enough to secure a prize ; but the apples are so round and slippery, so aggravatingly illusive, that, unless you thrust your head and neck beneath the cold water, regardless of consequences, and drive an apple to the bottom, the feat cannot be accomplished. The girls can seldom be induced to try their luck in this game, but usually content themselves with looking on, immensely enjoying the frantic endeavors of the boys to succeed at any cost.

The Apple and Candle Game

is another favorite sport for Halloween, and is played as follows : From the ceiling is suspended a stout cord, the lower end of which is securely tied to the centre of a stick about a foot and a half long. On one end of the stick is fastened an apple, on the other a lighted candle. The string is set in motion, swinging back and forth like a pendulum, and the contestants for the prize stand ready, each in turn, to make a grab for the apple, which must be caught in the teeth before it can be won. Frequently the candle is caught instead of the apple, which mishap sends the spectators off into shouts of merriment ; but although funny, it is at the same time a little dangerous to catch a lighted candle in one's teeth, and we would suggest that a bag made of cheese-cloth, or like thin material, be filled with flour and tied to the stick in place of the candle. When the person essaying to snatch the fruit is struck in the face with the bag, and is covered with flour instead of the glory anticipated, as much mirth will result as can possibly arise when the old and dangerous practice of using a candle is clung to.

The Ghostly Fire

should not be lit unless all of the party have strong nerves, for the light it produces is rather unearthly, and may affect some members unpleasantly. We, at our Halloween parties, never omitted this rite, however, its very weirdness proving its strongest attraction. Salt and alcohol were put in a dish, with a few raisins, and set on fire. As soon as the flame leaped up we clasped hands and gayly danced around the table, upon which burned our mystic fire. The laughing eyes and lips looked in strange contrast to the pale faces of their owners, from which the greenish light had taken every vestige of color. The dance was not prolonged, for it was our duty, before the fire was spent, to snatch from the flames the raisins we had put in the dish. This can be done, if one is careful, without as much as scorching the fingers, and I never knew of anyone burning themselves while making the attempt.

Trying for a Raisin

is a very laughable performance. The raisin, which must be a good-sized one, is strung on and pushed exactly to the middle of a soft cotton string about one yard long. Two aspirants for the prize then take each an end of the string, which they put in their mouths and commence to chew, taking it up as fast as they can—the raisin falling to the share of the person who succeeds in reaching it first.

A Lighted Candle

is again used in a game which is exceedingly amusing. The candle is placed upon a table in full view of everyone ; then one of the players is blindfolded, turned around several times, and set free to seek for the candle and blow out the light, if possible.

To see girls, with their hands clasped behind them, going crazily about the room, blowing at anything and everything, is very ludicrous. They seldom find the candle, and even when the table is reached it is difficult to blow in such a direction as to extinguish the flame.

The Fairy's Gifts

are suggested as a new and original ending of a Halloween frolic.

The Fairy Godmother, in Mother Hubbard costume, carries a large basket under her cloak or shawl. She enters the room and announces that she has a certain number of gifts which she proposes to distribute among the company. After cautioning all that the contents must be kept secret, she passes to each person a folded paper. On one is written "*Wealth*," on another "*Honor*," on the third "*Fame*," etc., and some of the papers are left blank.

Those whose papers contain the names of gifts are then blindfolded, preparatory to receiving their behests.

The first is led up and made to kneel before the Fairy Godmother, to whom she repeats these words :

> Most gracious Fairy, the gift you give
> I shall treasure and keep as long as I live.

Then the paper containing the name of the gift is handed the Fairy, who reads it aloud very solemnly : " *Wealth*"—and, turning to her basket, she takes from it a new dust-pan, to which is attached a ribbon-loop, at the same time reciting these lines :

Your choice is bad when you intrust
Your happiness where moth and rust,
In time, turn all your wealth to dust.

From a paper-bag the Fairy pours a small amount of dust over the kneeling girl, and hangs the dust-pan around her neck.

The next person who has drawn a prize is then brought forward and the performance is repeated, only altering the Fairy's speech. For "*Honor*," she will say:

Your honor crowds shall loud declare,
But in your heart, no crowd is there,
You'll find, like *Falstaff*, " honor's air."

The present here is a pair of bellows, from which the Fairy blows a blast on the bowed head before her as she utters the word *air*. The bellows, like the dust-pan, are hung by a ribbon around the recipient's neck.

For "*Fame*," the Fairy gives a wreath of roses, and says, as she adjusts the crown:

When Fame doth weave a laurel-wreath,
He weaves this subtle charm beneath ;
" For every evil thought that's born
The laurel grows a prickly thorn ;
But where pure thought and love reposes,
The laurel-wreath's a wreath of roses."

Buckeye Portière.

CHAPTER XVIII.

NATURE'S FALL DECORA-TIONS, AND HOW TO USE THEM.

THESE beautiful decorations are free to all who care to possess them. Every autumn comes to us laden with orna-ments which no skilled workman can rival. The graceful golden-rod, so rich in color, sways and bends over the low stone walls, and in the fields wild flowers of all kinds grow in great profusion. White, spreading wild carrot, yellow and white dai-sies, light and dark purple asters, and sumach, with its varied hues, give color to the landscape on our bright fall days. There are also the queer-shaped pods and feathery, silky seeds peculiar to some wild plants ; among others the poor "vagabond thistle," which has donned its robe of glistening white, although some of its tribe still wear their faded purple gowns. The latter may be gathered for thistle-puffs, and all the objects mentioned can be used in home decorations.

We cannot pass by unnoticed the brown milk-weed pods, for within the shells, full well we know, are hidden the silvery, downy seeds which make such pretty milk-weed balls. Here, too, we notice the rich coloring of bark as well as foliage, the bright scarlet berries contrasting with the brown, yellow, and green leaves. The vine, once a fresh green, is now changed to deep crimson ; even the tiny leaves of the wild strawberry and some grasses have touches of red on their edges.

How the rich coloring of autumn differs from the delicate tints of spring, when the promise was made in bud and leaf, which is now realized in the bountiful harvests !

Having such a wealth to glean from, we scarcely know what to take first ; but for decorations to last only a few hours it would be difficult to imagine anything more brilliantly appropriate than

Fresh Autumn Wild Flowers

and small branches of brilliant fall leaves. At the time of this writing wild flowers are very popular ; one of our daily papers records a wedding which recently took place, where the display of wild flowers was beautiful in the extreme. Curtains of wood-ferns were caught back with golden-rod, and a bower of holly and oak was fringed with clusters of scarlet bitter-sweet berries. Daisies were also used in abundance, while the beauty of the little church was enhanced by the masses of white blossoms and oak-branches.

This idea can be used advantageously in decorating the house for evening parties and receptions, or afternoon teas and coffees. Have the flowers and foliage in masses, the effect is much better ; and if you gather very large, hardy ferns with their roots attached they will make exceedingly graceful decorations, and placed in water or wet sand they will remain fresh for days.

When golden-rod is gathered in its prime it will keep nearly all winter without fading. Do not put it in water ; all that is necessary is to keep it dry. The rich brown cat-tails should be treated in the same manner ; these must be gathered at their best, before they are too ripe. Bitter-sweet berries will last for months and retain a bright red. The old-fashioned honesty, with its white, satiny pods, keeps perfectly for any length of time. The wild rose-bush in the fall is decked with seed-coverings, which closely resemble scarlet berries; these will last for many weeks. The wild clematis, with its festoons of hazy fluff, will keep for a long time, and always looks well when thrown over and on the top corner of a portière and allowed to hang naturally down a little on one side, or arranged in a similar manner over the tops of windows, doors, pictures, or wherever it will look graceful. It should hang out of harm's way, as it is brittle and easily broken when dry.

For entertainments, the more elaborate and bountiful the decorations of fresh wild flowers the more beautiful will the house appear; but for every-day life during the cold weather, when we have only the dried fall plants, we may almost make up for the lack of fresh flowers by using judgment and taste in arranging the dried ones. Though wild flowers

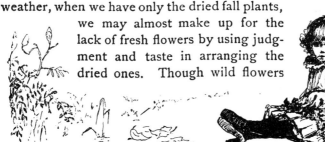

A Young Decorator.

are beautiful, you must use taste in their arrangement and not mingle them together promiscuously, but make a judicious selection, for where a light bunch of golden-rod would be the very thing needed to give color to a particular spot, should the dark cat-tails be placed there the effect might be lost. There are places where some high, stiff decoration would look best, and others where the soft, swaying clematis seems to belong. As with everything else, so with our decorations, we must seek to have harmony.

Who has not admired the dark-brown, glossy buckeyes and horse-chestnuts, and wondered what use could be made of them? Children love to gather them and come home with their pockets and baskets full, only to play with them for awhile, and then the pretty dark balls, each marked with a spot of light cream-color, are thrown away or lost.

Now, the next time the buckeyes are collected save every one and make a

Buckeye Portière.

The writer assures you that you will find it much easier to do this than she did to make a picture of the curtain, for it is difficult with a pen-and-ink drawing to give an idea of the richness of color in the handsome hangings these horse-chestnuts make when properly fashioned into a portière for hall or doorway. Two full bushels of buckeyes will be needed to make a curtain two yards and a half long and one yard and a quarter wide.

Take a very large, long needle and a strong, waxed thread a little longer than you desire to have your curtain, make a large knot in the end of the thread, and commence to string your buckeyes in the same way as stringing beads or buttons. Continue until the thread in the needle is exhausted, then tie the thread in a large knot close to the last buckeye, leaving a length of three inches of thread. Make your other strands in the same way. When all are finished, fasten as many small screw-eyes in a straight line on a curtain-pole, or a rustic pole if desired, as there are strands of buckeyes, and tie securely to each screw-eye one string of buckeyes   When all are fastened

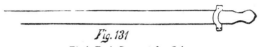

Fig. 131
Birch-Bark Support for Pole.

on, your portière is finished and ready to be hung.   This is easily accomplished if the pole used is a regular curtain-pole, as they always come with brackets ; but should your pole be rustic, it must be supported by bands of strong birch-bark, or leather, as in Fig. 131.   Our illustration shows over the portière a

Panel of Fall Decorations.

These also look handsome over windows and doors, and you are at liberty to use ornaments of all styles, for the panels are placed where there is no danger of anything coming in contact with them to break off the decorations or mar their beauty. Any kind of board will do for the panel, rough or smooth, as you like.   Paint the board a pure white, then decide on your ornaments, which may be a chestnut-branch with bursting burs attached, sprays of common wayside velvet-leaf with clusters of pods clinging to them, a piece of black-berry vine with its twigs, thorns, and dried berries, or branches of buckeyes with some of the nuts falling from their horned shells.

Select according to your fancy, and gild the decorations chosen, then tack them on the panel.   It is best to place the ornaments on the board while the paint is soft and wet, for then it will help to fasten the decoration more securely ; if the paint be put on thick where the ornaments are to be placed, they will lie partially embedded in the paint, and when it dries they will appear as if carved from the wood.*

A white and gold panel made in this way is very pretty and inexpensive.

The fall decorations also enable us to make a very effective

Louis Quinze Screen.

For this it is necessary to have two small wooden hoops, such as children roll along the streets; fasten these together with a

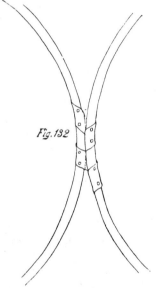

Fig. 132

Hinge for Louis Quinze Screen.

strong piece of white tape, two or three inches wide, cut the end of the tape bias, tack this on the side of one of the hoops, bring it around between and over the other hoop, and tack it again, repeat the operation and the hinge will be finished (Fig. 132). If you look at the hinge on a wooden clothes-horse you will understand how to make one. Fig. 133 shows the hoops fastened together. Now cut two pieces of coarse, strong cotton cloth, a little larger around than the hoops, and place one of the pieces smoothly over one of the hoops; tack it down, driving the tacks in far apart, and so that they can be easily extracted; if the cloth wrinkles, keep changing it until the surface is perfectly even; when this is accomplished carefully tack the covering securely down, keeping it smooth and

---

* For this work the staple-tacks used for tacking down matting will be found very convenient.

without wrinkles. In like manner tack the remaining piece of cloth on the other hoop. Next get four broomsticks and cut a notch on each one, at exactly the same distance from the top, for the hoops to fit in. Then measure where you wish the hoops to be placed and cut another notch on each stick a certain distance from the bottom ; all the sticks must be of the same length and have the notches cut in the same places, so each one may be a duplicate of the others. Mark the hoops where the sticks are to fit, and then fasten them firmly on with small screws. Make

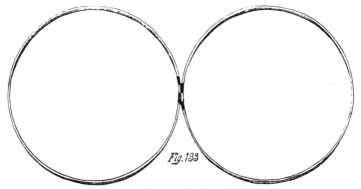

Fig. 133.

Hoops Fastened Together for Louis Quinze Screen.

the screen strong, so that there will not be any danger of its coming apart. Give each cloth a sizing of common flour-paste on both sides, then scrape off all the paste with a knife ; in this way the cloth will be starched and prepared to receive the paint. When the screen is thoroughly dry, sew a branch across one of the disks and some waxed fall leaves in the places where they would naturally lie on the branch ; when these are securely attached, decorate the other disk with something different ; acorns can be used if cut in halves ; but never place any ornaments on the screen which will not lie flat, for if they stand out they will be broken off or injured by persons passing and brushing against them. Now give the screen a coat of white paint all over, including the branch and leaves, but do not paint the hinge. Set the screen away until it is perfectly dry, then gild the branches and leaves, connecting the latter with the twigs by painting a line of

Louis Quinze Screen.

gold between the two. Gild a ring around each pole near the top and another near the bottom, and cover the edges of the hoops where the cloth has been fastened on by tacking white gimp around each one, using fancy brass-headed tacks and placing them at equal distances apart; this completes the ornamental screen.

Should you desire it, the screen can be painted black or any other color, and the decorations bronzed instead of gilded. The bronzes come in different shades, and the color of real bronze can be easily copied.

As an ornament for the dining-room

A Panel of Field-Corn

is very decorative and easy to make. When the corn ripens, select some nice, firm, golden ears, with husks and without ; then break off pieces of corn-stalk and group them together, as in the illustration; cover a board of

requisite size with a piece of old black velvet ; if you have no velvet, paint the board black, and after tying the corn firmly together, tack it securely on the board, and the dark background will bring out the many yellow tints of the decoration beautifully ; fasten two screw-eyes in the back of the board, by which to attach the wire, and the panel will be ready to hang on the wall.

The corn can also be fastened to a rough board of the desired size and the panel and decoration bronzed, using green bronze for the background and portions of the group, while all the edges and prominent points should be of copper-colored bronze.

Early in November the many varieties of gourds ripen, and their odd and fantastic forms seem like nature's suggestions of the unique in ornamentation. So suggestive are they that it needs but little originality to make them into many useful and beautiful articles. As a decoration for looping over the poles of portières, and for holding back draperies, these

Ornamental Gourds

are convenient. They must first be allowed to become perfectly dry ; then they can be made into tasselled festoons. Take six mock-oranges, which imitate so closely our real oranges in color, size, and form, and cut a hole about the size of a silver dime in the top and bottom of each one ; then shake out the seeds. To make the openings in the gourds, first bore a small hole with the point of a large needle, then twist the needle around and around until it will easily pass through. Next, carefully enlarge the opening with a sharp penknife until it is of the stated size. Make a rope two yards and a half long of Persian colored wools or worsted ; on the end fasten a slender tassel, six or seven inches long, made of the same worsted ; now

string one of the bright orange-gourds on the rope down against
the tassel, which should be large enough to prevent the gourd
from slipping off ; make another similar tassel, and attach it to
the rope about twelve inches from the first one, and thread another gourd on the rope, bringing it down against the second
tassel ; proceed in like manner with the remaining gourds,
making a tassel for each one, and you will have a decoration
unlike any to be found elsewhere.

We are all more or less familiar with the

Gourd-Dippers

so common in the South, where, in olden times, scarcely a spring
bubbled in a rustic nook that was not supplied with its drinking-
gourd.   These dippers are made by sawing an opening in the
large part of the gourd, scraping out the contents, and making
the inside as smooth as possible with sand-paper.   They need
no ornamentation.

The kind of gourds resembling flattened globes can be made
into graceful and unique

Bowls.

The gourds must be sawed into two parts, with the inside of
each sand-papered, and flowers painted, with oil-colors, on the
outside.   After they have thoroughly dried, give a coat of white
varnish to both the inside and outside.   A pretty

Bonbon-Box

can be fashioned of one of these gourds.   Saw off the top, which
will serve as a lid, and fasten it to the bowl with narrow ribbons
tied through holes at the back of each ; line both lid and box
with satin by gluing it along the edges with stiff glue put on

sparingly, and cover the raw edge of the satin with chenille ; this is also put on with a little glue. Do not allow the chenille to interfere with the closing of the box, but place it along the inside edge of the box and lid.

Another form is the

Bottle-Gourd.

Ornament this with ivy-leaves painted as if twined around bowl and neck, and when the paint is dry varnish the gourd all over; if you wish it for use as well as decoration, saw off the top about two or three inches deep, shake out the seeds, then fit a cork in the piece cut off, and so glue it in that the cork may extend an inch downward to fit in the bottle.

The large egg-shaped gourds look well as

Vases.

Select a deep-colored gourd, saw off the top and scrape out the inside ; then varnish the vase and mount it on feet of

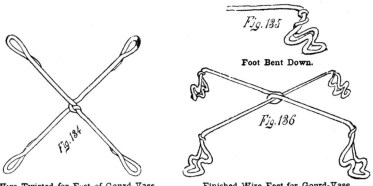

Foot Bent Down.

Fig. 135

Fig. 136

Fig. 134

Wire Twisted for Feet of Gourd-Vase.

Finished Wire Feet for Gourd-Vase.

twisted wire, made according to Fig. 134 ; bend down the feet, as in Fig. 135, when the wire will be formed into Fig. 136. To

fasten this on the vase, first bore holes in the bottom of the
gourd, then sew the feet firmly on, passing the needle through

Ornamental and Useful Gourds.

the holes previously made and bending the wire a little to fit to
the gourd. Gild the wire feet, and your vase is finished. An-

other way is to save the top sawed off, fasten an ornament of twisted wire on the top of it, and then, after making the vase as the one just described, add bands of gilded cardboard made to fit the gourd, fastening them to the vase with glue. Handles can also be fashioned of cardboard and sewed to the upper band before it is glued to the vase, as in the illustration.

There are many other ways of utilizing gourds, but we will leave it to your ingenuity to think up new and pretty conceits.

Pine-cones, large and small, acorns, and balls from the sweet-gum tree, can be used as

Small Decorations.

Never try to fasten them by the natural stems, for these will soon break off, but place in each one a small screw-eye, and when tied in groups they form ornaments for waste-baskets and fancy baskets of all kinds. We have seen chandeliers with gilded cones hanging from the different points, and being the identical color of the chandelier, they seemed of the same metal, and added novelty and grace to its appearance.

There are some varieties of the tree-fungi which make dark, rich-colored

Brackets.

Use heavy cardboard or thin board as a covering for the back ; have this fit the fungus perfectly, and fasten it securely in position with very stiff glue or nails. Paint the back the same color as the fungus, and on either side of the upper edge place screw-eyes by which to fasten up the bracket.

Many of the curiously formed galls and oak-apples to be found on different trees can also be employed as ornaments.

Nothing can be finer than our brilliant autumn season, which is said to be more beautiful in this than in other countries, with its crisp mornings and bright sunny afternoons.

When the weather is too lovely to remain in-doors, and all nature invites us out, then is the time to gather our fall decorations.

The Little Brown Squirrel.

CHAPTER XIX.

NUTTING-PARTIES.

OFF they go with bright, laughing eyes and glowing cheeks, each one carrying a light little basket or fancy bag slung carelessly on her arm. The girls are full of life and spirits as they walk briskly along toward the woods in the delightful fall weather, talking and laughing in a happy, thoughtless fashion, now telling where the best nuts are to be found, the shortest route to take, or where the prettiest walks lead, and again lingering or stopping to admire the many wonderful beauties of autumn. Leaving the road they enter the woods, where the dry leaves rustle pleasantly beneath their feet, and in some places the gold and brown leaves through which they walk lie ankle-deep.

All this is fully enjoyed by the party as they proceed on their way discussing the best place for lunch, which consideration is quite important, as it is necessary, if possible, to be near a clear. cool spring ; otherwise the water must be transported.

Arriving at the selected spot about noon, all bring forward their baskets and bags to contribute the contents to their " nutting-dinner." Soon the white cloth is laid and the tempting feast spread, when the hungry but merry maidens gather around to relish their repast in the forest, where, all about, are seen sure signs of coming winter.

The airy dining-hall is carpeted with the softest moss, and the gorgeous coloring of the surrounding foliage is far more beautiful than the most costly tapestry, while the sky forming the roof is of the serenest blue.

Now and then the sound of falling nuts is heard as they drop from the trees. This is music in the ears of the girls, and they hurry through their lunch, collect the empty baskets, and are soon busy gathering the glossy brown chestnuts, which are thrashed down from the branches by some of the party, who use long poles for the purpose. Down comes the shower of nuts and burs, and away the party scamper to patiently wait until it is over, as the prickly burs are things to be avoided. Some wise girls have brought tweezers to use in pulling open these thorny coverings. Others have their hands well protected by heavy gloves which cannot easily be penetrated with the bristling spikes.

It does not take long to fill their bags, and the one who first succeeds in the feat receives the title of "Little Brown Squirrel." Then all the others, for the rest of the day, obey her wishes. Nor is this difficult, for their Little Brown Squirrel is blithe and gay, generous and kind, and does all in her power to render her subjects happy.

As they turn their faces homeward the girls plan for another nutting-party to come off soon, for they wish to make the most of the glorious Indian summer, which belongs, we claim, exclusively to our country, and which may last a week or only a few days.

The chestnuts are brought home, where in the evening some are eaten raw, others have the shells slit and are then roasted or boiled, making a sort of chestnut festival, as in the North of Italy, only of course on a very much smaller scale, for there the peasants gather chestnuts all day long and have a merry-making when the sun goes down. This harvest lasts over three weeks and is a very important one to the dark-eyed Italians, who dry the nuts and grind them to flour, which is used for bread and cakes during the barren season. The harvest in the Apennines is quite an event, as the trees are plentiful, the fruit is good, and the people gladly celebrate the season.

Our thin, white-shelled shag-bark hickory-nut is peculiarly American, and many a nutting-party have found its delicate and agreeable flavor very welcome when, gathered around a large rock, they crack a few to sample their fruit before returning home.

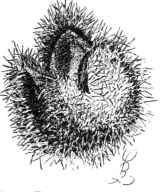

Blossom and Fruit of the Chestnut-Tree.

These nuts are only cooked by covering the kernels with hot candy, and thus prepared, they make a delicious sweetmeat.

When cracking hickory-nuts, hold each nut firmly by the

flat sides, bringing uppermost one of the narrow sides; strike this and the nut will open so that the halves fall out, or may be easily extracted, and occasionally the kernels will come out whole. We have seen quaint little figures, with the heads made of hickory-nuts, the pointed end forming the nose, and the eyes and mouth marked with ink, giving a comical expression to the peaked face.

The neat little three-cornered beech-nut is easy and pleasant to gather, making a desirable change for the "nutters" after going for other kinds, and the trees with their beautiful foliage render the scene very attractive. But not more so than do the lofty and stately walnut-trees with their rich, brown fruit encased in such rough shells, whose outside covering is so juicy that, unless we are very cautious, it will stain our hands its own dark color. The black-walnut tree (J. nigra) is indigenous to the United States, and we are informed that a celebrated specimen is still standing at Roslyn, L. I., where the seed was planted in 1713. The tree measures twenty-five feet in circumference at three feet from the ground.

Butter-nuts, so significant during our civil war, also belong to America; the meat, though quite oily, is sweet and agreeable.

Butter-nuts will repay anyone for gathering them, though, like the walnut, the outer husk is apt to stain the fingers; but this may be avoided by wearing gloves while handling the fruit. The cross-sections of the shells, when properly polished, make pretty ornaments.

Although we are all fond of the round little hazel-nut, they do not seem to be as plentiful as could be wished, and it is seldom we have the pleasure of going hazel-nutting, yet when the opportunity occurs, it is rare sport and an event to be talked of afterward.

Nuts are to be found in all portions of the country, and the varieties depend upon the section in which you live.

Rules for Nutting-Parties.

1. In selecting the members of a nutting-party be careful to choose only those on whom you can safely depend for cheerfulness, kindly feeling, and a willingness on their part to do all in their power to assist, should occasion arise, in letting down the bars of a fence, going for water, or anything which might happen to require their services.

2. Decide by majority any case of controversy in regard to destination, the best place and way of crossing a brook, which route to take, or in fact any question concerning the comfort and pleasure of the party, until the "Little Brown Squirrel" wins her title. Then she rules absolutely and settles all questions according to her best judgment, giving council and friendly advice to those who ask it. All

Pea-Nut Vine and Fruit.

differences being referred to her, the decision is considered final, and the party must obey when their Little Brown Squir-rel directs.

3. The one who gathers the greatest quantity of nuts in a given time wins, and receives the above much-desired title. The standard of measure being previously decided upon by the party, the time may be either long or short, as desired.

4. The badge given to the successful competitor may consist of fall leaves or nuts tied with a brown ribbon. This she keeps in remembrance of the delightful day spent nutting in the woods when she was a Little Brown Squirrel.

Select, if possible, a day in Indian summer for your nutting-party, and it is well to wear a gown that will not easily tear, catch the dust, or spot—not that these accidents are always to be met with on such excursions, but they might happen, and we must be on the safe side, so that no thought or anxiety need be given to the clothing.

If your party contemplates a series of nutting-picnics, pro-pose that they shall go for different varieties each time. This will add novelty and zest to the excursions ; and should the distance in some cases be too great for a walk, secure a vehicle with a good reliable driver, and the ride will be particularly enjoyed. This mode of travelling procures another change in the programme, which should be as varied as you can make it. Let the plates for your dinner be of wood or paper, to avoid the necessity of carrying them home. A table-cloth made of large sheets of white paper is a good substitute for damask, and after doing service the paper may be thrown away, leaving your baskets entirely empty to be filled with nuts.

There grows a nut, highly prized, that is never gathered by nutting-parties. Nor could they see it if they examined every tree throughout the country. Yet it flourishes in this climate, and may be seen any day at the fruit-stores and corner-stands. The shells of these furnish odd fancies for little trifles made by girlish fingers. Cut in the shape of slippers and glued to a card, they seem suitable for a wood-nymph, and the card is used as a birthday or *menu* card. Strung together with needle and thread, and dressed in costume with black thread for hair, they make quite a good-looking Japanese.

Glued on a twig and marked with ink in representation of the birds, they look not unlike owls perched on a limb. When divided in halves the shells are transformed into tiny boats with tissue-paper sails. This nut boasts of four names: gouber, pindar, ground-nut, and the familiar name of pea-nut.

CHAPTER XX.

HOW TO MAKE A TELEPHONE.

ELLO! Hello! What is it you say? You can really make a telephone? What fun! How far will it work? You think it can be heard a long distance? Very good. Could we manage to construct such a one? How, pray tell us?

The answer which came back over the line we give in a more concise form, as follows:

The best way to make a simple telephone is to procure two round, medium-sized tin baking-powder boxes, and remove the bottoms with a pair of pinchers; then soak two pieces of Whatman's drawing-paper, or any other strong paper, in a basin of water for a few moments, and when thoroughly wet take them out and place one smoothly over the end of each box. Fasten these down by winding a waxed cotton twine securely over the paper and box, and tying it tightly (Fig. 137). This done, allow the drums to become wholly dry, when they should be firm, even, and without wrinkles. Next cut away that portion of the paper which stands out, frill-like, beyond the string, and paste a narrow strip of paper around over the twine (Fig. 138). Wax a piece of string of the desired length, and with a large needle or pin carefully punch a hole in the centre of each drum; thread one end of the waxed string through one of the holes and make a large knot in the end, then cautiously pull the string until the knot rests on the inside surface of the paper.

Connect the other box to the string in like manner, so that the twine will have a box fastened on each end.

The telephone is now ready for use ; and if the distance is short, the line may be stretched taut from point to point. But should the space be great, supports will be needed and loops must be made of the twine and fastened at intervals on trees, corners of the houses, or any available points, with the connecting cord passed through these loops (Fig. 139), which act as supports. Keep the course of the waxed string as straight as possible, and, as far as practicable, avoid sharp angles. This style of telephone we know, from personal experience, works perfectly at the distance of

Fig.137

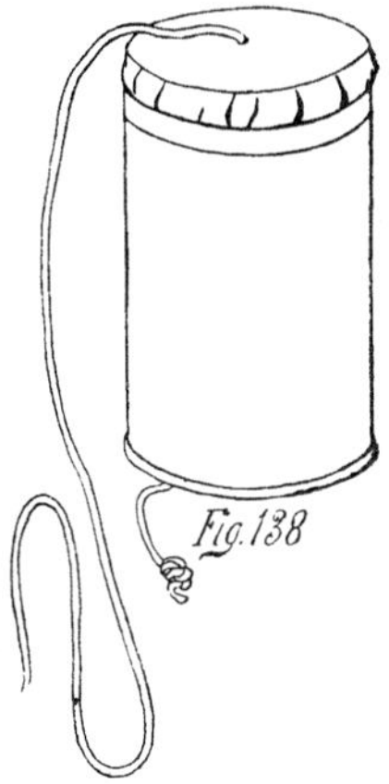

Fig.138

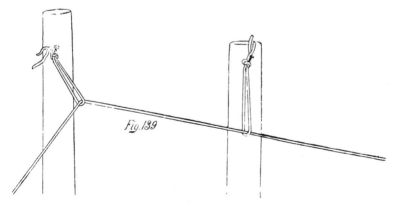

Fig.139

fifty yards, and doubtless it will do as well when the line is stretched much farther. Be particular, in selecting the tin baking-powder boxes, to have them round and even ; if they are old and battered the experiment may not prove satisfactory.

Listening.

We find the telephone very useful and convenient, besides affording any amount of amusement and fun ; with its aid we converse with acquaintances, even though they be at a distance. The friendly little instrument carries the voice all along the slender line to the very ears of our best friend, and we can chat away as freely and almost as easily as if side by side. What a comfort to be able, when seated in your own room, to listen to the voice of some companion, living perhaps blocks away, and it is such a pleasure, too, to have questions answered immediately, which is impossible in communications made by letter. Nor is this a pleasure to be enjoyed at rare intervals, for as long as the telephone lasts it can be used at any time for a short or long talk, as one may feel inclined. The consultations, the plans, the sport, and merriment to be had with the telephone can scarcely be appreciated by one who is not the happy possessor of such an instrument.

When the weather will not permit of a walk or a visit, the telephone brings us, if not face to face, at least within speaking distance of those to whom we desire to talk.

There are many other easy methods of making telephones. They can be manufactured as described without waxing the string, or the boxes may be used unaltered, in which case the tin bottoms serve as drums, and the holes for the string are made in the centre of each by driving a small tack through. With these instruments the voice cannot be sent a great distance, but when only a short line is needed they succeed very well.

More complicated telephones are made with the drums of bladder and the line of soft, flexible wire. Though good and serviceable, they are more difficult to make and require more time and labor.

The two beef-bladders used for such a telephone must first be blown up, tied, and left about thirty hours, or until they are stretched, but not dried. When in proper condition, cut off the necks and portion of the ends, then soak them in warm water, and they will become very pliable and light in color. Having previously prepared two square pieces of board by very carefully cutting out a perfect circle in the centre of each, about as large as a medium-sized pie-pan or a tea-plate, place the bladders smoothly but not tightly over the

Speaking.

openings, allowing the outside of the bladder to come on the bottom, and fasten it all around the circle, a little distance

from the edge, with tacks so driven in that they may be easily removed.

Try the drums with your finger; if they stretch evenly they are correct, if they wrinkle, change them until they stretch perfectly smooth. Then tack a piece of firm tape securely around the edge of the circle, and cut off the bladder reaching beyond the tape. Next fasten four feet of soft, flexible wire to a large-sized gutta-percha button by threading it through the two opposite holes in the centre of the button; pass the other end of the wire through the middle of the bladder, bringing the button flat against its surface.

After attaching a weight of about seven pounds to the end of the wire, place the drum in the sun until perfectly dry. Proceed with the other in the same manner, and when both are well dried, fasten one on each end of the line and attach the drum-wires to the principal wire by loops; then stretch it firm and tight. This telephone will also need loops for supports, which should be of wire. When the instrument is carefully and properly made it will carry the voice three or four miles or more, giving every word and tone distinctly and clearly.

CHAPTER XXI.

HOW TO DRAW.*

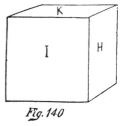

OULD you like to learn to draw, to sketch from nature ? Don't you think that it would be delightful to be able to take out your pencils and paper and copy some scene you want to remember, or produce a likeness of any bird or animal which strikes your fancy ?

Many will say, " I'd like it very well, but I *can't* draw."

You can write, can hold a pencil, and trace lines upon the paper ; and if you can do this, you can draw a little. A girl who can learn anything can learn to draw if she will give the same attention to it that she gives to other things.

Now we are not going to talk about copying pictures which someone else has already drawn, for there is not much sat-isfaction in making imitations of other

Fig. 140

people's work ; it is much more gratifying to make the original drawings ourselves ; but to do this we need some direction.

---

* The material for this chapter is from an article written by Professor Frank Beard for Harper's Young People. By permission of Harper & Brothers.

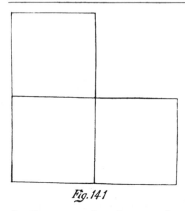

Fig. 141

The reason it is easier to copy a picture than to draw the real object is because the lines to be copied are all laid out on the flat surface of the picture ; but to draw the object we must find out where to trace the lines for ourselves.

For instance, suppose we are to draw a flower-pot and plant. If we have the picture before us, we can readily see where all the lines are placed upon the paper, but in viewing a real plant and pot we are apt to become confused in trying to discover the directions and proportions of the lines.

Fig. 142

Therefore we must learn *to see things as they appear*, not as they really are. This may seem strange to you, because one is apt to think that a thing must appear as it is; but let us look into the matter.

We will take a square box (Fig. 140). Now, we know that all the sides are the same size, that the top is as large as the side, and that one side is as large as an-

other; but if you try to draw it so, you will find it impossible, because, although you know that the top and sides are the same size as the front, they do not look so, and you draw things as they look, not as they really are.

What would our cube look like if we tried to make the sides K and H just like the side I? Why, like Fig. 141. Don't you see that would be no box at all?

Take another example. We all know that a man's leg is longer than his arm, but it doesn't always appear so. Measure the arms and legs of Fig. 142, and you will see by actual measurement the arms are longer than the legs, and yet it looks right, because the legs are projected toward you; in other words, the legs are *fore-shortened.*

Fig. 143

The great secret of drawing from nature is to train the eye to see a real object just like a picture.

Now let us return to our flower-pot again. We will suppose we are drawing from a real flower-pot and plant. We determine how large we will make our sketch, and begin operations by drawing a vertical line (a straight upright line). Along this line we will mark out the proportions of the plant and pot, as in Fig. 143.

We may easily discover that the plant is longer than the pot. This can be done by holding the pencil upright before the eye at arm's length, as in Fig. 144, so that it will cover the pot, and measuring by the thumb the height of the pot, then raising the arm so as to cover the plant, and comparing the measurement of the pot with the plant. The lines drawn from the eye Fig. 144) show how the pencil makes the measurement on the object.

After settling the question of the height of the flower-pot and plant, we will mark the measurements on the line. And

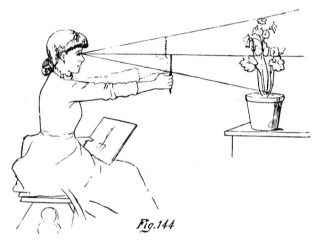

Fig. 144

now we will draw in the pot, leaving the straight line through its centre.

On observing the plant we will see that it is not exactly straight, and here again the straight line will be of assistance.

By holding up our pencil, which represents the straight line, we will discover that the main stem of the plant leans considerably to the left. Guided by the line, we can get the curve of the stem about right. Now we sketch the stem. Along the straight line we again measure the distance from the top of each leaf and flower to the pot, as in Fig. 145. We can see several leaves, each reaching a certain height. Observing the same plan of measurement, we find that the top of the lowest leaf is about the same height from the pot as the height of the pot itself, and again from the top of the lowest leaf to the top of the plant measures the same distance.

By drawing another vertical line just touching the right side of the pot, we find that it touches the extreme edge of the leaf. Thus we find the exact situation of the leaf. By the same method we find the right places for the other leaves and flowers, and after we know just where they belong, we draw them in, and find that we have produced a very creditable outline from nature.

Fig. 145

We need not confine ourselves to one or two guiding lines in sketching an object ; in fact, we may use as many straight lines as will help us to get the correct proportions ; not only vertical and horizontal lines, but slanting lines will also assist us in most cases.

The sketch of a dog (Fig. 146) will give an idea of the way to employ all lines necessary in sketching from nature. A few words will be all that is necessary to explain this illustration.

There lies the dog on the floor, and we seat ourselves at a little distance from it with pencil and paper. We will start off with a horizontal line (A) ; then we can form some idea as to whether the little dog lies along a straight line, or in case the bottom line slants, how much it slants. Then draw the vertical line (B E). Now suppose we hold our pencil upright, in such a position as to touch the back of the knee-joint of the foreleg, we will find that it passes through the middle of the dog's back,

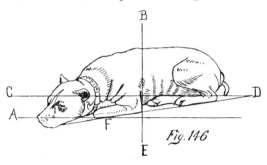

Fig. 146

as represented by the line (B E); so we have found the places for these parts.

Another horizontal line (C D) drawn above the first will touch just over the right eye, pass through the middle of the left ear, through the middle of the neck, cut off the foreleg, and run along the top of the two hind legs, passing through the knee of the left one. This will show us that the top of the right eye, the ear, and the top of both hindlegs are on a line. It will also help us to get the proportions above and below the line ; then by drawing a line from D to the point F on the horizontal line A, we find that the lower edges of the left hind and fore legs are on the same line, which, if extended a little farther down, will touch the edge of the dog's mouth. With these lines to guide us we cannot go far astray in our proportions.

One of the chief difficulties in following this method of drawing from nature is to hold our measuring-stick exactly vertical or horizontal. This difficulty can be overcome by providing yourself with a T-square (Fig. 147) and attaching to it, at the point P, a *Fig. 147*

string with a weight tied on the other end so that it will hang plumb. By using this we can be sure whether we hold it straight or not, for in case we tip it too much on one side or the other the string will swerve from the middle of the upright stick. Of course, whenever we hold the T-square perfectly straight, the string will fall straight down the middle of the upright, and the top of the T will then give us a true horizontal line. A little thought and practice will lead you to thoroughly understand this method, and when you really understand it you will have an unerring guide to assist you. Of course, as the eye and hand become more trained, with practice and observation, the work will become easier, and you will not need the T-square.

In beginning the practice of drawing from nature, we had better confine our first efforts to things that will stand still, for without a practised hand it will be almost impossible to sketch a restless subject ; but if we attempt to do so, we should follow the methods before taught as nearly as possible.

Now, suppose we step out of doors in search of something to sketch. The first moving object our eyes rest upon is a goose, and we decide to use him as a model.

But he is so restless, will not keep still an instant. First we have a front view, then a side view, and again he turns his back upon us. If we really must have his picture, the only way is to catch him and tie him up.

Yet even now he is a difficult subject, twisting and turning, and bobbing his head about. Determined on sketching him, however, we observe the position in which he remains the longest time, or assumes oftenest, and begin our work.

We first note the general proportions. Is his body as thick as it is long ? Is his neck as long as his body ? Are his legs nearest the head or tail ? Is the head as long as the neck ? What part reaches the highest, or what part the lowest ? We hastily but carefully consider these questions and determine in our own mind the answers, for we must get an idea of the proportions before we begin our sketch.

Now we draw a horizontal line along our paper, and then hold up our pencil horizontally, so that it will answer for a straight line drawn across the body of the real goose (Fig. 148). This will represent the horizontal line on the paper. Noticing then the directions the outlines of the goose

Fig. 148

take from the horizontal line (represented by the pencil), we sketch them in on the paper, remembering that one of the most important things is to get the right directions of the lines.

Observe that in Fig. 149 the line G is directed to too high a point, and makes the body too thick and out of proportion.

Fig. 149   Fig. 150

In sketching it is best to make all lines straight instead of curves, for in this way we are more likely to get the right direc-

tions. Our first rough sketch of the goose ought to have something of the appearance of Fig. 150, and as we work it up more
carefully it will become as nicely rounded as we could desire.

One of the most common faults a beginner is apt to commit
is to try to do too much, either by choosing too great a subject,
such as a large landscape, or by putting too many little things
into the composition. Take care of the large things, and the
little things will take care of themselves.

If our subject be a clump of trees at some distance, we
should not attempt to draw in separate leaves, but endeavor to
get the true shape of the tree, simply indicating the leaves by a
few lines. Neither must we attempt, in our first sketches, to put
in all the shadows we see ; the strong principal ones are all that
are necessary. A background of hills and trees should be
merely suggested by a few lines, because the light striking upon
them gives a very light appearance.

Draw as simply as possible. Ten pictures are spoiled by
putting in too much work, where one is spoiled by too little.

Don't be discouraged. Every effort will show improvement,
if you really put your mind and heart in your work. As for

Materials,

a sheet of drawing-paper, a No. 2 lead-pencil, and a piece of soft
rubber are all you really need to commence with. Later it will
be well to have a drawing-pad and several more pencils.

CHAPTER XXII.

HOW TO PAINT IN WATER-COLORS.

HERE is a certain charm in water-color painting—a charm distinctly its own—which lies, as Penley says, " in the beauty and truthfulness of its aerial tones." Without this quality a water-color, as a water-color, is a failure.

This transparency of effect does not depend alone upon the manner of painting or the colors employed, but much rests with the paper we use. In the days when our mothers and grandmothers were taught painting at school, the finest, smoothest cardboard was thought necessary ; but we have since learned that the flat, smooth paper tends decidedly toward producing a flat, smooth effect in the picture painted upon it, while the rough, uneven surface of the paper now in use helps to produce depth and atmosphere. Therefore it is always best to have *rough* paper to paint upon. We give below the

Materials for Water-Color Painting.

1. A block of rough drawing or water-color paper.

It is better to buy it in blocks than by the sheet, as it is much more easily handled, and is always ready for use.

2. Brushes. The best brushes are made of sable, and although costing more to begin with, it is really more econom.

ical to purchase them than to choose the less expensive camel's-hair ; for the sable are by far the most satisfactory, and will last much longer.   Three or four brushes are sufficient.   As Devoe & Co. number them, they should range between No. 3, which is small enough for ordinary painting, and No. 19, for clouds, backgrounds, etc.

3. Colors. A tin sketching-box of moist colors, which also contains a palette, is very useful, but the colors can be bought separately in tubes or pans.

Water-color painting seems by its qualities to be especially adapted to flowers and landscapes, and as this is to be a chapter, not a book, on water-colors, we will confine ourselves to the principal points to be observed in these two departments, and will commence with the

Flowers.

Few oil-paintings, however well executed, give the delicate, exquisite texture of a flower as nearly as water-colors. The semitransparency of a rose-petal, the juicy, translucent green of the young leaf, it is difficult to truthfully represent in other than these colors, whose essential quality is transparency.   To preserve this transparency of color, everything about the painting must be kept exceedingly neat.   The brushes must be thoroughly washed before using them for a different tint from that already upon them, and plenty of water, changed frequently, is necessary.

Having arranged your materials conveniently upon a table, place your paper so that it will lie at an angle slanting toward you, not perfectly flat upon the table; this can be done by putting books under the edge farthest from you, thus raising it up. Stand the flowers you wish to copy in such a position that the light will fall upon them only from one direction and produce decided shadows; the effect will then be much better than when the light is more diffused.

Always arrange your model exactly as you want to paint it, and leave nothing to your idea of how it ought to look. If you do not intend to have any background other than the white paper, place something white behind your flowers. If you want a colored background, arrange the color you have chosen behind the flowers, and paint it as you see it. Commence your work by sketching lightly, as correctly and rapidly as you can, the outline of your flower. Try

Painting in Water-Colors.

something simple at first; say a bunch of heart's-ease or pansies, and when drawing them try to get the character of both flower and leaf. Observe how the stem curves where it is attached to the flower, and at what angles the stems of the flowers and the leaves join the main stalk. Given character, an outline drawing painted in flat tints will closely resemble nature; without it, the most beautifully finished painting will not look like the flower it is intended to represent.

When your outline is drawn in, dip your largest brush in clear water, and go over the whole surface of your paper;

then place a piece of blotting-paper over the paper to soak up the water, leaving it simply damp, not wet.

If you are using tube colors, have ready on a porcelain palette, or ordinary dinner-plate, these colors : crimson lake, cobalt blue, indigo, Prussian blue, and gamboge. Put in your lightest tints first, leaving the white paper for the highest light ; then paint in your darker tints and shadows, and get the effect.

If your flower is what we call the johnny-jump-up, the lowest petal will be yellow. Paint this in with a light wash of gamboge, leaving, as we have said, the white paper for touches of high light. The two upper petals will probably be a deep claret-color ; this is made by mixing crimson lake and cobalt blue, the crimson lake predominating. The two central petals may be a bluish lavender, and this color is made by mixing a little crimson lake with cobalt blue. Use plenty of water ; but do not let it run, and keep the colors of the petals distinct.

Paint the stems and leaves, where they are a rich green, with a mixture of gamboge and Prussian blue, and where they appear gray as the light touches them, a pale wash of indigo will give the desired effect.

Keep your shadows broad and distinct, and your tints as flat as you can. Leave out details altogether in your first paintings, and add them afterward only when you can do so without spoiling the effect.

When a tinted background is desired, put it in quickly in a flat tint, before commencing the flowers. It is best not to bring the tint quite up to the outline, as a narrow edge of white left around the flower gives a pleasant, sketchy look to the painting.

Landscapes.

In your first studies from nature keep to simple subjects, and treat them simply, without any attempt at elaboration.

Choose, for instance, a picturesque corner of an old fence, with perhaps a bit of field and sky for the background. Sketch in the principal features in the foreground in outline, and indicate the horizon, if it comes in the picture.

Penley says, in his "System of Water-Color Painting," "White paper is too opaque to paint upon without some wash of color being first passed over it," and he recommends a thin wash of *yellow ochre* and *brown madder*, which should be put all over the surface of the paper except on the high lights in the foreground, which are best left crisp and white.

Notwithstanding what Penley says in this matter, it must be borne in mind that some artists do not believe in successive washes, but claim that the color desired should be put upon the white paper at once.

If the yellow tint is used, let it become quite dry and then wash it over with a large brush and *clean* water ; then, as in the flower painting, soak up the water with blotting-paper ; the blotting-paper must also be quite clean. While the paper is damp, not wet, begin with a blue tint—a light wash of cobalt will give it—and put in the sky *in a flat tint ;* bring the same color down all over your sketch except in the high lights. The blue tint gives atmosphere and distance. Let your paper again become quite dry, and then wash it over as before, in clear water.

The process of laying on color and lightly washing over it afterward should be repeated several times, "and the result will be a transparent aerial tone."

Keep your extreme distance bluish, your middle distance warmer in tone, but not too strong, and the principal objects in your foreground strong.

Leave out small objects, and with light and shade seek to obtain the effect.

Keep your colors pure or your sketch will be dull.

Contrast has much to do in producing strength and character.

Phillips says that, " in aiming at opposition of color, we must select that which gives force to the foreground, and consequently communicates the appearance of air in the distance. Thus, if the general tone of the light be warm and yellow, we should have blues and purples in the foreground ; if the lights be cool, reds and yellows in the foreground give atmosphere to distance, as neither of these colors in a positive state is found in the middle or remote distance."

The three principal contrasts are blue opposed to orange, red to green, and yellow to purple ; and " a good first lesson in sketching in color will be to put in your shadows with color opposite to the object in light ; and by carrying out this principle of opposition throughout the scale you will obtain an endless variety of contrasts." It is the general rule in most painting to have cool shadows to warm lights, and warm shadows to cool lights. We all know that a *green* picture is very disagreeable, and although a green field *is* green, it must not be made intensely so. An untrained eye will not see how nature tones down the vivid color with shadows, and softens it with the atmosphere ; but when the eye has learned to look at nature in the right way this difficulty will be overcome. Howard says, " green must be sparingly used, even in landscapes, whose greatest charm consists of vegetation."

Foliage in some form will present itself in almost every landscape, and it is therefore necessary to have a few general principles to guide you in this important feature. In sketching trees be sure to get the character of their trunks, limbs, branches, and general form ; also the texture of the bark, rough or smooth. You will see that the foliage appears in layers, one above another. Sketch in the outlines of the principal layers, where they are tipped with light ; then go over the whole tree with a local color, and afterward separate the light from shadow. Each mass is edged with light, while its base is in shadow, as a rule. Omit *details*, and keep to your *masses* of light and shade. If your tree is in the foreground, leave the white paper for crisp touches of high light. The tone of your fence will probably be gray, but do not take it for granted that it is *all* gray ; look for other colors, and you will find brown, blue, green, and sometimes red. Put these in as you see them, letting the edges melt into each other, as they will do when the paper is damp ; but have each color pure, and do not try to mix them.

Painting from Notes

is not as difficult as one might imagine. With a little practice it is easily learned. The following directions will tell how to paint a sunset on the meadows, from notes made at sunset on the meadows on Long Island.

Take a piece of Whatman's rough drawing-paper, or a kind that is termed egg-shell cartoon, the size decided upon for your picture. Have ready a large dish of clean water, brushes, and paints. Draw a pencil-line along the centre of your paper for your horizon, Fig. 151 ; then directly on the line paint a streak of vermilion. Put the color on quite damp, and make it about half an inch broad, extending one-fourth of an inch on either side of the horizon-line, Fig. 152. Next, quickly paint a yellow streak above and below the red one, making each streak of the same size and parallel, and leaving a little white paper between the different colors, Fig. 153. With a clean brush dipped in clean water carefully moisten the paper between the streaks, and allow the edges of the colors to mingle, Fig. 154. Before this has time to dry, paint a blue streak above and below, about half an inch from the yellow, Fig. 155 ; then with the clean brush dampen the white paper between, being careful not to get it too wet ; there should be just enough moisture to en-able the colors to flow and mingle at the edges, Fig. 156. This may be aided by holding the paper first one side up and then the other, until the edges are evenly blended. Now, before the horizon is quite dry, while it is still damp enough to cause

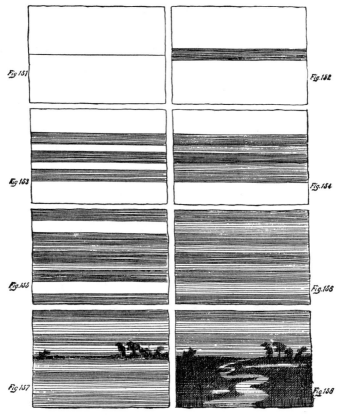

How to Paint a Sunset in Water-Colors.

the paint to spread, fill a brush with Payne's gray, which should be rather dark and not too wet, touch the point of your brush here and there along the horizon, now a little above and now a little below, and you will find that the paint will spread and make

ex c e l l e n t
trees for the
distance, Fig.
157.

W h e n
your work is
dry enough
to paint over
w i t h o u t
spreading the
color, mix
some green
and b l a c k,
and green

Fig. 159

and brown; paint in the meadow, using the color made of green
and black for the extreme and middle distance, the color made

of green and
brown for the
f o r e g r o u n d,
leavingspaces
for s t r e a m s
and p o n d s,
and your sun-
set upon the
m e a d o w is
finished. A
pretty little
sketch it is,
too, Fig. 158.

A differ-
ent composi-

Rosetinted sky

Cadmium Dark Cloud

Rose tint & Paynes gray

Rose tint & Paynes gray

Shirking

Orange
Rose-tint Horizon line

Sunset on New York Bay

Fig. 160
Leaf from an Artist's Note-Book.

tion can be made by proceeding as directed as far as **Fig. 156,**

and then, instead of putting in trees on the horizon, hills running to points in the water can be painted in a flat tint with
the Payne's gray, and a vessel with masts painted in the foreground, as in Fig. 159.   This also makes a pretty and effective
little sketch.

Fig. 160 shows sunset notes taken while aboard a ferryboat
in the winter of 1886-87.   From these you can see just how the
notes are made ; but you must make *your own notes*, because
what is perfectly intelligible to the writer of the sunset memoranda is an enigma to another person.   For example, in Fig.
160, " Rose-tinted sky " may mean almost any shade of red, or
blue and red mixed, but " Rose-tinted sky " no doubt brings
before the mind's eye of the writer of the notes the exact color
of the sky at the time the notes were made.

A Study in Oil.

CHAPTER XXIII.

HOW TO PAINT IN OIL-COLORS.

THE difference between oil- and water-color painting lies in the fact that, although especially well adapted to the portrayal of some subjects, water-color has its limitations, while with oil-colors any subject, from the simplest study in still-life to the grandest conception of a great artist, can be represented, and no limit has yet been reached in its possibilities.

But there are first steps to be taken in all things, and the greatest artist who ever lived had to make a beginning and learn the preliminaries of painting before he could produce a picture. To these steps, then, we will turn our attention, and the first will be the necessary

Materials.

The following list of colors, with their combinations, will be found sufficient for most purposes.

YELLOWS.	REDS.	BLUES.	GREENS.
Yellow Ochre,	Vermilion,	Permanent Blue,	Terre Verte,
Naples Yellow,	Light Red,	Cobalt,	Emerald Green,
Light Cadmium,	Indian Red,	Antwerp Blue.	Light Zinnober
Orange Cadmium.	Venetian Red,		Green.

Burnt Sienna,

Rose Madder.

Silver White,   Raw Umber,   Vandyke Brown, Ivory Black.

Winsor & Newton's colors are acknowledged by most artists to be the best, but the writer personally prefers German white, as in her opinion it is not so stiff, and mixes better with other colors than the Winsor & Newton.

The Easel

may be simply a pine one, which can be purchased from any dealer at the cost of about one dollar. More elaborate easels are, of course, more expensive ; but as the merits of a picture do not depend upon the easel which holds it, a common pine one will do.

The Palette

should be light in weight and not too small; oiled and not varnished. A very light-colored wood is not desirable ; one of walnut or cedar, about eighteen inches long, is the best to use, and will cost from thirty to sixty cents.

Brushes,

both of sable and bristles, are used, but we would advise a beginner to work with bristle brushes only, for the first attempt should be to obtain a broad style of painting, without the finished details which the sable brushes are used for.

About four different sizes of flat bristle brushes are needed to commence with ; there should be two of each size, the largest one inch wide, and the smallest not more than a quarter of an inch in width.

The Palette-Knife

is used for taking up color on the palette, for cleaning the palette, and sometimes for scraping a picture after its first painting.

It should be flexible, but not too limber. The cost will be from twenty-five cents upward.

Oil-Cups

are fastened on to the palette, and are used for oil and turpentine. The double ones range in price from eight cents to twenty. The single ones, without cover, can be bought for five cents.

A Paint-Box

for holding colors, palette, and brushes will cost from one dollar and twenty-five cents up. It is convenient to have one, and necessary when going out sketching, but for painting at home any kind of tin box will answer for the paints. The palette can be hung up, and the brushes put in a vase or jar, handles downward, which will keep them nicely.

Mediums.

Boiled linseed-oil or poppy-oil, siccatif Courtray, and turpentine.

Canvas.

In selecting canvas choose that of a warm-gray or creamy tone, for it is difficult to give warmth to a picture painted on a cold-gray canvas. The German sketching-canvas is quite cheap, and does very well to commence on. It is best to buy it on the stretcher, as a girl's fingers are seldom strong enough to stretch the canvas as tight as it should be. A very good sketching-canvas, 18 × 24, can be bought in New York City for twenty-five cents.

Several clean pieces of old white cotton-cloth are necessary for wiping brushes, cleaning knife and palette, etc.

The Light

in the studio, or room in which you paint, should come from one direction only, and fall from above. This can be managed by covering the lower sash of the window with dark muslin, or anything that will shut out the light. A shawl will answer for a temporary curtain.

Most artists prefer that while painting the light should come from behind over the left shoulder.

Our advice to beginners in all the departments of art is the same : commence with simple subjects.

Your first study should be from still-life (which means any inanimate object used for artistic study), and let the object selected be of a shape that requires but little drawing ; for your aim now is to learn to handle your colors, and it is not desirable to have your mind distracted by complicated drawing. A vase placed on a piece of drapery, which is also brought up to form the background, is a good subject ; the drapery should be of one color, and of a tone that will contrast agreeably with the vase and give it prominence.

Arrange whatever object you have decided to paint so that it will show decided masses of light and shade ; place your easel at a sufficient distance from it to obtain the general effect of shape and color without seeing too much detail ; arrange your canvas on the easel so that you will neither have to look up nor down upon it, but straight before you ; then sketch in the object you are about to copy in outline. Observe the edges of the heaviest shadows, and draw them also in outline. Charcoal is better than a pencil for sketching on canvas, as it can be easily rubbed off with a clean cloth if the drawing is incorrect. When the sketch is finished, dust off the charcoal lightly and go over the lines again with a camel's-hair brush and India ink.

Setting the Palette

is a term used for arranging the colors in a convenient manner upon the palette. The colors should always occupy the same position, so that, the places once learned, you will never be at a loss to find the color you want. Fig. 161 shows a con-

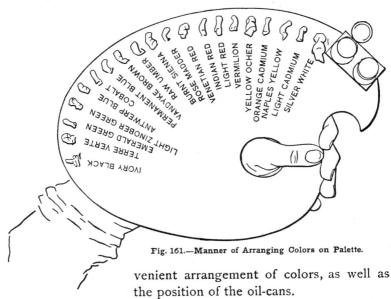

Fig. 161.—Manner of Arranging Colors on Palette.

venient arrangement of colors, as well as the position of the oil-cans.

Fill one of your oil-cans one-third full of turpentine, to which add enough siccatif Courtray to turn it the color of strong coffee. Dip one of your good-sized brushes in this mixture and scrape it off on the edge of the can, that the brush may not be too wet; then take up some burnt sienna on the brush and put it on your palette about an inch or so below the terre verte, add some terre verte, and mix the two with your brush. Lay in all the shadows of the vase, or whatever object you are about to paint, in a flat, even tone with the color thus formed, keeping it thin with the turpentine and siccatif.

Mix a tint as near the required color as you can, and go over the whole background without regard to light or shade ; cover all the background ; do not leave any white or bare canvas showing.

The general effect being thus obtained, it is easier to see what colors are needed for further painting.

Select a medium tint between the high lights and half-tones, and paint in the lights of the vase in a flat, even tint ; then go over the shadows again with a medium tone, still keeping them in one flat, even mass. Should you lose the outline at any time, dip a rag in turpentine and wash off the paint that covers it.

Having progressed this far, the painting should be left to dry.

The turpentine and siccatif Courtray have such drying properties that by the next day you may work again on the study.

Begin the second painting by putting in the half-tints. These unite the decided light and shade, and should be dragged over their edges, but not blended with them. Once more go over the shadows, strengthening them and putting in the reflected lights.

Add more color in the lights where it is needed, and put in the high lights with clear, crisp touches. Work on your background in this second painting. Indicate the shadows, but do not make them strong, except the one which will probably be cast by the object; that can be strengthened, as it helps to set the object out from the background and gives the idea of space. Do not make the background strong ; keep it toned down, that it may not become too prominent. Drag the background a little over the edges of the vase, or whatever it may be you are painting, and then paint over it again with the colors of the vase. Do this while working around the edges of the vase, or object, to prevent its looking flat, as if it were pasted on.

These directions are to be applied to painting any subject; but after you have learned how to manage the colors and wish to really paint a picture, the medium must be changed from turpentine and siccatif Courtray to oil, either linseed or poppy, using the turpentine only for the first effect of shadow.

When oil is used it will require two or three days for the picture to dry. Many advise the use of but little oil, and there are artists who dissapprove of any medium at all.

Before commencing the second painting, a coating of poppy-oil should be put all over the canvas with a large, flat camel's-hair brush. Every bit should be covered without touching the brush twice to the same spot. This softens the first coat of paint sufficiently to allow of its blending with the next. If a raw potato be cut in half and rubbed over the painting before the oil is put on, it will prevent the oil from crawling, or separating into drops on the canvas.

Do not use the same brushes for dark and light tints, but keep them separate. Mix your tints on your palette, the dark tint below the dark colors, and the light tint below the light colors.

In putting away your work after painting, be sure that the tops are screwed on to all your color-tubes, and arrange them neatly in their box. Clean your palette with the palette-knife, and then wipe it off with a rag. Dip your brushes, one by one, in turpentine and wipe them on a rag; this removes most of the paint and makes them easier to wash. Warm, not hot, water should be used for washing the brushes. The best way is to hold several brushes in the right hand, their sticks being in an upright position, dip them in the water, rub them on a piece of common soap, and then scrub them round and round on the palm of the left hand; rinse them in clear water, and wipe dry with a clean rag.

Our limited space will not allow of our going more fully into the details of painting ; but we hope that these directions will give some idea of how to make a beginning as a painter in oil-colors, and after you have made a start you will find two good professors at your elbow to help you along and encourage you —Prof. Judgment and Prof. Experience.

CHAPTER XXIV.

HOW TO MODEL IN CLAY AND WAX.

A N eminent artist once remarked within the writer's hearing that, should he bring into his studio the first dozen boys he happened to meet on the street, taking them as they came, he would probably be able to teach at least half of them to model within six months, whereas there might not be one of them who could be taught to paint at all. Possibly none of these boys would ever become great sculptors, but they could learn to model moderately well. If that is the case with boys, who are apt to be so awkward and clumsy, how quickly could a girl's deft fingers learn to mould and form the plastic clay or wax into life-like forms. In some of the institutions for the blind, deaf and dumb, modelling is taught with great success. Quickly the sensitive fingers of the young inmates run over the object to be copied, and skilfully they reproduce in their clay the form conveyed to them by touch alone. It is pleasant to think that these silent little workers have this new pleasure added to their somewhat limited stock; but at the same time the fact puts to shame some of us who, having all our faculties, the use of all our senses, and not infrequently artistic ability in addition, do so little with the talents intrusted to our care.

Let us to work then, girls, and see if we cannot accomplish at least as much as our unfortunate sisters, who have neither sight nor hearing to guide them.

Modelling in Clay.

The great difficulty we encounter in learning to draw—which is representing things as they appear, not as they really are—will not trouble us in this other department of art, for in modelling it must be our aim to do precisely the reverse, and reproduce an object exactly *as it is*, not as it appears.

Modelling, besides its own worth, is of value as an aid to drawing, for it teaches form, and the shadows on an object can be drawn more intelligently and correctly when it is known just what formations produce them.

A great deal can be done in modelling without the aid of a teacher. So, not waiting to look up a professor, suppose we commence by ourselves and see what we can do. It is very fascinating work, and if a few failures are the result of our first attempt, we need not be discouraged, for what others can do, we also can accomplish.

The writer has lately been initiated into the mysteries of this art, and since, as they say, the person just graduated from a primary department is best fitted to teach in that department, perhaps the hints given here may be better suited to the understanding of beginners than if they were written by a great sculptor, who might forget that everyone does not know, as well as he does himself, the preliminary steps necessary even in accomplishing the grandest results.

Instead of entering into the later and more artistically finished processes we will confine ourselves to the prelude or introduction to modelling ; and then, girls, with the object before you, your only guide and instructor, you must work out the rest for yourselves.

The first thing to do is to provide your

Materials,

and here is a list of all you will need :

1. Clay, such as is used by potters, perfectly free from grit.

2. Modelling-tools. These can be bought at any artists' material store, and the simplest ones might be made at home of hard wood. Only a few tools are necessary for a beginner ; Fig. 162 shows those most useful. The fingers and thumbs are the best of all tools, and a great deal can be done with them, though for fine, delicate modelling tools must be used.

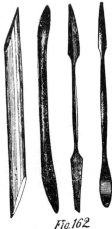

Fig. 162
Modelling Tools

3. Modelling-stand. A regular modelling-stand with rotary platform will cost from eight to twelve dollars and the expense may be an objection ; but the writer has found that an ordinary high office-stool with revolving seat makes a good substitute. If the stool is not high enough it can be raised by placing on the seat a drawing- or pastry-board, and on top of that a square wooden box about one foot high and broad enough to allow sufficient room for a good-sized head and bust.

4. Basin of water and towel for washing and drying the hands.

How to Manage Clay.

Clay costs, near New York, from one to three cents per pound, and about fifty pounds will be required. If possible buy it moist, but if dry, put it into an earthenware jar, or anything that will hold water, and cover with clear water. Let it remain until thoroughly moistened ; then with a stick stir the clay around as, when a small girl, you did the mud while making mud-pies, until it is free from lumps and is perfectly smooth ; clear away from the sides of the jar and pile it up in the centre.

When it is dry enough not to be muddy and is still pliable, it is in a fit condition to work with. It is necessary to keep your hands perfectly clean and conveniences for washing them should be handy.

Do not use muddy water or a dusty towel.

Use any tools that will produce the result desired with the greatest ease ; a little experience will soon determine what they are, but as a rule the largest are best.

When leaving unfinished work cover it with a damp cloth to keep it moist.

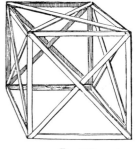

Fig. 163

If you are working on a head, and the features have been commenced, stick a small wooden tool in the head just above the forehead to hold the cloth away from the face, for it is liable to soften the nose and push it out of shape if it rests upon it.

A frame made of laths (Fig. 163) covered with oil-cloth or rubber (an old gossamer water-proof will be just the thing), placed over the modelling, will keep it better than the cloth, as

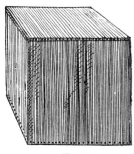

Fig. 164

it excludes the air and prevents its drying (Fig. 164). When using the frame, sprinkle your work by dipping a clean whisk-broom into water and shaking it over the clay. Remember, the clay must always be kept moist and pliable and never allowed to dry. If it does become dry and hard there is nothing to do but to put it back into the jar, and go through the process of damping it again.

Keep your tools clean, and do not allow the metal ones to become rusty, as they will if carelessly left on the modelling-stand when not in use. To avoid trouble of this kind it is best to put your tools in a box where they will be perfectly dry. Unless you wish to go through one of the writer's first experiences, when she was obliged to let her tools lie in a pan of kerosene oil for two days, and then clean them with knife-brick.

How to Preserve Modelled Clay.

If terra-cotta clay is used, it can be baked in a kiln, which will, while hardening, turn it a fine buff terra-cotta color, and make the object, if well modelled, ornamental enough for almost any use.

From the other clay, plaster casts can be taken, and the article reproduced in plaster as many times as desired.

Hints for Modelling a Head.

Always work from a model, and it is best to try copying plaster casts before attempting to model from life.

Place on the centre of your stand a wooden or tin box (a

Fig. 165   Fig. 166   Fig 167

How to Model a Head.

cigar-box will do) to form the base ; cover this with clay in the form of Fig. 165, and stick a support in the middle, as shown in diagram. The support may be a piece of kindling-wood eight inches long and about one inch thick.

Build up the clay around this stick, as in Fig. 166, and with your hands mould the clay, piecing it out here, and cutting off there, until it bears some resemblance to a head, as in Fig. 167.

Still using your hands, get the general proportions of the head, and then commence the features. Begin with the profile, using tools when necessary, and try for character without detail; then turn the head a little and work from that point of view; always look at your model from the same point of view as you do your work. Turn the head in the opposite direction and model the other side, keeping the face evenly balanced. Continue turning your work little by little, until each outline it presents is as near as you can get like the corresponding outline of your model, and then work up the detail.

In modelling any object the same process, of viewing the model from all points, must be gone through with.

Do not strive to obtain a likeness at first, but be careful to have all of your outlines correct, and the likeness will come of itself.

How to Model in Wax.

Modelling-wax prepared at home is much better than any that can be purchased. The following recipe is a very good one :

Modelling-wax.

1 pound pure yellow beeswax.
½ pound corn-starch.
4 ounces Venice turpentine.
1½ ounce Venetian red powder.
½ ounce sweet-oil.
Put the wax on the stove in a saucepan and let it melt ; *take*

off and pour in the turpentine. Never attempt to add this while the wax is near the fire, as it is extremely dangerous. It is a good idea, when buying the ingredients, to have the oil and turpentine put in the same bottle (which should have a wide neck), then they can be poured into the wax at the same time. Warm the bottle of oil and turpentine in hot water to soften before mixing with the wax. Keep stirring all the time. Pour in the corn-starch and Venetian red. When the corn-starch is dissolved the wax is ready for use.

Bas-relief Figure in Wax.

Modelling-wax is much more expensive than clay; it is used principally for small objects and those that require fine workmanship. It is quite useful for sketchy work, as it may be carried about almost like a sketch-book, and being so much cleaner than clay, it can be used even in the parlor without damage to table or carpet. With the wax on a small board one can sit at a table and work very comfortably. The tools for clay modelling may also be used for wax ; probably the smallest will be most useful.

As cold weather advances, we like to pass the evenings in some agreeable occupation, that may be carried on without disturbing the family group around the fireside. For such occasions, modelling in wax will make a pleasant pastime. Sitting quietly, taking part in the general conversation, or listening while someone reads aloud, one may model the wax into many pretty forms to be preserved afterward in plaster, or, obtaining a profile view, a likeness

Bas-relief Head in Wax.

of one of the group may be done in bas-relief. If a slate is used to work on, it will make a good foundation, and the head can first be drawn on it in outline and the wax built over it, using the drawing as a guide. The slate is smooth and firm, and it is a good idea to use it as a foundation for all wax bas-relief, especially when plaster casts are to be taken from the modelling, for in that case the panel forming the background must be perfectly even.

Making Plaster Casts.

CHAPTER XXV.

HOW TO MAKE PLASTER CASTS.

I T is not at all difficult ; anyone can succeed in it who will take the pains to follow carefully the directions given here for making plaster casts. Without the knowledge of drawing or modelling you can in this way reproduce almost any article in a very short time.

Casting in plaster is really so simple a process that even a child can soon learn to manage it nicely.

You will need a board, about a foot and a half square, upon which to work, fifteen or twenty pounds of clay, five pounds of plaster-of-Paris, a cup of warm melted lard, and several small wooden pegs ; these can be made of wooden tooth-picks or matches broken in two.

Select an object with few angles and a smooth surface to experiment on ; a firm round apple will do. Rub the lard all over the apple until every particle is greased ; then lay it in the centre of your board. Take some clay and pack it around it just as high as the middle of the apple, forming a square, as in Fig. 168. Smooth the clay off on the edges and stick pegs in diagonal opposite corners (Fig. 168) ; then with more clay build a wall close around the apple and its case, making the sides one inch higher than the top of the apple (Fig. 169). Put a cupful of clear water into a pan or dish, and stir in enough plaster of Paris to make it like batter ; pour the plaster over the apple, filling the clay box to the top. This makes a half mould of

Fig. 168

Fig. 169

Fig. 170

clay and a half mould of plaster.

When the plaster is hard, which will be in a very short time, pull away your clay wall, and take out the apple and half plaster mould together, lifting the apple from its half clay mould.

Remove the clay from your board and set the plaster mould containing the apple in the centre. Rub lard over the apple and upper edge of the mould, build around it the clay wall, as you did the first time ; roll a small piece of clay into a slender conical shape and stand it upright on top of the apple, as in Fig. 169. This will make a hole through which to pour the plaster when filling the completed mould, and it must stand high enough to reach above the top of the clay wall.

Pour the plaster over the apple as at first, and let it set or harden. Take away the wall of clay once more, and carefully separate the two parts of the mould with the blade of a table-knife ; remove the apple, and all is ready for the final cast which is to produce your plaster fruit (Fig. 170).

Thoroughly grease the inside of your mould, fit the two parts together, and wrap and tie them with string to hold them in place.

Pour in the plaster, through the hole left in one-half of the mould, until it is quite full ; then gently shake it to send the plaster into all small crevices.

Let your mould stand without moving again until sufficient time has elapsed for the plaster to harden ; then gently separate the two parts and you will find a perfect cast of the apple.

The ridge made by the joining of the mould you must scrape off with a sharp knife, or rub with sand-paper.

In taking casts of almost any object not too complicated, this same method must be employed. The only difficulty lies in deciding just where to place the dividing-line, which must be exactly at the broadest part of your model, otherwise you will break your mould in taking the object out.

In casting a hand the clay must be built up around each finger to precisely its widest part ; therefore it is a good plan, before commencing, to mark on the hand, with a fine paint-brush and ink, the line that is to be observed.

When making casts of long objects, or those that are larger at one end than the other, such as vases, always lay them on one side, as a much better mould can be obtained in that way.

I have read that if milk-and-water is used for mixing the plaster, or, after the cast has hardened, if a little oil, in which wax has been dissolved, be applied to the surface, it will take a high polish ; and if left for a while in a smoky room it will acquire the look of old ivory.

The same writer also states, without giving the proportions, that liquid gum-arabic and sufficient alum in solution, mixed and put into the slip or soft plaster, will make the cast so hard that it can be set as a panel in a cabinet.

The dead white of plaster-casts is frequently objected to when they are wanted for ornaments ; but that difficulty is easily overcome by mixing dry colors with the plaster before wetting it.

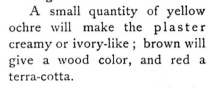
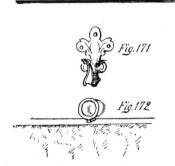

Fig. 171

Fig. 172

A small quantity of yellow ochre will make the plaster creamy or ivory-like ; brown will give a wood color, and red a terra-cotta.

Plaster-casts can also be bronzed with gold, red, or green bronze, which makes quite handsome ornaments of them. A plaster panel in bass-relief, bronzed with gold bronze and mounted on black or dark-colored velvet, is an exceedingly rich wall decoration.

To mount a panel of this kind you must first secure a smooth, flat piece of board, not more than half an inch thick, and just large enough to allow about four inches of the background to show all around the panel when it is mounted. Cover the board with velvet or velveteen, bringing it smoothly over the edges, and tacking it down at the back. Fasten on it a small brass hook. Fig. 171 is the best kind to use, which is tacked to the board with small, brass tacks.

Make a ring or loop for hanging the panel in this way :

Take a piece of wire about three inches long, form a small loop in the middle, and give the wire several twists ; then bend the ends out on each side.

Scrape a narrow place in the top edge of the panel, just long enough to admit the wire, and about half an inch deep ; then place the wire in this little ditch and fill up the hole to the top with soft plaster. When this hardens the ring will be quite secure. Fig. 172.

CHAPTER XXVI.

CHINA PAINTING.

ERTAINLY you can paint on china; have confidence, and do not hesitate because you may never have studied art, but select the china you wish to decorate and we will go to work. First, take what is needed for present use from the following

List of Materials.

PALETTE.

A common square, white china tile is the best palette for mineral colors; but in case you have no tile, an old white plate will answer the purpose.

BRUSHES.

These are of camel's-hair, Figs. 173 and 174, are broad and flat, and are used in placing the color on the china when the surface is to be tinted. Fig. 175 is for blending the color after it is on the china; it is called a blender, and is useful where borders and surfaces are to be tinted. Figs. 176 and 178 are for general use. Fig. 177, with its long, slender point, is for gilding, another similar brush is needed for India-ink. Mark the two brushes in some way to distinguish them one from the other, and never use either for any paint except that for which it is intended. Fig. 179 is a stipple for blending the colors when painting a face, a fish, the sky of a landscape, or wherever delicate, fine blending is needed.

To clean the brushes after using : dip them in turpentine and wipe off the paint on a cotton cloth, repeating the operation until the brushes are perfectly clean ; then dip them in fat oil, and bring them out smooth to a fine point. Do not allow the brushes to become bent over, if the box is not long enough

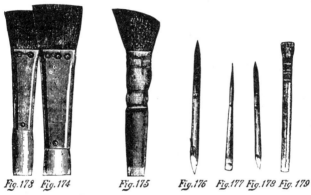

Fig. 173   Fig. 174   Fig. 175   Fig. 176   Fig. 177 Fig. 178 Fig. 179

Brushes for China Painting (about one-half actual size).

for them to lie out straight, remove the quills from the wooden handles and they can easily be replaced when needed. Should the brushes seem a little stiff at the next painting, immerse them in turpentine ; this will make them soft and pliable.

To save the expensive gold paint, the gilder should be kept exclusively for gilding, and need not be cleaned, as it will not be injured if the hairs are carefully straightened out and the brush put away with the gold.

KNIVES.

Fig. 180 is a horn palette-knife for mixing Lacroix white, the yellows, and all such colors as are injured by contact with metal. It is the only knife used with the mat paints for Royal Worcester decoration. Fig. 181 is a steel palette-knife for general use. Fig. 182 is a steel scraper for removing paint from the china when necessary. Always clean the knives after mixing one color, before using them for another.

Fig. 180
Horn Palette-
knife.

Fig. 181 *Fig. 182*
Steel Palette- Steel
knife. Scraper.
(Reduced sizes.)

PAD.

This is made of a ball of cotton tied in a piece of soft lining-silk, fine linen, or cotton-cloth (Fig. 183) and is used for tinting.

THE PAINTS

are Lacroix's colors; they come in tubes and should be squeezed out on the palette and used as in oil painting, with a little turpentine and fat oil when desired. To moisten the colors while painting dip your brush, carefully, without shaking or moving it around, into the turpentine or oil, and then in the color. Allow the paint to lie on the palette as it comes from the tube, except when two colors are mixed, or when using the stipple for blending one tint with another, or when tinting, then the paint must be mixed and rubbed down with oil and turpentine. Keep the colors in a *cool* place, and when

Fig. 183.
Printer's Pad.

returning them to the box, after you have finished painting, do not lay them back on the same side. Always remember to turn them over so that the color will not separate from the oil. If you are careful and follow these hints, your colors will keep in a good condition. We would advise you to purchase the paints as they are needed, thereby avoiding all unnecessary expenditure.

OILS.

Fat oil is for general use in painting. Clove oil is used in its place when two or more tints are to be blended together, as in painting a face, etc. Capavia oil is always mixed with the colors for grounding.

TURPENTINE

is in constant demand in china painting. It is used with all the different oils, paints, bronzes, and gilt, and should be poured in a small cup or any little vessel, and kept convenient while painting.

TAR PASTE

comes in bottles, and is used to take the color off of tinted backgrounds, in order to leave a clean surface of the china in which to paint the design in different colors. The paste should be rubbed down smooth on the tile with the palette-knife ; if it is too hard, a little tar oil may be added. A small brush is best to use for the paste in covering the design you wish to wash out ; but be very careful to keep within the outlines, for this mixture will take off the color wherever it touches. When the tint is light the paste may be wiped off in a few moments ; but when it is dark, the paste must be allowed to remain on for perhaps hours before the paint will be sufficiently softened to remove.

Use small balls of raw cotton-batting in wiping off the paste, and take a fresh piece for every stroke. If any of the tar paste is left on the tile after using, scrape it off with your palette-knife, and return it to the bottle.

MAT GOLD

is for gilding, and can be either burnished or highly polished. It comes on a little square of glass inclosed in a box. This gold can also be used as solid ornamentation or for delicate tracery, and is sometimes used over colors, greens excepted, but is then never so bright as when on the plain white china.

The gold is prepared for painting on a tile kept expressly for the purpose, and which must not be used for any other paint. Place some of the gold on the palette with your palette-knife, and mix a little turpentine with it by dipping your palette-knife in the turpentine and rubbing down the gold with the turpentine on the knife. If more is needed, again dip your knife in the liquid, and do so as often as it is necessary ; but you must use the utmost care not to have the gold too thin ; gild with it as stiff as it can be smoothly applied.

Should any gold remain on the palette after the gilding is finished, mix in a little turpentine and scrape it all up with your palette-knife, then replace the gold on the square of glass.

Silver is used the same as gold.

The bronzes are for handles and conventional flowers or figures ; they are rich and pleasing in effect.

PURE GOLD

cannot be employed for gilding plain white china. It also comes on a little square of glass and is used for gilding over colors. It can be applied over any mineral paint or relief, and may be polished or burnished as desired.

This gold is mixed with turpentine, for use in the same manner as mat gold.

RELIEF.

The best is mat relief, which comes in a powder, and is used for both tube and mat colors. It is prepared by mixing with a very little fat oil and turpentine, and should be applied stiff enough to make a raised line. It is useful where a small raised surface is desired, as on the edge of a leaf or the petals of flowers. A fish-net is much more effective if the gilt be put on over the relief. Should the relief dry and become too stiff while using, soften it from time to time with a little turpentine, always using the horn knife for mixing, as the steel knife should never be used with the relief, and the relief must always be fired before the gilt is applied.

Enamel white can be mixed with delicate tints, turpentine, and a very little fat oil for raised flowers; or the white alone may be used for pearls, imitation of lace, or embroidery, but its use is limited and it will not stand two firings, so should always be the last paint applied.

MAT COLORS

are for Royal Worcester decorations. They come in powders, and when mixed with a little oil and turpentine are used in the same way as the Lacroix tube paints.

BOX FOR MATERIALS.

Select a light wooden box, or one of strong pasteboard; have the box of a convenient size to contain all your painting materials.

PIECES OF SOFT, OLD MUSLIN,

torn in different sizes, and plenty of them, are very essential for cleaning brushes and rubbing paint off the tile or china; the demand for clean pieces will be constant while painting.

CHINA.

Have this of the very finest French ware, without spots or other imperfections of the surface, and never attempt to decorate china after it has been used, for it seldom proves satisfactory.

A Monochrome Painting.

For this we will need a tile, a pad, a broad flat brush (Fig. 173), some turpentine, capavia, two tubes of paint—one copper-water green, the other brown green—a palette-knife, and some pieces of cotton cloth. Now be sure your china is perfectly clean and dry, then mix your copper-water green for

Tinting.

Place enough color on your palette to cover the entire surface to be tinted; dip your palette-knife in the capavia oil and tap it off the knife on the tile; in the same way place turpentine on the tile with the oil, and use your palette-knife to *thoroughly* mix the paint, oil, and turpentine. If the mixture seems too stiff add a little more oil and turpentine, but be careful not to have the paint too thin so that it will run; test its consistency with a brush on a clean place on the tile.

As a rule, the proportions for tinting should be five drops of paint to three of capavia, mixed with a little turpentine.

The paint being prepared, take the flat brush and begin to paint; rapidly cover the entire surface with color. Then go over the tinting with a pad, touching lightly and gently, not letting the pad rest a moment on the paint, nor touching it twice in the same place in succession. Continue going over and over it until the grounding is even and of a uniform tint. Then set the china away to dry, in a safe place, where it will be free from dust. Always make a fresh pad every time you tint, and a separate one for each color used, as a pad cannot do service more than once.

All tinted grounds and borders are made in this way, the capavia oil and turpentine being mixed with any of the grounding colors you may wish to use. Tinting is very easily and quickly done ; but should anything happen to spot or mar the evenness of the grounding, the paint must all be washed off with turpentine, and the china tinted over again.

When your green-tinted china is perfectly dry, gather some maple leaves and with the brown-green paint try a

New Method of Decorating China.

The leaves must be free from dust and moisture and perfectly fresh. Place a small quantity of paint on the palette, do not mix the paint with oil or turpentine, but rub it down well on the tile as it comes from the tube ; make the paint perfectly smooth, now press a small clean pad down lightly, lifting and again pressing until the paint is smoothly distributed on the pad ; next select a leaf and place it face or right side downward on a piece of folded newspaper, then press the pad down on the under side of the leaf, which is now lying upward, repeating the operation until the leaf is sufficiently covered with paint. This done, carefully place the leaf painted side downward on the china, over it lay a piece of common wrapping-paper, and rub your finger gently all over the covered leaf. Then remove the outside paper and very carefully take up the leaf, when an exact impress of the natural leaf will be printed on the china. Repeat the operation with another leaf either larger or smaller, and still another, using as many as you wish ; connect the leaves to a central branch by making the stems and branch in the same color with a small paint-brush. To do this paint a long line for the branch and other smaller ones for the stems of the leaves. Set the china away to dry, and it will be ready for firing. Very pretty effects may be secured by using two shades of one color for the tinting and designs. First tint the china, and when it is perfectly dry, ornament it with the same paint in the manner described, making the ground of a lighter tint than the decorations. The colors of fall leaves can be used on white china, or you may make the combinations and designs of whatever is most pleasing.

It is well to have some idea of what your decoration is to be like before commencing with the leaves. If you desire a spray, try to place the leaves as they are on the natural spray, or as represented in some picture taken for a guide. The prints also look well used in a conventional style. As any kind of leaves or grasses that will print can be employed, your decorations will always be original and true to nature.

Flowers are more difficult to print, yet when the impressions are successful they are very beautiful.

You will find this new idea an interesting method of ornamenting china, while the decorations may be made in much less time than is usually required. The style is suitable for dinner-sets, vases, tiles, plaques, and lamps, and it requires no knowledge of drawing or painting to decorate china in this simple yet effective manner.

Tracing.

Lay a piece of tracing-paper over the design to be copied and trace the outlines very carefully with a hard lead-pencil. Then have your china perfectly clean and dry, and give it a wash all over with a clean cotton cloth wet with clear turpentine. Place a piece of red transfer-paper on the china, and having determined exactly where you wish the design, lay the tracing-paper over the transfer-paper on the space for decoration. Use bits of gummed paper on the corners of the transfer- and trac·ing-paper to hold them in place, and carefully go over the lines with a lead-pencil, remove the papers, and the design will be clearly outlined on the ware. Now rub a little India-ink on a common individual butter-plate of white china, and using a fine brush, very carefully paint over the red marks with the India-ink, making your lines as distinct and delicate as possible. When this is finished, again wash the china with turpentine to remove any of the red coloring which may be apparent on its surface. Thus prepared the design can be painted, or the china may first be tinted and allowed to dry, when the outlines will be plainly visible through the tinting, and the color can be re-moved from the design with tar paste. Use the scraper to take the grounding off of minute spaces. For those skilled in draw-ing it will not be necessary to trace the design, as it can readily be sketched on the china with a lead-pencil after the ware has first received a coat of turpentine, and when tinted the decora-tion can be drawn on after the grounding has thoroughly dried, and the color may be removed as before.

Mottled Grounds.

Prepare the paint as for tinting, only make it more moist, and dab it lightly over the china by means of a piece of cotton cloth on the end of your finger ; this will give the china a mot·tled appearance which in some cases is preferred to the plain grounding.

Snow Landscape.

We will take for example Fig. 184.

After tracing the design, paint a streak across the sky, just back and a little above the trees, with carnation No. 1 mixed with clove oil and turpentine, then another narrow streak above it of a lighter shade, and another still lighter of the same color, allowing each tint to meet. Next mix light sky-blue with clove oil and turpentine, and paint as deep a tint as it will make across the sky at the top of the plate, graduating it down to the

Fig. 184

red ; use the stipple immediately while the paint is wet to blend the colors and tints ; this finished, make the reflections on the ice, beginning with carnation No. 1 for the ice nearest the castle, and ending near the bottom of the plate with the deepest shade of light sky-blue, using the colors mixed for the sky. Paint the foliage in the background with neutral gray and sky-blue mixed with turpentine and fat oil for the darker tones, and turquoise-blue with neutral gray, turpentine and fat oil for the lighter parts, also for shading the darker portions of the snow. Then take brown No. 4 as it comes from the tube, with a little turpentine when necessary, for the shading of the trees in the foreground, the outlining of the castle, and the tufts of grass and edges of the ice in places where the copy requires it.

Leave the white china for the high lights and the white snow on the roof of the castle, on the trees, and here and there on the ground.

Paint the castle with neutral gray and yellow ochre mixed with turpentine and fat oil, and its windows with brown No. 4, using the color as it comes from the tube. Now allow the plate to dry and then have it fired, after which mix carnation No. 1 with clove oil and turpentine, and touch up the sky and reflections on the ice, using the stipple if necessary; then mix light sky-blue with clove oil and turpentine and paint the sky where that color is required and the light shadows on the snow; then take yellow ochre for portions of the trees, places in the foreground, and touching up the castle; mix this color with fat-oil and turpentine.

Again strengthen the trees and other places, where the painting requires it, with brown No. 4, unmixed, except with a little turpentine when necessary; for the last touches mix relief-white with fat oil and clean turpentine, using the horn-palette knife always when mixing the white; this is to be laid on, in little raised places, where the snow is whitest on the ground and where the snow has lodged in the trees.

Now inclose the snow scene with a gilt band, using the stipple to make an uneven edge of gilt on the surrounding white rim; the gold next to the picture must be perfectly smooth and even; put this on with your fine long-haired brush;

then make a similar band on the edge of the plate and it will be finished and ready for its last firing.

Almost any snow landscape with a sunset sky may be painted in this way.

Often you can find Christmas cards which will furnish very good copies.

Fig. 185

How to Paint a Head on China.

Select a pretty copy from some photograph, as in Fig. 185 ; very carefully trace the head on a plate and go over the lines with Indian ink; next give the plate another wash with turpentine, to remove all remains of the color from the transfer paper ; then mix thoroughly two parts of carnation No. 2 with one part of ivory-yellow, adding a little turpentine and clove oil ; give the face and neck a wash with this color and touch up the cheeks with carnation No. 1 mixed with clove oil and turpentine ; now lay on the shadows with neutral gray, five parts, mixed with deep chrome-green, one part, using clove oil and turpentine in mixing the colors ; last, the deepest shadows with brown No. 4, two parts, to one of ivory-black, mixed together with clove oil and turpentine, and immediately before any of the paint dries use the stipple to blend the colors, making the face round out and have the blending soft and true to nature ; set your copy before you and try to have the shadows on the face you paint correspond exactly with those in the copy.

Now leave the face and neck, and place some brown No. 4 on the tile ; do not mix it with anything ; use it as it comes from the tube, dipping your brush in turpentine when it becomes necessary to thin the paint a little ; with this paint the shading of the hair and follow with your brush, as nearly as possible, the sway of the masses. That finished, paint the eyes, eyebrows, and nostrils with brown No. 4 and ivory-black mixed together as they come from the tubes, using when necessary a little turpentine ; then mix a little carnation No. 1 with fat oil for the lips. Next turn your attention to the drapery ; shade the white material with gray No. 1, unmixed, and gray No. 2 for the deeper shadows, mixed with fat oil and turpentine.

For the handkerchief on the head mix emerald-green with fat-oil and turpentine ; put it on in a light tint, so that the handkerchief can be shaded, when dry, with the same color.

When the plate is dry, it is ready to be fired. After it has been fired touch up the shading on the face and neck with two parts of carnation No. 2 mixed with one of brown No. 4, using clove oil and turpentine while mixing; and for the deepest shadows mix two parts of brown and one of ivory-black together with clove oil and turpentine. This must be put on carefully, so that the shadows will not be too dark. Use the stipple to blend the shadows ; then give the hair a wash of yellow ochre all over, and touch up the handkerchief on the head with emerald green, the same you used before.

For the background of the head mix light coffee, turpentine, and capavia oil ; make it an even tint with the blender (Fig. 175); the brush must be clean and dry, and used in the same manner as the pad in tinting, then, for the outer border, mix celestial-blue with capavia and turpentine, and with your large flat brush paint the border and blend it to an even tint with your pad. When this is finished wipe off the paint around the edge as evenly as possible, so that the bare china may be left to receive a band of gold. Roll up a piece of white cotton cloth into a small point and with this remove the paint around the inner edge of the blue border, making an even narrow white band ; this is also to be gilded.

On a clean tile mix the mat gold with turpentine, and using the slender, fine, long-haired brush, carefully cover the white bands of china with gold ; when this is finished the plate is ready for the second and last firing. If a fairer complexion be desired, make the flesh-tints of the same colors, only lighter in tint ; try the paint on the edge of the tile until the tint is correct. Always try your colors this way when painting any design. For blue eyes use sky-blue shaded with black ; the high light of the eye may be left the white of the china. If you wish the hair very light, take ivory-yellow and shade with sepia and black.

Once more we say, be *very* careful in tracing not to get the head or features out of drawing, as so much depends upon the correct outlines. Before sending china to be fired, paint in small figures the date on which it was decorated and add your name or initials.

How to Paint a Carp, Sea-weed, and Fish-net on China.

Having traced in your design very carefully, mix one part of neutral gray with two parts of sky-blue, some clove oil, and turpentine ; with this paint the upper edge of the back of the fish dark, graduating to white along near the centre of the fish ; stipple this so that it will look even, soft, and rounding, keeping it dark on the edge and tinting down to the white china ; paint the tail and dorsal fins a flat tint of gray No. 2 mixed with fat oil and turpentine ; then mix carnation No. 2 with fat oil and turpentine for a flat tint on gills, mouth, and ventral fin ; shade the mouth with the same color and paint the anal and pectoral fins a flat tint of car-

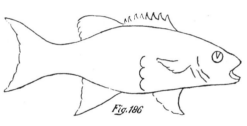

Fig. 196

nation No. 2 mixed with sepia ; when dry shade with the same color, and also shade the gills and fins painted carnation with carnation, and the dorsal fins and tail shade with ivory-black mixed with fat oil and turpentine ; try the paint with your brush until you get rather a gray tint instead of black, and use this for the shading ; now paint the rows of spots along the back of the fish ivory-black, making the dots smaller as they approach the tail ; and with your eraser take the paint off of the eye, leaving a clean white spot of china ; paint a fine circle around this in ivory-black ; then paint a portion of the eye black, leaving the white china for the high lights ; in painting the scales and lower part of the fish use gray No. 1 as it comes from the tube, mark an outline of gray along the lower edge of the fish and stipple it off in the white, remembering this gray must occupy only a narrow line along the lower edge of the fish.

Commence to mark the scales in gray No. 1 by making a line of them with a fine-pointed brush downward across the body of the fish (Fig. 186) and this will be a guide to build out from (Fig. 187); after the painting has thoroughly dried begin again by marking, on the head and around the eye, the tiny scales in gray No. 2, with a little fat oil and turpentine, and paint a line along the upper edge of the head and back with brown No. 4, and another lighter line of the same color along the back just below and adjoining the first one; paint the eye and markings on the head brown and strengthen the tail and dorsal fins with gray No. 2; touch up around the gills with sky blue, also with yellow ochre where the copy requires it. Then

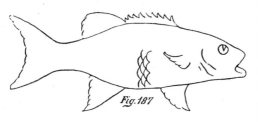

Fig. 187

turn your attention to the sea-weeds; mark the thread-like branches of these in different colors, using carnation, brown No. 4, gray No. 2, and brown-green; paint each weed in one color, place the sea-weeds on one side or corner of the plate, making them branch out this way and that, as in nature. Now clean off your palette and mix some mat relief for the fish-net, which is to be placed over and across a portion of the plate; with a lead-pencil mark the netting on the plate, but do not touch the fish; then with a very fine brush follow the markings with the relief, when it is necessary to paint across the fish, your eye and the copy must be your guides, as it would take the paint off the fish to attempt any marking on it. The relief on the fish cannot be altered, so be careful to have it correct the first time. Should the line of relief be too broad in other places, remove it with your scraper and make another trial. When the plate is perfectly dry it must be fired, after which put in a background of warm gray mixed with capavia and turpentine ; bring this to an even tint with the blender, and if any paint blends over on the fish wipe it off while the color is damp ; also remove the paint from the netting and set the china away to allow the color to thoroughly dry ; next paint broad sweeps across the plate, but not over the fish, with gray No. 2 mixed with fat oil and turpentine, to represent the different tints of the water, and again remove the paint from the net ; now touch up the sea-weed and the fish where they need strengthening, then give the fish a very light wash of gray No. 1.

Here and there along the upper edges of the water colored gray No. 2 make a very fine line with enamel or relief-white mixed with a little fat oil and turpentine ; gild the fish-net, using either pure gold or mat gold, cover the relief carefully with the gold, and put it on thick but in fine lines ; this accomplished, finish by gilding the edges of the plate with mat gold, and when dry send it to be fired. To avoid mistakes when sending china to be fired, state whether you wish the gold burnished, dull, or polished.

Foliage on China Made With a Sponge.

Prepare the paint with fat oil and turpentine, rub it down smooth, then with a small sponge apply the colors, using different shades as the first dry, and touching up afterward with a brush ; in this way you can also paint backgrounds which cannot be made with the brush.

Mixing Colors.

The best way to paint with safety when you are in doubt what colors will mix, is to test them yourself. For this purpose take a French china plate and make experiments with different colors on the plate ; at the same time write down a memorandum of the paints used and of those mixed, have the plate fired ; then paste your memorandum on the back. Use this for reference, and with experience will come the full knowledge of the use of all the paints.

Royal Worcester Ware

is very delicate and dainty and something quite novel for amateurs in the way of china decorations.

Very beautiful pieces of this ware may be seen now in all the leading china establishments in New York City, and so choice is it that even some of the largest jewelry stores have rare Royal Worcester vases among their most valuable articles on exhibition.

We know of no book that teaches this art of decoration, and although we have seen some amateur work which only an expert could distinguish from the genuine article itself, we think our exposition of the method is the first of its kind printed in this country ; and girls, if you would know the secret, so that you also may be able to paint and gild in this beautiful fashion, you have only to listen while the writer tells how to decorate a Royal Worcester vase as she did ; then you will have a practicable and detailed method which we know to be good, having tried it.

Select a vase of the finest French china, and be sure that it is perfectly clean, dry, and free from dust. Then with a clean white cotton cloth give the vase a wash all over with clear turpentine, and having chosen your design, make a tracing of it on the vase, and it will be ready for grounding. Mix enough mat lemon-yellow to cover the entire surface of the vase. First place a little of the powder on the tile, then dip your palette-knife in the capavia oil and tap it off on the tile ; in the same way drop turpentine on the tile with the oil. Use a horn palette-knife and *thoroughly* mix the paint, oil, and turpentine ; if the mixture seems too stiff, add a little more oil and turpentine, but be careful not to have the paint too thin, so that it will run ; try the paint with a brush on a clean place on the tile to see if it is of the right consistency and shade ; do not let the color be too intense ; it should be of a delicate tint, and if it is too dark add a very little more oil. Take a broad, flat brush and begin to paint at the top of the vase, passing around with short strokes rapidly over its whole surface ; go over the tinting with a pad, touching lightly and gently ; then set the vase away to dry in a dry place free from dust. The Indian-ink outlines will be plainly visible through the paint, and when the grounding or tinting has *thoroughly* hardened, to remove the color from the design, mix a little of the tar paste upon a clean tile by working it with

Fig. 188.—Royal Worcester Vase.

your palette-knife until it is smooth. Use a small brush and go over the design with this mixture, covering every part except the stems and fine grasses ; be very careful not to go outside of the lines. When the design is all painted with the paste, begin at that first covered and wipe off the tar paste with small pieces of cotton batting rolled into little balls, using a fresh wad for each stroke ; clean it all off carefully and the vase will present vacant white china spots where the flowers, leaves, and bird are soon to appear. For a guide we will take Fig. 188. Now mix a little mat pink with fat oil and turpentine in the same way you prepared the grounding yellow, only this time fat oil takes the place of capavia ; use the horn palette-knife as before ; the steel knife should never be used with the Royal Worcester colors, as the metal is apt to rub in with the paint, dulling and spoiling the colors. Paint all the flowers a flat tint of light pink. Always try the color first on the tile until you have the desired shade. By the time all the flowers have received their tint of color, those first painted will be dry enough for shading. Observe attentively the copy, and notice where the different flowers are shaded ; then shade yours with the same color, following as nearly as possible the copy before you.

For painting the leaves, mix separately with turpentine and fat oil, mat light yellow-green, mat dark-green, and mat blue green. These colors can be used separately or any two mixed if desired. Shade the leaves with mat yellow-brown mixed with the different greens. Paint the body of the bird a flat tint of mat gold-yellow and the top of its head and back green ; the edges of wing and tail and eye must be of mat black. When the bird is dry, shade its breast with broad sweeps of mat gold-yellow, according to the copy ; then mix black with yellow-brown for the other shading on the bird's breast, and mix black with blue for painting and shading the wings and tail.

While the paint is drying on the vase mix the mat relief for the raised edges of bird, flowers, and stems. Mix the relief with turpentine and fat oil, making it as stiff as it can be used. With a very fine brush outline the bird, its wings, and tail ; also a few strokes on its breast, tail, and back ; be sure the relief is stiff enough to make a fine raised line ; then outline the flowers and the stems ; the leaves are not raised on the edges. When this is finished the vase is ready for its first firing. Allow the ware to become perfectly dry before sending it to the firers.

As great care should be taken with the firing of royal Worcester china, send your vase to the most reliable firers you know of, and when it is fired and returned, all that remains to be done is to carefully gild the vase. Mix pure gold with turpentine, but do not have it too thin, as the gold should be applied as thick as possible. For fine gilding use a fine small brush with long hairs ; this will make a distinct thread-like line ; first cover all the relief with the gold, next outline the leaves, veining them if necessary ; then with thick gold make your grasses according to the copy. When the gold becomes too stiff work in a little more turpentine. After you have finished this gilding, mix some mat gold with turpentine and gild the top rim of the vase ; use the small stipple brush cut off square at the end (Fig. 179), and bring the border down unevenly along its lower edge, making it the same way on the inside of the vase ; then with the fine long-haired gilder cover the upper edge of the vase thick with gold. This finished, gild the bottom of the vase in like manner and make the handle solid gilt ; after it is all dry the vase is ready for its second and last firing, and when it returns again from the firers you will have a piece of beautiful Royal Worcester ware similar to that seen at Tiffany's.

The mat colors used, remove all the gloss from the china, and when mat lemon-yellow forms the grounding, the china comes from the firing having the appearance of beautiful decorated ivory without any glaze.

This ware must be seen to be appreciated, and is suitable for vases and ornaments, but the Royal Worcester colors cannot be used on table china, for any grease coming in contact with the colors would spoil them.

Exquisite little vases of all shapes are decorated in this manner ; the delicate gold tracery and outlining brings the designs out effectively. In this style of painting the decoration is more conventional, and does not require the same amount of working up and shading, but is as a rule, treated simply, flat tints with a little shading being all that is required. Almost any floral design can be used on royal Worcester, when outlined with relief and gold ; there are, however, copies which come expressly for the purpose.

CHAPTER XXVII.

A CHAPTER ON FRAMES.

AFTER the foregoing chapters on drawing and painting, it is surely our duty to provide the means
of framing the various pictures which we hope
will be the result of their teachings. Un-
framed, a picture is apt to be tucked away out
of sight, or it becomes rumpled and spoiled
when left lying about, and a picture-frame, as a rule, is quite an
expensive article ; but with a little ingenuity and good taste
almost any girl may manufacture frames, if not of equal finish,
at least as durable and quite as artistic as any the dealer can
produce.

The cost ? The cost is the price of a wooden stretcher and
a bottle of gold paint.

The first sketch shown here (Fig. 189) will give some idea
of the appearance of a frame decorated appropriately for a
marine picture. The articles necessary for this frame are a
stretcher, some rope, a piece of fish-net, several dried starfish,
and gold paint. The stretcher must first be gilded ; then the
rope, upon which the fish-net has been strung, should be fastened with small tacks around the outer edge, joining it at the
corner, where the starfish will hide the ends. The net must
be large enough to drape gracefully across one corner, along
the top, and fall a short distance down the other side of the
frame. When the starfish, graduating in size, are tacked

around the draped corner, and they, as well as the rope and net, are given a coat of gilt, a pretty, unique, and substantial frame is the result.

If starfish are not to be had, sea-shells may be used instead (these of course will have to be glued in place), and if fish-net

Original Design—Marine Picture Frame.

is also out of reach, a piece of fine netted hammock can be used as a substitute.

For the benefit of those who spend their summers at the sea-shore where such things are obtainable, I would advise that a small collection be made of the quaint and pretty products of the place, as they will be found useful in various ways for decorative purposes.

The next sketch (Fig. 190) shows a corner section of frame especially appropriate for a flower piece. The open lattice-like border is cut with a sharp penknife from stiff pasteboard and tacked along the edge of the frame.

The pattern shown in diagram (Fig. 191) is simple, quite easily made, and well suited for a border, though other and more elaborate ones may be used. This border must, of course, be made in sections. The edges to be connected should be cut to fit exactly, then after tacking them upon the frame the whole may be laid upon a table, face downward, and strips of paper pasted across the joints (see Fig. 192), which will hold them securely together. If the work is neatly done, when the gilt is applied all traces of the joints will disappear. The decorations of this frame consist of a spray of artificial rosebuds and leaves, gilded and tacked on the upper left-hand corner. A few scattered rosebuds look well upon the lower part of the frame near the right-hand side.

Fig. 190.—Section of Decorated Frame.

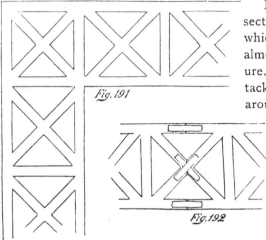

Fig. 191

Fig. 192

Section of Border for Decorated Frame.

Figure 193 is the section of a frame which will look well on almost any kind of picture. It is made by tacking a small rope around the inside edge and then covering it and the frame with crumpled tin-foil, which, after it is pressed to fit the rope, is brought around and tacked on the wrong side of the frame, joining that edge which is turned over the top. Care should be taken while handling the tin-foil not to flatten it, as its beauty depends upon its roughness. The pieces are joined by simply lapping one edge over the other, the uneven surface hiding all seams. This frame like the others must be gilded.

A very effective rough surface on a frame can be produced by dabbing on it with a palette-knife the scrapings of the palette. Of course this frame can-

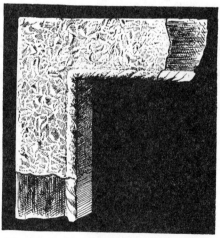

Fig. 193.—Section of Frame covered with Tin-foil

not be made in a day, but if every time the palette is cleaned the paint is used in this way it will not be long before the surface is covered and ready for gilding.

The cork paper used in packing bottles makes quite a handsome frame for black and white pictures or photographs (Fig. 194). This paper is sprinkled all over with small bits of cork, making a rough surface and one admirably suited to the purpose.

First the foundation of the frame is cut of stiff pasteboard exactly the size and shape desired ; then the cork paper is cut the width of the frame and glued securely to it, the corners being joined as in Fig. 195. The frame is very pretty when left its natural color, as it resembles carved wood at a little distance, but it can be gilded if preferred.

The inside mat is made of white or gray-tinted cardboard, cut with the open space for the picture, from half an inch to an inch smaller

Fig. 194.
Cork Frame.

than the opening of the frame. The mat is pasted to the back of the frame and then the entire back is covered with strong paper pasted at the top and two side edges, and left open at the bottom until the picture is shoved in place, when the lower edge is fastened also. The mat will look well if the inside edge is gilded.

Another frame is made in the same manner as the one just

described, only instead of using cork paper a thick coating of glue is put all over the face of the foundation, and sand or small pebbles are sprinkled over the entire surface. This must be quickly done before the glue has time to harden.

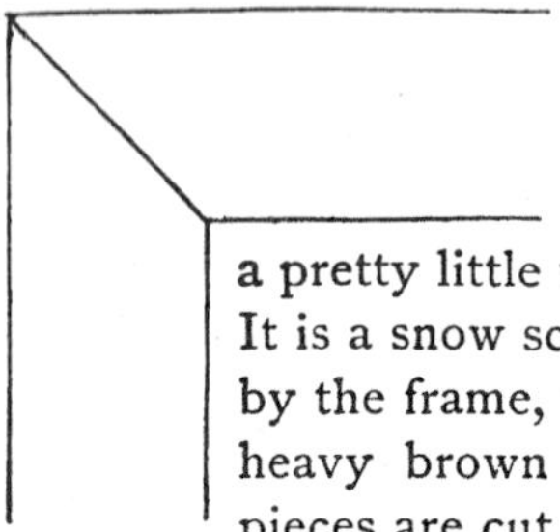

Fig. 195.

The writer has in her possession a pretty little winter landscape done in water-colors. It is a snow scene, and its light effect is well set off by the frame, which is made simply of two pieces of heavy brown strawboard or pasteboard. The two pieces are cut exactly the same size ; then the centre is cut out of one, leaving a broad frame of equal width on all sides. The picture is placed between these two boards, which are then glued together. The cord for hanging it is fastened to two small brass rings which are attached to pieces of tape glued to the back of the frame, as in Fig. 196. Fig. 197 shows how a piece of paper is pasted over the tape to hold it more securely.

When making a frame of this kind the picture to be framed should first be measured and the width of the frame decided upon ; then cutting a piece of paper the size the open space is to be, or one-half inch smaller all round than the picture, it must be laid upon the pasteboard and a mark drawn around it showing its exact size and proportion (Fig. 198). The width of the frame can then be measured from these lines, which will place the opening exactly in the centre (Fig. 199). The lines must be perfectly straight and the measurements correct or a lop-sided frame will be the result.

Fig. 196 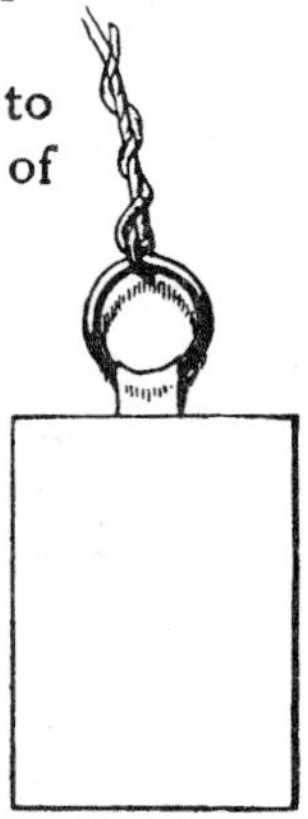   Fig 197

In cutting out the frame a sharp knife should be used, and
it will be a great help in keeping the lines straight if a ruler is

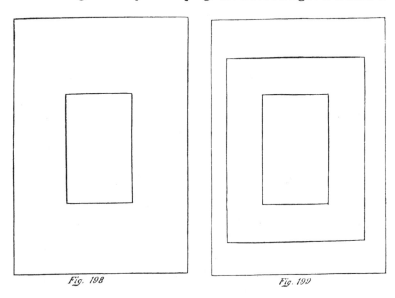

Fig. 198   Fig. 199

held down firmly close to the line to be cut, and the knife
guided by that.

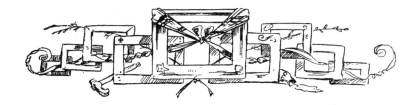

CHAPTER XXVIII.

THANKSGIVING.

NOT to Pagan ancestors in far-away countries, but to our own Pilgrim Fathers do we trace the origin of Thanksgiving Day—as purely American as our Independence Day. Instituted by William Bradford, the Governor of Plymouth, and first observed by the Puritans, who, suffering from hunger and privation, were truly thankful when the first harvest brought them the means of support for the approaching winter, it has come to us as " the religious and social festival that converts every family mansion into a family meeting-house." The pleasant New England custom of the gathering together of families to celebrate Thanksgiving is now observed in most of our States. From far and near they come, filling the cars with merry family parties, who chatter away of anticipated pleasures to be found in the old home. Little children taught to lisp grandma and grandpa are instructed by their mammas not to be afraid of the old gentleman who will meet them at the depot, nor the dear old lady who waits with open arms at the door of grandpa's house.

Children old enough to know what a Thanksgiving at grandpa's is like are wild with delight at the prospect before them.

Their eyes brighten at the thought of the great pantry where grandma keeps her doughnuts and cookies ; of the cellar with its bins of sweet and juicy apples ; of the nuts and popcorn, all of which taste so much nicer at grandma's than anywhere else.

And then what fun the games will be which they will play with cousins, who, though rather shy at first, will soon make friends. The lovely young aunties, too, who help grandma entertain all these guests, will join in the games and suggest and carry out schemes of amusements which the children would never think of.

One Little Indian.

What a happy holiday it is, how social and pleasant and comfortable and easy ! How near and dear all the bright faces gathered around the long table at the Thanksgiving-dinner, seem to be. Truly, we should all be thankful that we have a Thanksgiving.

However, this chapter is not written merely to generalize upon the pleasures of the day, but in order that we may offer something new, in the way of amusement, which will add to the fund of merriment on this occasion. The series of

Pilgrim's Spectacles.

Impromptu Burlesque Tableaux

illustrating some of the principal events in our history will be appropriate for this national holiday, and will prove a mirth-provoking entertainment.

When two rooms are connected by folding-doors, a whole room may be used for the stage. In this case no curtains are necessary, as the doors take their place, and, for impromptu tableaux, answer very well. When there are no such connecting rooms, one end of a large room can be curtained off with sheets, or any kind of drapery, suspended from a rope or wire stretched from one wall to the other. It is best to keep the audience as

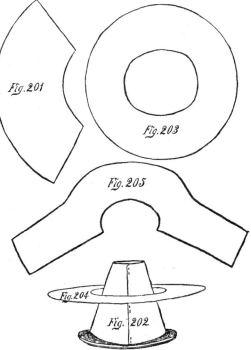

Patterns of Pilgrim Father's Hat and Collar.

far away from this improvised stage as the room will admit of, for distance greatly assists the effect.

Landing of the Pilgrims.

TABLEAU I.—The good ship Mayflower has just touched Plymouth Rock. Pilgrim Father stands upon the rock, and reaches down to help Pilgrim Mother to land. A number of Indians sit upon the edge of the rock, fishing unconcernedly over the side, while the Pilgrims take possession. In the ship Pilgrim children are standing, with outstretched arms, waiting to be taken ashore.

COSTUMES.

PILGRIM FATHER.—Cape, a broad-brimmed, high-crowned hat and large, white collar, over ordinary boy's dress, spectacles—cut from black paper (Fig. 200). The cape may be of any material, so that it is of a dark color.

The hat can be made by cutting from stiff brown paper a crown (Fig. 201), fitting it around the crown of an ordinary flat-brimmed hat, bringing it

Costume of Pilgrim Father.

into a conical shape, and pinning it in place (Fig. 202). The brim should be cut from the same paper in a large circle (Fig. 203), the hole in the centre being just large enough to fit nicely around the crown, over which it is slipped, and pushed down until it rests upon the real hat-brim (Fig. 204). The paper brim should be about seven inches wide, and the crown nine inches high. Figure 205 is the pattern of collar, which can be made of white paper or muslin.

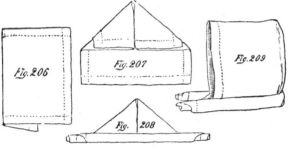

Manner of Making Pilgrim Mother's Cap.

PILGRIM MOTHER.— Full, plain skirt, white kerchief, small white cap, and large spectacles. A gentleman's linen handkerchief, put around the neck and crossed over the bosom, answers for a kerchief. The cap, too, can be made of a large handkerchief in this way.

Fold the handkerchief in the manner shown in Fig. 206 ; lay it flat upon a table, and turn the folded corners over as in Fig. 207 ; turn up the bottom edge over the other, and roll over about three times (Fig. 208) ; take the handkerchief up by the ends and the cap (Fig. 209) is made.

CHILDREN.—The young Pilgrims' costumes are like the others, on a smaller scale, but they wear no spectacles.

INDIANS. — Bright-colored shawls for blankets, and feather-dusters for head-dresses. The duster is tied on to the back of

Costume of Pilgrim Mother.

the Indian's neck with a ribbon which passes under the chin, and the shawl is placed over the handle, partially covering the head and enveloping the figure.

PROPERTIES.

The ship is a large wash-tub, which is placed in the centre of the stage; its sail is a towel, fastened with pins to a stick, the stick being tied to a broom, as shown in illustration. It is held aloft by one of the children in the tub.

Plymouth Rock is a table, occupying a position near the tub. On top of it is a chair, placed on its side to give an uneven surface, and over both chair and table is thrown a gray table-cover. The fishing-poles of the Indians are walking-canes with strings tied to the ends.

The Good Ship Mayflower.

First Harvest.

TABLEAU 2.—Pilgrim families, grouped in the centre of the stage, examining an ear of corn and rejoicing over their first harvest.

PROPERTIES.

A broom, upon which is tied one ear of dried corn, or popcorn, it doesn't matter which, and if neither is to be had, an imitation ear of corn can be made by rolling paper into the

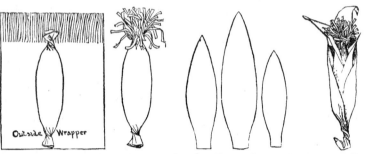

Fig. 210.—Paper Ear of Corn.   Fig. 211.—Pattern for Outside   Fig. 212.—Ear o
Husks of Corn.   Corn Finished.

The Corn-field.

shape of Fig. 210, cutting husks after the pattern Fig. 211, and putting them together like Fig. 212. The broom is held erect, with the handle resting on the floor, by Pilgrim Father.

Devastation by the Indians.

TABLEAU 3.—A long table reaches across centre of stage ; upon it are empty dishes, and the remains of a feast.

At each end and at back of table are grouped the Indians, who are gnawing large turkey-bones and eating huge pieces of bread and pie. The Pilgrim family stand at each side, and view with horror the destruction of their dinner.

PROPERTIES.

The table is a board placed across the backs of two chairs. In the centre of the table is a large pie-plate, with only a very small piece of pie remaining in it ; most of the other dishes are empty.

The Revolution.

TABLEAU 4.—This is represented by the revolution of a wheel. Pilgrim Mother stands in the centre of the stage, at a spinning-wheel, which is set in motion just as the curtain is parted.

PROPERTIES.

If a real spinning-wheel cannot be obtained, a velocipede, baby-carriage, or child's wagon, turned upside down, will answer

The Spinning-wheel.

the purpose. In the illustration the curtain has been made transparent, to show how the two back wheels of a velocipede are disposed of. A broom is fastened in an upright position to the velocipede, and on the handle is tied a piece of gray linen (a handkerchief will do), to represent flax. A string tied to the linen is held by Pilgrim Mother. The curtain must be dropped before the wheel ceases to revolve.

Slavery.

TABLEAU 5.—Pilgrim Mother is bending over a wash-tub, with sleeves rolled up to shoulders, washing ; a great pile of clothes lies on the floor at her side ; she looks angrily at the Pilgrim Father, who sits opposite to her with his legs crossed, calmly reading a newspaper.*

PROPERTIES.

The tub used for the ship, placed on two chairs ; a washboard and a pile of clothes, white predominating. A rocking-chair for the Pilgrim Father.

Rebellion.

TABLEAU 6.—Pilgrim Mother stands in defiant attitude, facing Pilgrim Father, who has just arisen from his chair.

The tub and one of the chairs upon which it stands are tipped over, and the clothes are scattered about.

PROPERTIES.

Same as in preceding tableau.

Peace and Plenty.

TABLEAU 7.—Table extending across the centre of stage is heaped with all sorts of edibles—whole pumpkins, vegetables,

---

* Of course we all know that our Pilgrim fathers did not have the daily papers, but this fact makes it the more absurd.

fruit, and flowers. At one end of the festive board stands Pilgrim Father, at the other Pilgrim Mother, smiling at each other.

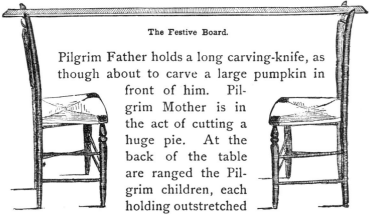

The Festive Board.

Pilgrim Father holds a long carving-knife, as though about to carve a large pumpkin in front of him. Pilgrim Mother is in the act of cutting a huge pie. At the back of the table are ranged the Pilgrim children, each holding outstretched an empty plate, waiting to be served, and all smiling. At each side of the stage, extending to the front, is a line of Indians

Side View.   Back View.   Front View.

Fig. 213.—Pumpkin Lantern.

sitting on the floor, smoking the pipes of peace. The Indians also are smiling.

PROPERTIES.

Table same as in Tableau 3 : Dishes, fruit, and vegetables. The Indians' pipes are canes with bent handles.

If, in arranging the stage, clothes-horses, with drapery thrown over them, are placed at the back, they will not only form a background for the pictures presented, but the space behind makes a nice dressing-room or retiring-place for those taking part.

Pumpkin lanterns, set in a row on the floor just inside the curtain, will be funny substitutes for footlights. They will decorate the stage appropriately, and at the same time be quite safe. Fig. 213 shows how they are made. The face is not

cut through, but the features are scraped thin enough to allow the light inside to make them visible. If they were cut, as in ordinary pumpkin lanterns, the light would shine out from instead of on to the stage.

The Game of the Headless Turkey.

Silhouette of the Headless Turkey.

A large silhouette, representing a headless turkey, is cut from black, or dark colored paper-muslin, and fastened upon a sheet stretched tightly across a door-way. To each member of the party is given a pin and a muslin head, which, if rightly placed, will fit the turkey. Then, one at a time, the players are blind-folded and placed at the end of the room opposite the sheet. After turning them around three times one way, then three times the other, they are started off to search for the turkey, that they may pin the head where they suppose it belongs. When the person going blindly about the room comes in contact with anything, no matter what, be it chair, table, wall, door, or another player, she must pin the turkey-head to the object touched. To the person who comes nearest to placing the head in its true place, a prize of a gilded wish-bone, tied to a card with a ribbon, is given. And she who makes the least successful effort is presented with a turkey-feather, which she must stick in her hair and wear for the remainder of the evening.

A Suggestion.

Amid all these bright and happy thoughts of feasting and merrymaking, comes an idea, so gently, yet persistently, forcing itself upon my notice, that it finally assumes the form of a definite plan which I will put to you in the form of a suggestion.

At this time, when, thinking over the numerous blessings, that most of you find to be thankful for, how would it do, girls, to form a society among yourselves, to be called the Thanksgiving Society, whose object will be to provide a real Thanksgiving for other and less fortunate girls, by giving them something to be thankful for before next year's Thanksgiving shall arrive?

There need be no formality about the society. The only necessary officer will be a secretary, to keep a record of what is done by the society, individually and collectively; which report the secretary will read at the grand annual meeting on Thanksgiving Day.

Many girls, young, like yourselves, to whom it is just as natural to be glad and happy, have little to make them so, and to bring some brightness into their lives would indeed be worth forming a society for.

There are various ways in which kindness may be done these girls, and so many avenues will open to those seeking to benefit them, that it is needless to attempt any instruction as to what work may be performed by the society ; if this suggestion is adopted, I know it will be safe to leave it to the quick sympathy and warm hearts of the girls to do the right thing at the right moment. What think you, girls, would it not be worth while to make of this last Thursday of November a Thanksgiving for others as well as for yourselves ? and would not your own pleasures be doubly enhanced when sweetened with the thought of having done what you could to make someone else happy ?

CHAPTER XXIX.

CHRISTMAS FESTIVITIES AND HOME-MADE CHRISTMAS GIFTS.

MONG all the days we celebrate Christmas stands first and foremost in our thoughts, the holiday of holidays. Coming in the season of frost and snow it brings a cheering warmth to our hearts that defies the icy atmosphere, and the feeling of kindliness and good will toward everyone, which it awakens, seems in response to the words the angels sang on our first Christmas, " On earth peace, good will toward men."

Christmas is not merely a day set apart for feasting, giving and receiving presents, and for merrymaking. The day on which we celebrate the birth of our Lord is a time of rejoicing for rich and poor alike, and Christmas is Christmas still, although we may receive and can offer no presents and our feast is humble indeed.

Feeling this, let us keep the Christmas festival as it should be kept, right happily and merrily. Let us decorate our homes to the best of our ability in honor of the day, and supply all deficiencies with happy hearts and smiling faces.

A friend of the writer's once remarked, as she busied herself with some Christmas-cards she was preparing to send to the hospitals, " I always like to tie a sprig of evergreen on each card ; it looks and smells so Christmasy." And so it does. Even a few pieces of evergreen, tacked over doorways or branching out from behind picture-frames, give a room a festive, Christmas-like appearance that nothing else can, and as evergreens are so plentiful here in America there are few houses that need be without their Christmas decorations. Holly, too, with its brilliant red berries peeping cheerily forth from their shelter of prickly leaves, adds brightness to the other adornments, and when the white-berried mistletoe can also be obtained all the time-honored materials for the Christmas decorations are supplied.

Though we are Americans, our ancestors came from many nations, and we have therefore a right and claim to any custom we may admire in other countries. We may take our Christmas celebrations from any people who observe the day and combining many, evolve a celebration which in its variety will be truly American.

From Germany we have already taken our Christmas-tree ; from Belgium our Christmas-stocking ; Santa Claus hails from Holland, and old England sends us the cheery greeting, Merry Christmas !

The custom the French children have of ranging their shoes on the hearth-stone on Christmas-Eve for the Christ-child to fill with toys or sweetmeats, is too much like our own Christmas stocking to offer any novelty. The Presepio, or Holy Manger, of the Roman Catholic countries, which represents the Holy Family at Bethlehem, with small wooden or wax figures for the characters, is more suitable for the church celebration, but in Sweden and Denmark they have a peculiar method of delivering their Christmas-presents which we might adopt to our advantage, for it would be great fun to present some of our gifts in their novel manner.

Instead of describing this custom we will tell you just how to carry it out and will call it the

Julklapp,

which in Denmark and Sweden means Christmas-box or gift.

Before Christmas-Day arrives all the presents intended for the Julklapp delivery must be prepared by enclosing them in a great many wrappings of various kinds, none of which should in any way suggest their contents.

If one of the presents is a pretty trinket, wrap it up in a fringed tissue paper, such as is used for motto candy or sugar-kisses ; place it in a small box, and tie the box with narrow ribbon ; then do it up in common, rough brown paper, and wrap the package with strips of cloth until it is round like a ball; cover the ball with a thin layer of dough, and brown in the oven. Pin it up in a napkin, wrap in white wrapping paper and tie with a pink string.

The more incongruous the coverings, the more suitable they are for the Julklapp. You may enclose others gifts in bundles of hay, rolls of cotton or wool, and use your own pleasure in choosing the inner wrappings. It will be the wisest plan to always use something soft for the outside covering, the reason of which you will understand when the manner of delivery is explained. Each package must be labelled with the name of the person for whom it is intended, and if an appropriate verse, epigram, or proverb be added it will be the cause of fresh mirth and laughter.

The Julklapp delivery may, and probably will commence very early Christmas morning, for the little folks, always early risers on this day, will no doubt be up betimes, and ready for the business of the day. The first intimation the less enterprising members of the family will have that Christmas has dawned, will be a loud bang at the chamber door, followed by a thump of something falling on the bed or the sleeper's chest. Then springing up and opening startled eyes, from which all sleep has been thus rudely banished, one will probably discover a large bundle of *something* on the bed or lying on the floor close beside it. It will be useless to rush to the door to find from whom or where this thing has come, for although a suppressed giggle may be heard outside the door just after feeling the thump, nothing will be met upon opening it, but dead silence, and nothing seen but the empty hall.

At any time during the day or evening the Julklapps may arrive and when all look toward the door, as a loud rap is heard, whizz ! something comes through the window and lands in the middle of the room. A sharp tap at the window is followed by the opening and closing of a door, and a bundle of straw, wool, paper, or cloth, as the case may be, lands in someone's lap. In short the Julklapps may come from any and every direction, and when one is least expecting them, and so the surprises and excitement are made to last until, weary with the fun and gayety of the day, the tired merrymakers seek their beds on Christmas-night.

If it has not been made plain enough who, or what causes the mysterious arrivals of the Julklapps we will say that the whole household join in the conspiracy, and the packages come from the hands of each of its members. The

Polish Custom

of searching for Christmas gifts, which have previously been hidden in all manner of places in the house, is one the children will delight in, and one that, introduced at a Christmas party, will provoke no end of merriment and fun.

The Bran Pie

is an English dish, but is quite as well suited to the American taste. It is an excellent means of distributing trifling gifts and may be new to some of you.

Use a large, deep brown dish for the pie. Put in it a gift for everyone who will be at the Christmas dinner, and cover them over thickly with bran, ornament the top by sticking a sprig of holly in the centre. After dinner have the bran pie put on the table with a spoon and plates beside it, and invite everyone to help her or himself, each spoonful bringing out whatever it touches. Comical little articles may be put in the pie, and the frequent inappropriateness of the gift to the receiver of it, helps to create laughter.

The Bran Pie should be the secret of not more than two persons, for, like all things pertaining to Christmas gifts, the greater the surprise, the more pleasure there will be in it.

The Blind Man's Stocking

may also be used for small gifts, or it may hold only candy and bonbons. Make the stocking of white or colored tissue-paper like the pattern given in Fig. 214.

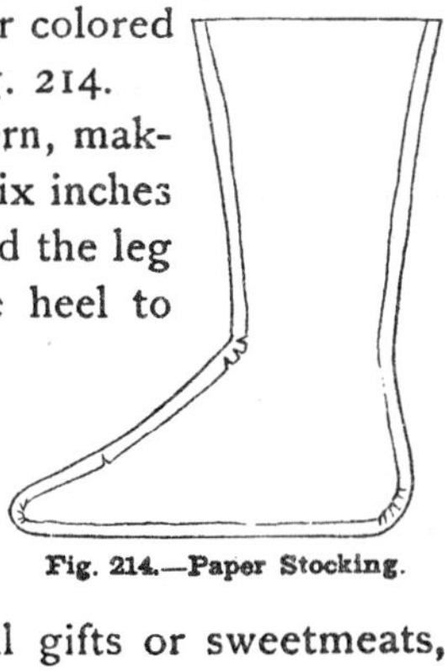

First cut out one piece like the pattern, making the foot thirteen inches long and six inches from the sole to the top of the instep, and the leg of the stocking sixteen inches from the heel to the top ; then cut another, one inch larger all around than the first. Place the two together fold the edge of the larger over the smaller piece and paste it down all around except at the top

Fig. 214.—Paper Stocking.

(Fig. 214). Fill the stocking with small gifts or sweetmeats, tie a string around the top to keep it fast, and suspend it from the centre of a doorway. Blindfold each player in turn, put a long, light stick in her hand, a bamboo cane will do, and lead her up within reach of the stocking and tell her to strike it. When anyone succeeds in striking the stocking and a hole is torn in it, the gifts or candy will scatter all over the floor to be scrambled for by all the players. Each player should be allowed three trials at striking the stocking.

Young children are always delighted with this Christmas custom, and the older ones by no means refuse to join in the sport.

Home-made Christmas Gifts.

That the children may do their share toward filling the Christmas stockings, adding to the fruit of the Christmas tree, helping with the Julklapps, contributing to the Bran Pie or Blind Man's Stocking, we give these hints on home-made Christmas gifts, all of which are inexpensive and easily constructed.

Chamois for Eye-glasses.

Fig. 215.—Chamois for Eye-glasses.

Cut out two circular pieces of chamois-skin about the size of a silver half-dollar, bind the edges with narrow ribbon, and fasten the two pieces together with a bow of the same. Print with a lead pencil on one piece of the chamois-skin, "I Make all Things Clear," and go over the lettering with a pen and India ink, or you may paint the letters in colors to match the ribbon. Fig. 215 shows how it should look when finished.

Glove Pen-wiper.

Cut four pieces from thin, soft chamois-skin, like the outline of Fig. 216. Stitch one with silk on the sewing-machine, according to the dotted lines. Cut two slits at the wrist through

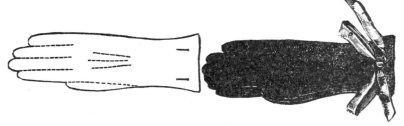

Fig. 216.—Pattern of Pen-wiper.   Fig. 217.—Pen-wiper.

all the pieces as shown in Fig. 216, and join them together by a narrow ribbon passed through the openings, and tied in a pretty bow, Fig. 217.

Sachet.

Open out an envelope, and cover it with white or cream-colored silk, refold carefully, joining the edges with stiff mucilage, using as little as possible. In place of a letter enclose a layer of cotton sprinkled with sachet-powder, fasten the envelope with sealing-wax as in an ordinary letter. Address it with pen and ink, to the one for whom it is intended. Print on it,

Fig. 218.—Sachet.

like a stamp, "Christmas, December 25," and fasten a cancelled stamp, taken from an old letter, on one corner. The finished sachet is shown in Fig. 218.

Fig. 219.—Book-mark.

A Book-mark.

Cut out the corner of a full-sized, linen-lined envelope, making the piece four inches long, and one and a half inches wide. Write on one side with pen and ink, or paint the lettering in color, " A Fresh Mind Keeps the Body Fresh." The book-mark will fit over the book-leaf like a cap, and is excellent for keeping the place. Fig. 219.

A Scrap-bag.

Scrap-bags have been fashioned in many shapes and sizes, and of all sorts of material, still it remains to be shown in what manner Christmas

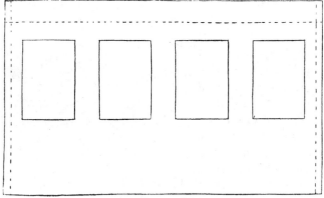

Fig. 220.—Pattern of Scrap-bag.

cards may add in decoration and beauty to these useful articles

From your collection choose four cards of the same size, then on a piece of bright silk or cloth sew the cards at equal distances apart, as in Fig. 220, stitching them around the edges on the sewing-machine. At the dotted line fold over the top of the bag as if for a hem, making the narrow fold lap just cover the upper edge of the card ; stitch this down to form a binding.

After joining the bag at the dotted lines on the sides, gather the bottom up tight and fasten to it a good-sized tassel ; then sew on each side a heavy cord with tassels placed where the cord joins the bag, as seen in Fig. 221. The cord and tassels of the example were made of scarlet worsted.

Fig. 221.—Scrap-bag.

A Walnut-shell Turtle.

For an ornament to be used on a pen-wiper, or simply as a pretty toy,

Fig. 222.—Pattern of Turtle.

the little turtle is appropriate. It is made of half an English walnut, which forms the turtle's back or shell, glued on a piece of card-board cut after the diagram given in Fig. 222. Paint the card-board as nearly as possible the color of the shell, and the eyes black. When perfectly dry glue the shell securely to the card-board, bend down and out the feet a little, in order to make the turtle stand ; bend the head up, and the tail down, as in Fig. 223.

Fig. 223.—Walnut-shell Turtle.

Here are some home-made toys which the children can make to give to one another.

Miss Nancy.

Miss Nancy (Fig. 226) is fashioned from a piece of pith taken out of a dried cornstalk. Cut away the stalk until the pith is reached ; then take a piece of the pith, about six inches

Fig. 224.   Fig. 225
Manner of Making Miss Nancy.   Fig. 226.—Miss Nancy.

long and whittle out one end to resemble a head as in Fig. 224, draw a face on the head with pen and ink, and glue half of a lead bullet on the lower end of the pith (Fig. 225). Make Miss Nancy's costume of a skirt, composed of some bright-colored Japanese paper, a shawl made of a piece of soft ribbon or silk, and a cap of white swiss. The peculiarity of the little lady is that she insists upon always standing upright, no matter in what position she is placed.

A Soft Ball.

A very pretty and safe return ball for the little ones to play with may be made of paper (Fig. 227), which, being soft, precludes all danger of " thumps and bumps."

Fig. 227.—Paper Ball.

Take a piece of newspaper, and, using both hands, roll it and fold it into something of the required shape. Then place it in the centre of a square piece of bright-colored tissue paper ; take the four corners of the tissue-paper up to the centre of the top of the ball, fold them over, also fold and smooth down what fulness there may be ; next place a small round piece of gold, silver, or some contrasting colored paper on the top of the ball. Secure all by winding a string around the ball, making six or eight divisions ; tie a piece of elastic to the string where it crosses on the top of the ball, then paste over this a small artificial flower. In the other end of the elastic, make a loop to fit over the finger, or tie on it a small brass ring.

If a tiny sleigh-bell be placed in the centre when the ball is being made, it will give a cheerful little tinkling noise whenever the ball is thrown.

A Lively Rooster.

To make the rooster (Fig. 228), cut out of stiff cardboard Figs. 229, 230, 231, and 232. Tie on Figs. 229 and 230 each a piece of string seven and one-half inches long. Then attach

the head and tail to the body by running a string through holes
at A in Fig. 230 and A in Fig. 231, and another through B in
Fig. 229 and B in Fig. 231. Bring the head and tail up close
to the body and fasten the ends of the strings down securely

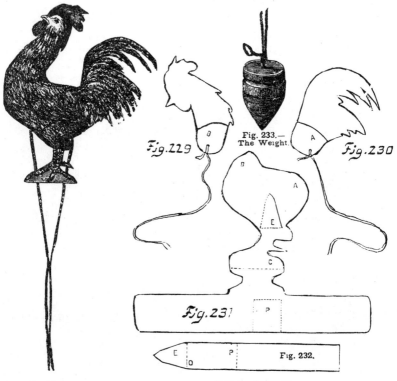

Fig. 233.—
The Weight.

Fig. 229

Fig. 230

Fig. 231

Fig. 232.

Fig. 228.—The Rooster.

Pattern of Rooster.

with court-plaster or pieces of paper pasted over them. Bend
Fig. 231 at dotted line C ; then on the space marked E, paste
the portion of Fig. 232 marked E after bending it at dotted line
O. Again bend Fig. 232 in the same direction at dotted line

P, and paste it across the space marked P, on Fig. 231. When all is fastened together, and the paste perfectly dry, paint the rooster to look as life-like as possible. Tie the strings of Figs. 229 and 230 together four inches from where they are fastened on, then again about three inches lower down, and attach a weight to the ends. A common wooden top, with a tack in the head (Fig. 233), will answer the purpose nicely. To bring

Fairy Dancers.

the rooster to life, place him on the mantel-piece, with a book serving as a weight on the projection of Fig. 232, swing the top and he will move his head and tail in the most amusing manner.

Fairy Dancers.

Among the gifts made by little hands, a box, containing a set of fairy dancers, will be a most novel and welcome addition. These little figures, when placed on the piano, will move as soon as the keys are touched, dancing fast or slow in perfect time to the music. They may all be made to resemble fairies as in Fig. 234, or a famous collection of figures in the costumes of different periods in history will be equally pretty and perhaps more interesting. Ladies in kirtles and tunics, gentlemen in slashed doublet and hose of the Tudor times, Queen Elizabeth's starched ruffs and farthingales, etc. All these dresses can be more easily copied from pictures of the period than from any written description of them. The materials used for the costume must be of the lightest kind, for a heavy dress will weigh down the dancer and hamper its movements. To

Fig. 234.—A Fairy Dancer.

Fig. 235.—Pattern of Fairy Dancer.

make the fairy (Fig. 234) trace Fig. 235 on cardboard and cut
it out, sew a piece of bonnet-wire down the back, as shown in
diagram. Mark the slippers on the feet with
ink or black paint, select a Christmas or advertising card representing a child, with a head
of a suitable size, cut the head out and paste
it on the fairy.

Gather two short skirts of tarlatan,
make a waist of the same, sew with a
few stitches to the doll, and cover the
stitches with a sash of bright
colored tissue paper; add a
strip of tarlatan for a floating
scarf, gluing it to the uplifted

Fig. 236.—Pattern of Chinaman.

hands. Bend back the
piece of cardboard pro-
jecting from the foot,
and glue to it a small
piece of bristle brush.

Fig. 237. Fig. 238.
Chinaman's
Queue.

The wire on
the doll should be long enough to pass
tightly around the brush, thus making
it more secure.

If you would like to have the
Chinaman (Fig. 239) in your troupe of
dancers, trace on cardboard Fig. 236,

Fig. 239 —The Chinaman.

draw a face with slanting eyes, or paint it; then take several
strands of black thread and tie them together in the centre with

another piece of thread (Fig. 237), bring the ends down together (Fig. 238), braid them and sew the braid to the back of the Chinaman's head (239). Cut a loose sacque from pattern Fig. 240, fold at the waved lines and sew together at the dotted lines ; cut an opening for the head as seen in pattern. Make the hat of dark green paper cut in the form of Fig. 241, and crimp it from the centre (Fig. 242). Sew the hat to the back of the Chinaman's head, bend the cardboard projection at the feet and glue it to a piece of brush.

Fig. 240.—Chinaman's Sacque.

Fig. 241. — Pattern of Chinaman's Hat.

Fig. 242. — Chinaman's Hat.

Butterflies of brilliant hues, all hovering and circling, may take the place of the fairies, or they may mingle with them in the dance, presenting a scene indeed fairy-like. To make a

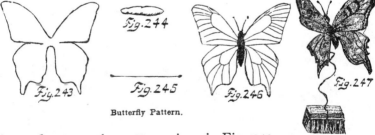

Butterfly Pattern.

Butterfly.

butterfly, trace the pattern given in Fig. 243, on brilliantly colored paper. Form a body by rolling a small piece of beeswax between the fingers until it assumes the desired shape (Fig. 244) ; then attach the wings to the body by softening the wax and sticking them to it. Wax a piece of black thread to stiffen it, and make a knot in each end (Fig. 245), bend this in the middle and stick it on to the head to form the antennæ (Fig. 246). Fasten one end of a very fine wire securely in the middle of the wax body, and wrap the other end around a small piece of brush as seen in Fig. 247. A number of these butterflies placed on the pianoforte will move, bend and sway with the music as if endowed with life.

Toys, also, which are small and light enough, can be made to " trip the light fantastic " in time to the music.

Select those most suitable and glue them to pieces of brush in the way described for the other dancers.

The children, generous little souls, always long to do their part towards making Christmas presents, and we hope that the suggestion we have offered will help them to manufacture, without other aid, many little gifts which their friends will prize the more highly for having been made by the loving little hands.

CHAPTER XXX.

AMUSEMENTS AND GAMES FOR THE CHRISTMAS HOLIDAYS.

 WINTER passed in-doors would be irksome indeed for a healthy, hearty girl, and even the most delicate are the better for an outing now and then. The keen northwest wind, the biting frosts, the crisp atmosphere and the glistening ice and snow are not without their attractions, and we hope that no American girl will neglect the opportunities this time of the year affords for healthy, enjoyable out-door pastime. It is well to follow the example of our Canadian sisters, and, clad in garments warm and appropriate, indulge in coasting, tobogganing, skating, sleighing, and walking.

The country, wrapped in its winter mantle, is very attractive. Many of our small animals and birds that city people are apt to associate only with a summer landscape, are to be found abroad in mid-winter, and upon a bright sunny day the birds are not only to be seen, but heard twittering and even singing in the hedges ; they do not feel the cold and are enjoying themselves heartily. The reason the birds and wild creatures are so comfortably content, is because they are prepared for the weather, their clothing is not only soft and warm, but fits them perfectly, without interfering with their movements. Take a lesson from them, girls, dress as becomingly as you choose, the birds always do that, but do not wear thin-soled shoes or anything that is uncomfortable ; wrap up warm and you can enjoy yourself out of doors in the coldest weather just as well as the birds. The cold winds will only bring the roses to your cheeks, and the keen, invigorating air, health and suppleness to your body.

We do not think any person ever learned to skate, coast, or walk on snow-shoes from reading the directions that can be given in a book. It is for that reason we have no chapter devoted to these sports and not because we do not believe in, and enjoy them, too. Therefore we will direct our attention to indoor sports, for they can be learned in this way and are quite as important as the others in filling out the list of winter amusements.

There are a great many days in winter when it is so stormy and disagreeable out-doors, one is glad enough to have the shelter of a roof and the warmth of a fire ; these are the days and evenings when in-doors games are in demand, and during the holiday season, when work has been put aside, and you have nothing to do but enjoy yourself, any new diversion is always welcome. It is here then that we will insert the

New Game of Bubble Bowling.

When the game of Bubble Bowling was played for the first time, it furnished an evening's entertainment, not only for the children, but for grown people also ; even a well known general and his staff, who graced the occasion with their presence, joined in the sport, and seemed to enjoy it equally with their youthful competitors. Loud was the chorus of " Bravo ! " and merry the laugh of exultation when the pretty crystal ball passed safely through its goal; and sympathy was freely ex pressed in many an " Oh ! " and " Too bad ! " as the way- ward bubble rolled gayly off toward the floor, or, reaching the goal, dashed itself against one of the stakes and instantly van- ished into thin air.

The game should be played upon a long, narrow table, made simply of a board about five feet long and eighteen inches wide, resting upon high wooden "horses." On top of the table, and at a distance of twelve inches from one end, should be fastened in an upright position, two stakes, twelve inches high; the space between the stakes should be eight inches, which will make each stand four inches from the nearest edge of the table. When finished, the table must be covered with some sort

Bubble Bowling.

of woollen cloth; an old shawl or a breadth of colored flannel will answer the purpose excellently. Small holes must be cut at the right distance for the stakes to pass through. The cloth should be allowed to fall over the edge of the table, and must not be fastened down, as it will sometimes be necessary to remove it in order to let it dry. It will be found more convenient, therefore, to use two covers, if they can be provided, as then there can always be a dry cloth ready to replace the one that has become too damp. The bubbles are apt to stick when they come upon wet spots, and the bowling can be carried on in a much more lively manner if the course is kept dry. Each of the stakes forming the goal should be wound with bright ribbons of contrasting colors, entwined from the bottom up, and ending in a bow at the top. This bow can be secured in place by driving a small brass-headed tack through the ribbon into the top of the stake. If the rough pine legs of the table seem too unsightly, they can easily be painted, or a curtain may be made of bright-colored cretonne—any other material will do as well, provided the colors are pleasing—and tacked around the edge of the table, so as to fall in folds to the floor. The illustration shows the top of the table, when ready for the game.

For an impromptu affair, a table can be made by placing a leaf of a dining-table across the backs of two chairs, and covering it with a shawl; lead pencils may be used for the stakes, and they can be held in an upright position by sticking them in the tubes of large spools. This sort of table the children can arrange themselves, and it answers the purpose very nicely. The other things to be provided for the game are a large bowl of strong soapsuds, made with hot water and common brown soap, and as many pipes as there are players.

The prizes for the winners of the game may consist of any trinkets or small articles that fancy or taste may suggest.

Bubble Bowling can be played in two ways. The first method requires an even number of players, and these must be divided into two equal parties. This is easily accomplished by selecting two children for captains, and allowing each captain to choose, alternately, a recruit for her party until the ranks are filled, or, in other words, until all the children have been chosen; then, ranked by age, or in any other manner preferred, they form in line on either side of the table. A pipe is given to each child, and they stand prepared for the contest. One of the captains first takes her place at the foot of the table, where she must remain while she is bowling, as a bubble passing between the stakes is not counted unless blown through the goal from the end of the table.

The bowl of soapsuds is placed upon a small stand by the side of the bowling-table, and the next in rank to the captain, belonging to same party, dips her pipe into the suds and blows a bubble, not too large, which she then tosses upon the table in front of the captain, who, as first bowler, stands ready to blow the bubble on its course down through the goal. Three successive trials are allowed each player ; the bubbles which break before the bowler has started them, are not counted.

The names of all the players, divided as they are into two parties, are written down on a slate or paper, and whenever a bubble is sent through the goal, a mark is set down opposite the name of the successful bowler.

When the captain has had her three trials, the captain on the other side becomes bowler, and the next in rank of her own party blows the bubbles for her. When this captain retires, the member of the opposite party, ranking next to the captain, takes the bowler's place and is assisted by the one whose name is next on the list of her own side ; after her the player next to the captain on the other side ; and so on until the last on the list has her turn, when the captain then becomes assistant and blows the bubbles.

The number of marks required for either side to win the game, must be decided by the number of players ; if there are twenty—ten players on each side—thirty marks would be a good limit for the winning score.

When the game has been decided, a prize is given to that member of the winning party who has the greatest number of marks attached to her name showing that she has sent the bubble through the goal a greater number of times than any player on the same side. Or, if preferred, prizes may be given to every child belonging to the winning party. The other way in which Bubble Bowling may be played is simpler, and does not require an even number of players as no sides are formed.

Each bowler plays for herself, and is allowed five successive trials ; if three bubbles out of the five be blown through the goal the player is entitled to a prize. The child acting as assistant becomes the next bowler, and so on until the last in turn becomes bowler, when the one who began the game takes the place of assistant.

When the evening lamps are lighted and the young folks, gathered cosily around the cheerful fire, begin to be at a loss how to amuse themselves, let them try the game of

Biographical Nonsense.

A paper must be written by one of the players which will read like the following :

The name of a noted man.

A date between the flood and the present year.

The name of a noted man.

A country.

The name of some body of water or river.

Some kind of a vessel.

A country.

A country.

The name of a school.

A city.

A city, town, or country.

A city, town, or country.

A number.

The names of two books.

The name of one book.

A wonderful performance.

The name of a well-known person.

A profession or trade.

A term expressing the feeling entertained for another person.

A term descriptive of someone's appearance.

A word denoting size.

A term describing form.

A color.

A word denoting size.

The name of an article of some decided color.

The name of any article.

The name of any article.

A number of years.

This paper is to be passed to each member of the party who in turn will fill up the blanks left, with the words, terms, and names indicated.

When the blanks have been filled, one player must read the following, and another supply the words, when she pauses, from the paper just prepared, being sure to read them in their true order.

A BIOGRAPHY.

———— was born in ———— the same year when ———— discovered ————, by sailing through the ———— in a ————. His father was a native of ———— ; his mother of ————. He was educated at ————, in the city of ————. His first voyage, which was a long one, was from ———— to ————. He wrote three books before he was ———— years of age. They are ————, and ————. He performed the miraculous feat of ———— with ————. He was a great ————, and one we shall ever ————. In appearance he was ———— being rather ———— of stature. His nose was ————, his eyes————, his mouth ————, and hair the color of   adorned his head. He invariably carried in his hand a ———— and a ————, by which he was always known, and with which he is represented to this day. He died at the advanced age of ———.

The ridiculous combinations found in this game make it very funny.

Comic Historical Tableaux

are very amusing, and being impromptu require no preparation beforehand.

As in charades, the company must divide into two parties. But instead of acting as in charades, one party decides what event in history they will represent, and then they form a tableau to illustrate the event, making it as ridiculous as possible. The other party must try and guess what the tableau is; if they are successful, it is their turn to produce a tableau, if not, the first party must try another subject, and continue to do so until the subject of their tableau is correctly guessed.

We will give a few suggestions for the tableaux.

BALBOA DISCOVERING THE PACIFIC OCEAN.

Place a pan of water on the floor in plain sight of the audience; then let someone dress up in a long cloak and high-crowned hat to personate Balboa, and stand on a table in the middle of the floor, while the rest of the performers, enveloped in shawls, crouch around. When the curtain is drawn aside, Balboa must be seen looking intently through one end of a tin horn, or one made of paper, at the pan of water.

NERO AT THE BURNING OF ROME.

Nero, in brilliant robes made of shawls, sits on a table, surrounded by his courtiers, who are also in fantastic costumes. Nero is in the act of fiddling, his fiddle being a small fire shovel, and the bow a poker. On the floor in front of the group is placed a large shallow pan or tray, in which is set a small house, which has been hastily cut from paper. A lighted match is put to the paper house just as the curtains are parted.

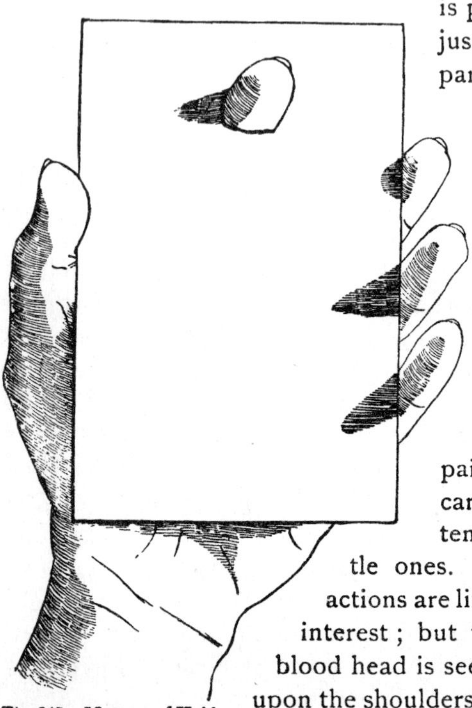

These two suggestions will no doubt be sufficient to show what the tableaux should be like and we need give no further illustrations.

Living Christmas Cards.

To impart seeming life to the little figures painted on the Christmas cards, is a performance intensely amusing to the little ones. A moving toy whose actions are life-like is always of great interest ; but when a little flesh-and-blood head is seen nodding and twisting upon the shoulders of a figure painted on a card, the children fairly shout with delight.

Fig. 248.—Manner of Holding Card.

Here is the method of bringing life into the bits of pasteboard.

Select cards with pretty or comical figures, whose faces are the size of the ends of your first or second finger. Carefully cut the face out of a card ; then with ink mark the features on your finger, and put it through the opening, as in Fig. 248. Place on this little live head a high peaked tissue-paper cap, and the effect will be exceedingly ludicrous (Fig. 249). A little Santa Claus who can really nod and bow to the children will be very amusing, and there are quite a number of Christmas cards which portray the funny, jolly little fellow.

Floral cards may have nodding fairies peeping out from among the petals of the flowers, whose heads are crowned with queer little fairy caps, as in Fig. 250. If among your collection you have a card with a picture of a house on it, it will be amusing to thrust a little head wearing a night-cap, out of one of the windows. Round holes will, of course, have to be cut in the cards wherever the heads are to appear.

Still another way of managing these living puppets is to cut in a piece of cardboard, five inches long and two inches wide, three round holes a little more than half an inch apart. Sew around the edge of the card-

Fig. 249.—Live Head with Peaked Cap.

board a gathered curtain of any soft material six inches deep. Sketch faces on three of your fingers, pass them under the curtain and through the holes in the cardboard. The curtain will fall around and conceal your hand, leaving the three heads appearing above (Fig. 251). On these heads place any kind of head-dress you choose, making them of paper; or

Fig. 250.—Nodding Fairies.

caps of white swiss look quaint, and wee doll hats may be worn.

It is best to use a little mucilage or paste in fastening the hats on, that there may be no danger of their falling off with the movement of the fingers.

The hair may be inked, or little wigs made of cotton can be used.

Fig. 251.—Living Puppets.

If the little faces are painted with water colors, giving color to the cheeks and lips, the life-like appearance will be enhanced.

These little personages can be made to carry on absurd conversations, and a great deal of expression be given to the bobbing and turning of their heads. One person can easily manage the whole thing, and entertain a roomful with the performance of the living puppets.

CHAPTER XXXI.

NEW YEAR'S AND A LEAP YEAR PARTY.

 **M**Y earliest recollection of New Year's day is of being awakened at midnight by the clangor of the fire bells, and the ringing of the church bells, as they swung and rocked in their high steeples and cupolas, shouting, Happy New Year! from their brazen throats to all the sleeping town. Not being thoroughly conversant with bell language, I was very much alarmed because they seemed to say " Come, get up— Come, get up—House on fire—House on fire ! " but, upon opening my eyes, I was assured that they were ringing in the New Year, and, as I again fell asleep, the bells were saying distinctly, " Wish you Happy New Year—Wish you Happy New Year."

Next day the table was decked with flowers, and was laden with roast turkey, fruits, salads, and mince-pies. Oh, my ! what delicious mince-pies they were ! None since have ever tasted as good as those made and baked by my grandmother.

I often wonder if the next generation of grandmammas will make such cookies, mince pies, and doughnuts as ours did ; but this was in Kentucky, and you know that we still observed the old-fashioned customs, and all day long the gentlemen came dropping in by twos and fours, and such handshaking and laughing, and such courtly compliments, and such a bowing and a wishing of Many Happy New Years, it does me good to think of. Who knows but that so many kind wishes of a long and happy life, sincerely given, may really help to bring it to pass.

Small as I was at the time, and little as I understood the customs or conversation, the spirit of the whole day was intelligible and appealed to the little child, perhaps more forcibly than to the grown-up people.

It is really too bad that the crowded states of our large cities tend to lead to the gradual decline of the custom of New Year's calls, so that now many people confine themselves to sending and receiving cards, making the always stiff and formal bits of engraved pasteboard, do all the calling and receiving ; but

New Year's Parties

are not out of date, so we will have one on New Year's Eve, because then young and old are privileged to sit up all night, that is, until after twelve o'clock midnight, and have all the fun possible. Let us begin our frolic with a

Pantomime of an Enchanted Girl.

For this a damp sheet must be fastened up across the room or between the folding doors of the parlor. First, fasten the corners of the sheet, next, the centre of each of the four sides, in order that the cloth may be perfectly smooth ; then place a lighted candle on the floor, about four or five feet from the centre of the curtain. When the lights in the room occupied by the audience are turned out, leaving it in total darkness, so the shadows of the actors behind the curtain may be seen on the screen, someone, standing outside of the curtain and facing the audience, should explain or relate the story of the play : of how a young girl, while walking out on the last day in November, meets Halloween, who presents her with three gifts to try her fortune, and how, when she is about to do so, a witch enchants her, etc. After the story is finished, and a lively overture has been performed on some musical instrument, the pantomime is played as follows :

The young girl personating the enchanted one, comes gayly forward from the side, when almost across the curtain she meets Halloween, who approaches from the opposite side, arrayed in short dress, with wings made of newspaper folded fan fashion, and fastened on the shoulders ; in her hand she carries a cane with a silhouette of a cat, or two or three stars and a crescent cut of stiff, brown paper and pasted on the end ; the cane is so held that the profiles of the figures are kept toward the curtain. Seeing this queer being the young girl clearly demonstrates, by her actions, that she is alarmed. When Halloween quiets her fears, by surely and plainly indicating with slow movements of the head, and downward motions of the arms that no harm is intended, they shake hands ; then Halloween shows the maiden three gifts, an apple, a hand-mirror, and an unlighted candle. Before presenting them she illustrates by gestures, the use to be made of each. Holding the mirror in front of her face, she bites the apple, then looks quickly around, as if expecting to see someone, and, again holding up the mirror in one hand and the candle in the other, she takes a few steps backward, when a boy enters by jumping over the light, which gives the appearance of his having fallen down from the sky, Halloween looks around, and the boy quickly disappears in the same manner as he came.

All this time the girl stands transfixed, with her hands raised and all the fingers spread out in astonishment ; she receives the presents which are given with many nods and gestures. As Halloween walks away the fortune-seeker turns and watches her with a telescope made of a roll of paper she finds at her feet on the floor. The maiden then proceeds to examine the gifts ; as she takes up the apple and mirror, her hand is stayed by a witch with flowing hair, who has approached unperceived, carrying under one arm a broom, and wearing on her head an ordinary hat with a piece of newspaper rolled up and pinned on to form a peaked crown. She motions to the girl to be seated ; then stands over her and makes passes in the air, and taking up her broom from the floor makes grand flourishes and departs walking back towards the candle, which causes her shadow to grow larger and larger. The poor girl looks anxiously around and discovers she has been enchanted, for there are three girls instead of one; this effect is produced by two more lighted candles being placed on the floor on either side of the first candle, and every movement the girl makes is mimicked by her other selves. The candles are removed and the Old Year instantly appears, his figure bent, a piece of fringed paper pasted on his chin for a flowing beard, and carrying in his hand a cane with a piece of stiff paper fastened on to represent a scythe. Discovering him the girl runs forward to tell her sorrows, and finds that it is only when alone that she is enchanted, for when she attempts to point out her other selves they have disappeared ; making many gestures she looks here and there for them, but in vain, then as the Old Year leaves she bids him a sorrowful adieu. Again alone, the facsimiles reappear and she grows desperate, so do the other two selves, she throws her arms about, skips, jumps, and dances wildly around, the other selves do likewise, and at the same time they are made to pass and repass her, by two persons taking up the two extra lights, and, keeping the lights facing the curtain, walking back and forth, passing, and repassing each other but never stepping in front of the candle on the floor. In the midst of the dancing the two extra candles are taken away and immediately the little New

Year enters, crowned with a paper star and wearing wings of paper. The young girl rushes to meet the New Year with a hearty greeting, she then tells him of her enchantment, counting the three selves by holding up the first finger of the right hand three times in succession, and while the New Year makes gestures that indicate advice the maiden listens with her hand to her ear, and, promising by signs to be a good girl, she kneels down, and the little New Year raises both hands above her head, then, kissing her hand to the maiden, departs.

The glad New Year has disenchanted her, she carefully looks this way and that, but seeing all is well she tosses her head, dances around, makes a courtesy, kisses both hands to the audience and disappears.

When the play is over, and just as the clock strikes twelve, the party can instantly change its character if it is leap-year and become a

Leap-Year Party

for the remaining hour or so, thereby creating a great deal more merriment and sport; the novelty of the fact that the girls exchange places with the boys makes everything appear strange. And when the music commences for dancing the girls look from one to another, no one at first having the courage to invite a partner to dance, so unaccustomed are they to even the thought of such a thing. The boys of course laugh, and make no move to assist their timid, would-be partners in the part they must play, but quietly await the expected invitation. When, however, someone takes the initiative step, the others follow, and all goes merrily.

The supper presents a new phase, but here the girls do their part perfectly, providing all the boys with a plentiful repast, and each one is made to feel that his presence is necessary to the success of the party, thereby insuring a happy, pleasant time for all.

In giving a leap-year party it is very essential that all the guests understand perfectly that the idea of the entertainment is to have the girls take upon themselves all the duties and courtesies properly belonging to the boys, and that the boys shall wait for an invitation before dancing, promenading, or partaking of refreshments, and that a boy should not cross the floor unattended, but wait for some fair friend to escort him. The girls are at liberty to go and come as they like, though they must remember not to leave a partner standing after the dance is over, but politely conduct him to a seat, and the girls must also endeavor to make the party pleasant and agreeable to all. The chaperons, of course, should have charge of the boys during the entertainment.

The leap-year party need not necessarily be a dancing party, as any social gathering can take the form of a leap-year party.

When an entertainment is given on the eve of a new leap-year, with a view to dancing the old year out and the new year in, just as the clock strikes twelve the party can immediately change into a leap-year party as described, or should the New Year be a common year, then as the time flies and the hands of the clock approach the hour of twelve all are on the qui vive to be the first to have the pleasure of greeting their friends with a Happy New Year.

CHAPTER XXXII.

HOME GYMNASIUM.

VERYONE *must* exercise to keep healthy and strong, for life is motion and activity. It is natural to be well and happy, and to keep so we must exercise all our muscles, as well as our moral and intellectual faculties, or they will dwindle and wither. The arm of the Hindoo devotee, not being used, at length becomes completely paralyzed, and fish in the Mammoth Cave having no use for eyes pass their life without them; so we find that *use* is the foundation of all things, otherwise they would cease to exist; then, girls, it lies within your power to become stronger and more graceful each day by regular and graduated bodily exercise, which will bring life and energy to every part of your system by causing the blood to circulate freely through all the body.

There are some simple methods of carrying this into effect in the most agreeable and salutary manner, but the exercises must be very light at first, and as you advance they may be increased a little each time, but always stop before you feel fatigued, for when the calisthenics cease to give pleasure it is doubtful if they are beneficial.

The best time for exercising is in the morning after having partaken of some light refreshments, though any time will do

except directly after hearty meals. Try and have a regular time set apart each day for your physical culture. Commence by exercising five or ten minutes, then for a little longer period next time, and so on until you can exercise with ease for half an hour or longer. You will feel refreshed, invigorated, and better prepared for the duties and pleasures which await you. Your clothing must not incommode the free action of the body, and it is essential that it be comfortable. What is suitable for lawn tennis is also well adapted for the gymnasium. An ordinary bathing-dress answers the purpose very well, as it is made for exercise.

The Egyptian water-carrier, with the jug of water poised so prettily on her head, and her figure so straight and beautiful, has always challenged admiration; her carriage is dignified, erect, and graceful, something worth striving for, especially when we have the certainty of success if we will only be faithful and persevering. The peasantry of foreign countries who carry all their burdens balanced on their heads have their reward in healthy, strong, straight figures, even in old age they do not stoop. Witness the emigrants landing at Castle Garden who carry their possessions done up in huge bundles on their heads with the utmost ease ; of this class, three generations—a grandmother, mother, and grown daughter—with baggage of the same weight on their heads, were lately seen at a New York ferry, each equally upright, strong, and vigorous.

A good straight back is an excellent thing ; and when the head is properly carried and all the movements are buoyant and elastic, then we may walk as it was intended we should, every step bringing a glow to the cheek and a sparkle to the eye. It requires only a few minutes' regular daily exercise for any girl to attain a carriage equal to that of the Egyptian water-carrier, and the only apparatus needed for

Exercise First

is a roll of paper. Now stand with your heels together, toes out, and shoulders well back ; then place on your head the roll of paper ; if your position is not perfectly erect the roll will fall off ; keep your chin straight and back against your neck, for it

Fig. 252.—Balancing a Roll of Paper.

is the *chin* which determines the poise of the body. You cannot stand straight unless the chin is straight ; throw out your chin and your shoulders will stoop forward, have your chin straight and your back will be straight ; bear this in mind in all your exercises. Now walk, keeping the roll balanced on your head (Fig. 252). Practice this walking back and forth until you can do so without the paper rolling off ; then try a tin cup full to the brim with water. Walk erect or the water will wash over, down on your head, and it will feel cold as it trickles through your hair ; soon, however, you will be able to carry the cup of water with ease and no danger of its spilling. But do not discontinue the practice on that account ; try something else in its place, until you are able to carry anything you wish on your head with no fear of it falling. The exercise affords amusement, and at the same time you will be acquiring a beautiful, dignified, and graceful carriage.

Exercise Second

is for gaining agility, suppleness, quickness of eye, hand, and foot. Standing as far from the wall as possible, take a common rubber hand-ball and toss it against the wall, catching it as it rebounds (see illustration), and again toss it against the wall. Vary this by allowing the ball to strike the floor, catching it on the rebound ; then try keeping the ball in constant motion by using first one hand and then the other as a bat for return-ing the ball to the wall. The exer-cise can also be changed by striking the ball against the floor, and on its return bound again striking it, thus keeping it in motion. You will find that activity is necessary, and the work so quick that it will keep you on the jump all through the exercise.

Exercise Third

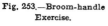

is with a broom-handle. Saw or cut off the broom and smooth down the sharp ends of the handle, and it will be ready for use. Stand erect, heels together, toes out, chin well back and straight, so as to throw out and expand the chest. Now grasp firmly each end of the broomstick and bring it up over the head (Fig. 253); repeat this motion six or seven times ; then change by carrying the broomstick over back of the head down across and

Fig. 253.—Broom-handle Exercise.

back of the shoulders ; then up above the head again, repeat-ing this, and all other motions in your calisthenics, half a dozen times. Another exercise is holding the stick down in front of you with both hands and bringing it up over the head and down back of the shoulders without stopping.

The side motion is made by grasping the broomstick at each end, holding it down in front of you, and swinging it sideways, thus bringing the right hand up when the left is down, and *vice versa.* Another way is to hold the stick by both ends above your head and swing it from one side to the other, which will cause the right arm to come in contact with the right side of the head, while the left arm is extended out horizontally to the left. Next carry the stick back of and against the shoulders ; then swing it from right to left, which gives another side movement. Vary all the movements in as many different ways as you can think of.

Exercise Fourth.

Stand erect always when in position for exercising, according to the directions given—heels together, toes out, etc. Now allow your arms to hang naturally down at your sides, raise your heels, and stand on your toes ; now lower the heels and repeat the motion ; then close your hands tightly and raise your arms out sideways at right angles with your body, next up straight above your head, and down again to the level of the shoulders, then back down to your sides as at first.

Again take position, close your hands tightly, and raise them up under the arms, bringing the elbows out to a level with the shoulders ; then bring your hands down at your sides again and repeat the movement vigorously ; resume position, firmly close your hands and carry them up to the shoulders, next extend them up straight above your head, down again to your shoulders, and back to the first position. A very good exercise is to extend both arms straight out in front of you, close your hands and bring them back to your chest, which will cause the bent elbows to project beyond your back.

Exercise Fifth.

Assume position, close your hands, and take one long step forward with your right foot, bend the right knee and stand with your weight resting on the right foot ; then extend your arms out sideways straight from the shoulders, now bring your hands together in front of you, still keeping the arms on a level with the shoulders, and while doing so throw the body back, straightening the right knee and bending the left so the weight of the body will rest on the left foot ; repeat this and vary it by taking one step forward with the left foot and going through with the same motions.

Resume position, and place your hands on your hips, with your thumbs turned forward and fingers backward. Now take a long step forward with your right foot, throwing the weight on that foot, then back again in position, and in the same manner step forward with your left foot and back again ; next take a step backward with your right foot, resume position, and then with your left.

Again stand with your hands on your hips, thumbs turned forward, and without bending your knees move the body, first bending it forward, then backward, and

Fig. 254.—Balancing Broom-handle.

resuming an upright position, bend over to the right and to the left.

Exercise Sixth.

In this the broomstick is used for balancing ; hold it in an upright position, and first try balancing it on the palm of your hand ; then on the back of your hand, next on each of the fingers in succession, commencing with the first finger (Fig. 254) ; be cautious, and when the stick wavers do not let it fall, but catch it with the other hand, and again balance it. This is an interesting, light, and diverting exercise, requiring all your attention, and, for the time being, your thoughts are concentrated on the effort to keep the broomstick properly balanced.

Exercise Seventh.

Pure blood means good health, and to purify the blood and keep the complexion clear it is essential that you breathe a sufficient quantity of *pure* air, and you cannot take in a proper amount of air unless your lungs are wholly extended. So take position with your hands correctly placed on your hips ; then very slowly draw in your breath until your chest and lungs are fully expanded ; next slowly exhale your breath, and repeat the exercise.

Exercise Eighth.

Screw in two large, *strong* hooks in the woodwork on each side of the doorway ; place the hooks as far above your head as you can conveniently reach ; slide the broomstick in so that it will extend across the doorway and be supported by the hooks ; have the apparatus on that side of the doorway where it will not interfere with the opening and closing of the door, and be sure that it is perfectly secure before attempting to exercise ; each time before commencing a new movement examine the stick, and be certain that it is not in any danger of slipping from the hooks. Unless you can be perfectly safe from liability to hurts or falls, do not include this in your list of exercises.

For the first movement grasp the bar firmly with both hands and swing the body forward and backward, standing first on the toes, then on the heels ; next, still grasping the bar, raise up on your toes, then back again. Change the movements in as many ways as you like, but do not try anything that may strain or hurt you. Now screw in two more hooks, on either side of the woodwork, below the first ones, placing them about two feet and eight inches from the floor ; take the stick from its elevated position and slide it across the doorway so it will rest securely on the two lower hooks. Standing in front of it, grasp the bar firmly with both hands and try to raise yourself up, feet and all, from the floor by bearing your weight down on the bar ; then let yourself gently back again. When you have finished exercising, remove the stick and put it away.

Exercise Ninth.

In the top part of the framework of the doorway fasten a very strong hook by screwing it into the wood ; then take a broomstick and, after shortening it so that when held in a

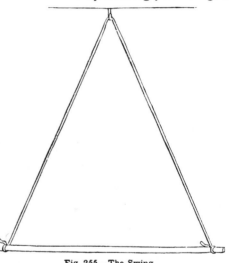

Fig. 255.—The Swing.

horizontal position it will readily pass through the doorway, cut notches in each end and securely tie the two ends of a rope across the notches ; suspend this swing by slipping the centre of the rope over the hook in the doorway (Fig. 255) ; have the apparatus strong and firm, capable of any amount of wear and tear. Stand facing the stick, which should be at the height of the chest, and take hold of it with both hands ; now bend the knees until they are within a short distance of the floor,

then rise and repeat the exercise.   Next, with both hands on
the stick, take a long step forward with the right foot, throwing
the weight on that foot ; return to your position and go through
the same exercise with your left foot.   Try different movements
which suggest themselves, and select those you like best.   When
not in use the swing can be slipped off the hook and put out of
the way.

Exercise Tenth.

To develop a weak voice and make it clear and sweet, and to
strengthen the lungs, reading aloud is an excellent exercise ; as
it requires both mental and muscular exertion and performs a
double duty, it should receive a full share of time and attention.   Begin with something you are interested in, then you
will find it much easier to read aloud than if you undertook a
book or an article which might be full of merit, but lack interest
for you.   When commencing this exercise read only ten minutes or less at a sitting, increasing the time as you practise and
the reading grows less difficult.   Do not be discouraged if your
voice sounds a little husky while reading ; stop a moment, and
then go on again.   After a few trials you will have no more
trouble in that way, for your voice will grow clear and distinct,
and the exercise will become a great pleasure as well as an attractive, useful accomplishment.

Let your reading matter be very choice and of the best ; do
not condescend to waste your time on other writings.

From the ten different exercises given, select those best
adapted to your size, age, and liking, and practise them for a
short time daily ; you can hardly realize the great advantage they
will prove to be.   In this way all parts of the system may be
strengthened and harmoniously developed.   But the constitu-
tion cannot be hurried : all must be accomplished little by little.
Allow yourselves to be happy and merry; be ready to enjoy

the little pleasures of life, and this, with kind and generous feelings for others, will do a great deal toward keeping you well
and strong.

Out-of-door exercise is always to be preferred to in-door
when one has a choice. Walking, tennis, archery, horseback,
and swimming are some of the athletic sports for girls, and they
all have their attractions. But there are times when we are de-
nied the pleasure of these pastimes, and then we are glad of a
little exercise in-doors, which also affords enjoyment and recreation.

CHAPTER XXXIII.

A DECORATIVE LANGUAGE.

HEN in olden times the warriors went around the country dressed in suits of clothes made by a blacksmith instead of a tailor, their hats were manufactured at the forge also, and had *iron front doors* that moved upon hinges. When danger was nigh these doors were closed, locked, and barred over the poor men's heads, leaving only a loop-hole or two for them to peep through. At such times in meeting Mr. Brown it was impossible to distinguish him from Mr. Smith, who was arrayed in like manner, and it might happen that Mr. Smith was the last man in the world that one cared to meet, not being on speaking terms or some such reason. Well, as we were saying, there was no chance whatever of telling one man from another unless he wore a distinguishing mark of some kind.

So to prevent such uncomfortable mistakes and to distinguish friend from foe, every gentleman had to be marked and labelled, like an express package, so one might read as he ran, " I am Earl Jenkins, of Thunderland, who married a Rhazor, of Stropshire." These names and addresses were not painted in words on their owners with a marking-brush, but worked and embroidered in translatable designs on cloaks, saddle-housings, and silken banners, or emblazoned on the shield they carried with which to meet the advances of their neighbors. Since that time our more recent ancestors in England have taken great pride in preserving and handing down from generation to generation these distinguishing marks, as a guarantee to their children that they came of gentle birth, which is very interesting and gratifying for European girls, but American girls need nothing of the kind ; it is sufficient that we are Americans.

Of course, some of us do take pleasure in knowing that our great-great-grandparents came over in the Mayflower, or that the name of an ancestor is among the signatures upon that Declaration of Independence which made such a stir a century ago, for that proves us to be Columbia's daughters.

When there was no other method of distinguishing a man his label became a very important item ; so these family devices were reduced to a science and protected by law.

The old countries' coats of arms may remain abroad, where they belong, but the ingenious scheme, that was gradually evolved, of picturing ideas, mottoes, and pretty sentiments we will adopt as our inheritance, with many thanks to our mediæval ancestors with the metallic clothes, who bequeathed them to us.

We propose to revive enough of this neglected knowledge of chivalry to serve our purpose in suggesting a method of designing devices which will not only be artistic decorations, but to the initiated can be made to portray almost any sentiment or set of principles the artist may choose.

The many uses to which these designs can be applied will, we hope, at once be seen by the quick-witted American girls, and we trust will interest the reader as much as they do the writer, who in this chapter can only give a few necessary, brief hints upon the subject, sufficient, however, to explain the application that can be made of this beautiful and perfect system of

Decorative Language.

In the following directions anyone can learn how to make a device which will not only be a decoration, artistic in form and color, but will at the same time express the peculiar traits, char·acteristics, and virtues of the friend for whom it is intended, or the precept, code, proverb, or creed of the designer. All technical terms, as far as practicable, are discarded, but the rules of heraldry strictly adhered to, with such simplifications as are necessary to render it intelligible.

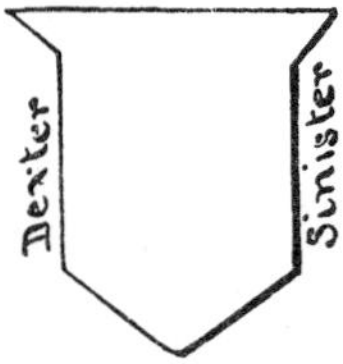

Fig. 256.—The Field.

The Field.

The surface on which the design is portrayed is called the field. This may be of any shape ; originally it was supposed to represent a warrior's shield, but you may use a circle, oval, square, diamond, or any other form.

The Points

on the surface of the shield locate the exact spot where a design or object in heraldry may be placed. Refer by numbers to Fig. 257.

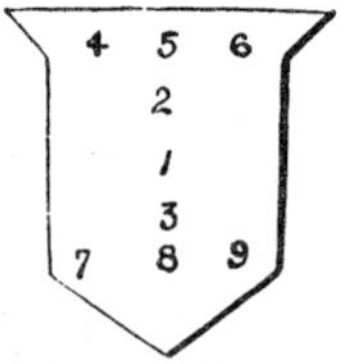

Fig. 257.—Points.

1. Fess point.
2. Honor point.
3. Nombril point.
4. Dexter chief point.
5. Middle or chief point.
6. Sinister chief point.
7. Dexter base point.
8. Middle base point.
9. Sinister base point.

If you desire to place a flower on the fess point, you find that it means the exact centre of the shield, and so on.

The devices take significance in accordance with the more or less importance of their position on the shield ; the honor point holds the highest grade, next to it the middle or chief point, and the right or dexter side is of more importance than the left or sinister.

The field may be divided, if desired, in any of the following

Divisions,

each of which has a significance, suggested generally by the form :

Fig. 258, the Chief, occupying the top or head of the

Fig. 258.—Chief.   Fig. 259.—Fess.   Fig. 260.—Parted per Fess.

shield, indicates pre-eminence, main object, intelligence, first principle.

Fig. 259, the Fess, denotes cause and effect, the central band containing the means by which the ends, in the other spaces, are accomplished.

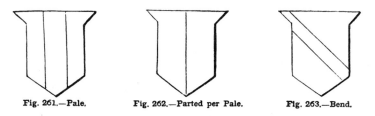

Fig. 261.—Pale.   Fig. 262.—Parted per Pale.   Fig. 263.—Bend.

Fig. 260 is a partition, and partakes of the meaning of the division, it is denoted by the term, parted per fess.

Fig. 261, the Pale, represents rectitude, uprightness; also union, the object in the central division uniting whatever occupies the dexter and sinister sides.

Fig. 262 is parted per pale.

Fig. 264.—Parted per Bend.   Fig. 265.—Chevron.   Fig. 266.—Cross.

Fig. 263, the Bend, is auspicious, meaning prosperity, success.

Fig. 264 is parted per bend.

Fig. 265, the Chevron, is indicative of aid, assistance, support.

Fig. 266, the Cross, suggests humility, devotion, patience, perseverance.

Fig. 267.—Saltire.   Fig. 268.—Pile.   Fig. 269.—Canton.

Fig. 267, the Saltire, a variation of the cross, is recognized as order, discipline.

Fig. 268, the Pile, being in the form of a wedge, means penetration, incision, entering to divide or distribute.

Fig. 269, the Canton, denotes an additional, separate idea or principle; also some characteristic that is added to the original design.

Colors.

These also have symbolical meanings.

Fig. 270.—Gold or yellow is expressed in black and white by means of dots, and is used in the sense of wealth, ability, or knowledge.

Fig. 271.—Silver or white is represented by a plain white

Fig. 270.—Gold.

Fig. 271.—Silver.

Fig. 272.—Red.

surface, and being the color of light, signifies brightness, pur ity, virtue, innocence.

Fig. 272.—Red, represented by perpendicular lines, means ardent affection, love.

Fig. 273.—Blue is represented by horizontal lines ; like the color in the heavens, it is truth, freedom, eternity.

Fig. 274.—Purple, represented by diagonal lines from sinister

Fig. 273.—Blue.

Fig. 274.—Purple.

Fig. 275.—Green.

chief to dexter base, being the royal color, is understood as authority, power, grandeur.

Fig. 275.—Green is represented by lines running diagonally across the shield from dexter chief to sinister base. Like spring foliage, it suggests hope, life, vitality, youth, freshness.

Fig. 276.—Orange is represented by horizontal lines crossed by diagonal lines from dexter base to sinister chief. It is the color of the king of beasts and signifies strength, honor, generosity.

Fig. 277.—Crimson, or blood-color, is represented by dia-

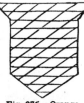

Fig. 276 —Orange. 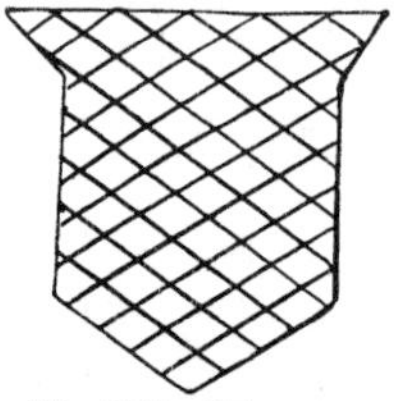　　Fig. 277.—Crimson. 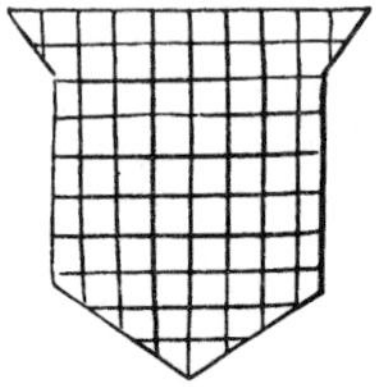　　Fig. 278.—Black.

gonal lines from dexter chief and sinister chief, crossing each other. It denotes boldness, enthusiasm, impetuosity.

Fig. 278.—Black is represented by horizontal and perpendicular lines crossed. It means darkness, doubt, ignorance, uncertainty.

To the principal design portrayed on the shield can be added such appendages as are appropriate—crest over the top and a scroll with a motto beneath the shield—but they are supplementary, and not of great importance; their colors should be those of the shield.

Thus far our plans have followed the exact science of heraldry, but at this point comes a departure, for in the place of other armorial devices we shall place Dame Nature's sweetest thoughts—flowers.

If we now add to the significance of the forms and colors already given the accepted and authentic language of flowers, we shall have a possibility of combinations practically inexhaustible, and with such a dictionary of symbols to draw upon, we can successfully translate almost any terse sentiment into a unique decorative design.

In order to give all the assistance in our power we have culled from the most generally accepted authorities and authentic sources a short floral vocabulary, and now that we have the material at hand let us test the system and learn

How to Make a Design in Decorative Language.

Suppose our Natural History Society desires an appropriate pin or badge.

First we turn to the floral vocabulary and there find that the magnolia means love of nature. The flower has a good

decorative form, its sentiment is exactly appropriate, and we unhesitatingly adopt it.

After trying various forms for the shield, we select a very plain one that the effect of the decorative form of the magnolia may not be lessened by too ornate surroundings, and to show the large size of the blossom we must have it occupy the entire field without any divisions. Next, as to color ; let us think. White, meaning brightness, purity, etc. ? No. Yellow or gold, sig

Fig. 279.

nifying wealth, ability, or—ah ! here we have it—*knowledge ?* Yes, that will do nicely—a love of nature on a field of knowlledge ; that certainly is appropriate. But the top of the shield

being so square and plain gives the device an unfinished appearance. Suppose we try a bar over it, and something not a flower.
As we wish this design to remain simple, a leaf of some kind
would be best; so we return to the floral vocabulary, and after
trying many and almost taking several, finally decide that the
oak leaf is just the form needed to give a finish to the top, and
its meaning, strength, will be an excellent element in the society.
There, our insignia is complete, good in form, attractive in color,
and appropriate in its meaning; but some of us prefer having
the motto written out in plain English, so we will add a decorative scroll, with the meaning of the design inscribed "True Love
of Nature." (See Fig. 279.)

To familiarize ourselves with the working of the method let
us try another experiment, and take the sentiment, "Wealth is
the Reward of Industry," to illustrate.

After deciding on the form of the shield, we turn to the divisions, and running them slowly over for something suitable, stop
at Fig. 259, the Fess, meaning cause and effect. That sounds
promising. Industry is the means by which the end, wealth,
is accomplished. Good so far. We can now see that a floral
emblem to represent industry should be placed in the central
division, and whatever signifies wealth on the other two spaces.
Among our legends of flowers we find industry portrayed by the
bee orchid, and wealth and prosperity are symbolized by wheat.
That is plain and easy. Now we have only to decide upon appropriate colors for the field to complete the design. Gold
would mean wealth, but that we have in the wheat; besides the
yellow of the wheat would not show well on the gold background,
while on white or silver the contrast is strong and the appearance agreeable. Silver denotes innocence and virtue, which
are so necessary that without them wealth would be undesirable.
Therefore silver or virtue shall be the groundwork for our wealth,
and for industry we will select purple as meaning power. In-

dustry possesses the power to acquire wealth. Thus we complete the emblematical design, as seen in Fig. 280.

The following is a problem given to us for solution : On a gold chevron in a black field is a scarlet lily, to which is added as a crest a sunflower, and under all a blank scroll. On this we must write a motto that will be appropriately symbolized by the design.

It would be excellent prac-

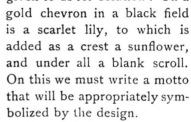

Fig. 280.

tice for the student in this new motif in decorative art to try, by application of the foregoing instructions, to decipher the meaning of this design before reading the analysis.

SOLUTION OF FIG. 281. —We do not think this is put together as scientifically as the system would admit of, but still it can be deciphered.

Fig. 281.

The scarlet lily (high-souled aspirations) on a gold (knowledge) chevron, which is aid, assistance, in a field of black (ignorance), surmounted by the sunflower (pure and lofty thoughts), freely translated, might be read : Aspirations after knowledge help to illumine the

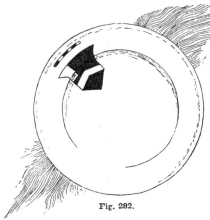

Fig. 282.

darkness of ignorance with pure and lofty thoughts. Aspirations (lily) after knowledge (gold) help (chevron) to illumine (the gold chevron and lily brighten up the dulness of the black field) the darkness of ignorance (black) with pure and lofty thoughts (sunflower).

For younger girls the plain shield of one color with an appropriate flower had best be used, which they may vary *ad infinitum.* A simple yet pretty shield can be made by placing a four-leaved clover, symbolical of good-luck, on a shield of one color, silver, meaning purity, innocence, showing that innocence, combined with the language of the clover, expresses good-fortune.

Fig. 283.

Fig. 284

We might go on forming innumerable designs, each more beautiful than the last, but enough hints have been given to enable the young people to make any style of design in this decorative language which may best suit their purpose. Young

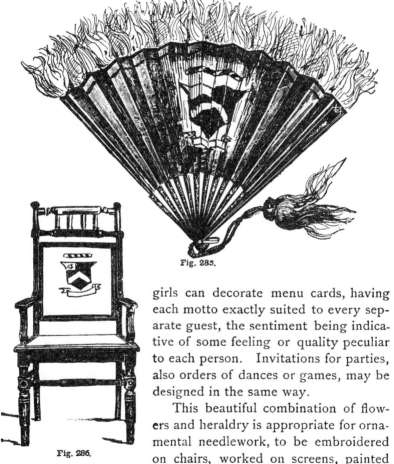

Fig. 285.

Fig. 286.

girls can decorate menu cards, having each motto exactly suited to every separate guest, the sentiment being indicative of some feeling or quality peculiar to each person. Invitations for parties, also orders of dances or games, may be designed in the same way.

This beautiful combination of flowers and heraldry is appropriate for ornamental needlework, to be embroidered on chairs, worked on screens, painted on velvet, wrought on scarfs, and adapted in innumerable ways to add to the refinement and attractiveness of home.

The idea can be utilized in stained-glass effects and in china-painting.

The chosen motto may be a decoration in marking personal

Fig. 287.   Fig. 288.

possessions, such as table china (Figs. 282, 283, 284), fan (Fig. 285), chair-back (Fig. 286), travelling satchel (Fig. 287), tidy (Fig. 288), handkerchief (Fig. 289), and sofa-cushion (Fig. 290).

Fig. 289.   Fig. 290.

These are only a few examples of the many articles which can be beautified and stamped with your individual mark. Portières offer a good ground for applique or embroidery in decorative language.

Book-Plates

seem to be regaining their popularity and usefulness. These book-plates are tablets in any style, which, when gummed inside on the front covers of books, have been used for many years to designate to whom the books belong.

There is a certain book-plate more interesting to us than all others. To the design on it we are indebted for our national shield and our Stars and Stripes. It was used by the Father of our Country, and we are glad to be able to give a print of the original in Fig. 291.

Fig. 291.

In the decorative language any style of book-plate can be designed, which, when pasted in a favorite book, will add to the value of the already treasured volume.

Floral Vocabulary.

Apple-blossom...............	Preference.
Almond.....................	Hope.
Acanthus...................	Art.
Arbor vitæ.................	Unchanging friendship.
Bulrush....................	Docility.
Balm	Social intercourse.
Balsamine..................	Impatience.

Blue violet....	Faithfulness.
Bay wreath................	Glory.
Box	Constancy.
Broom....................	Humility.
Buttercup.................	Riches.
Camellia japonica..........	Unpretending excellence.
Cherry................. ...	A good education.
Canterbury-bell.............	Gratitude.
Chestnut....................	Do me justice.
China aster................	Love of variety.
Cabbage..................	Profit.
Coreopsis.................	Always cheerful.
Clover, red................	Industry
Cowslip...................	Winning grace.
Clover, white..............	I promise.
Daffodil	Uncertainty.
Dahlia....................	Elegance and dignity.
Dandelion.................	Coquetry.
Fennel....................	Strength.
Geranium	Gentility.
Grass....................	Submission.
Heliotrope	Devotion.
House-leek...............	Domestic economy.
Hollyhock	Ambition.
Ivy......................	Dependence.
Laurestine................	A token
Lichen............	Solitude.
Lettuce...................	Cold-hearted.
Lemon-blossom............	Discretion.
Lilac, purple...............	Fastidiousness.
Lily, white................	Purity.
Mullein	Good-nature.
Mignonette...............	Worth.

May-flower	Welcome.
Nasturtium	Patriotism.
Oats	Music.
Olive	Peace.
Ox-eye	Patience.
Poppy, white	Dreams.
Snowdrop	Consolation.
Straw	United.
Sensitive-plant	Sensitiveness.
Star of Bethlehem	Reconciliation.
Sweetbrier	Simplicity.
Thyme	Thriftiness.
Thorn-apple	Disguise.
Tulip-tree	Fame.
Witch-hazel	A spell.
Winged seeds of all kinds	Messengers.
White violet	Modesty.
White rose	Silence.

CHAPTER XXXIV.

A FEW ITEMS ON OLD-FASHIONED NEEDLE-WORK, WITH SOME NEW AND ORIGINAL PATTERNS.

 OME around early this afternoon and bring your fancy-work; we will have a nice, cosey time; all the girls will be there, and we can read that last new book." Such is the familiar and welcome invitation given and received, from time to time, by most young girls, and they find quiet but real recreation in these informal meetings, where, while listening to a friend read aloud, they believe it much easier to keep their minds on the subject if their hands are employed with dainty needle-work. Then, too, sewing is a real pleasure when one becomes interested in the work, and anyone who thoroughly understands plain sewing can with ease learn fancy stitches of all kinds, for good old-fashioned

Plain Sewing

is the foundation—the A B C—of all the more elaborate drawn work, embroideries, and some of the laces. As a rule we think

OVERHANDING.

comes first on the list of plain stitches; this is exactly the same as sewing over and over. Hold the two edges of the material firmly together between the first finger and thumb of the left hand, while with the right hand you take the stitches very close together and as near the edge as possible, sewing from right to left (Fig. 292). It is well to keep the edge nearest to you a little tighter than the outer edge, to prevent its puckering. Always baste the seam before sewing, and when the seam is finished open it and flatten out the stitches (Fig. 293), so that

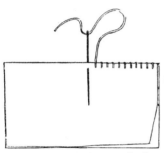

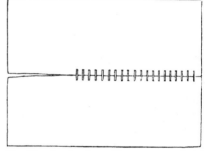

Fig. 292.—Overhanding; or Sewing over and over.

Fig. 293 —Overhanding. The seam opened with stitches flattened out.

the edges of the material will not overlap, but just meet together and lie smooth and flat.

OVERCASTING

is the same as overhanding, except the stitches slant, are farther apart, taken down deeper in the material, and the seam is not opened.

HEMMING.

First turn in the raw edge four or five threads, according to the kind of goods to be hemmed, then turn it down again to the desired width ; this done, baste the hem down evenly and neatly—it must be of the same width throughout—hold the sewing over the first finger of your left hand, and have the stitches small, even, and very near the edge of the hem (Fig. 294).

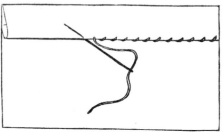

Fig. 294.—Hemming

RUNNING.

Pass the needle in and out of the material in a straight line (Fig. 295), making all the stitches the same size. We believe the rule is to take up two threads and leave two; but the length of the stitch should be regulated by the kind of material used.

BASTING

is to take long stitches in the same manner as running.

GATHERING

does not differ much from running; the stitches are taken on the needle in the same manner, but in this case two threads are taken up and four left; the line should be kept perfectly straight.

If you wish to gather an apron or a skirt divide it into halves, then into quarters, in order to make the fulness even on each half of the band; mark the four places and gather on the right side; when finished draw the stitches

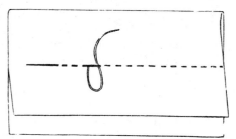

Fig. 295.—Running.

tightly together on the thread and stroke down evenly with a

needle. To sew in the
gathers, back-stitch each
one in separately.

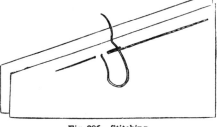

Fig. 296.—Stitching.

STITCHING.

Take two threads
back of the needle and
two before, having each
stitch meet the last one, as in Fig. 296 ; keep the stitches even
and in a straight line.

BACK-STITCHING.

Proceed as in stitching, only make the stitches longer and
do not have them meet.

FELLING.

First baste up the seam, allowing the upper edge to extend
five threads beyond the lower edge (Fig. 296) ; then back-
stitch or stitch the two edges together ; next turn the upper
edge down over the lower one and lay open the seam so that
the fell will lie down flat
like a hem (Fig. 297) ;
then hem it down neatly.

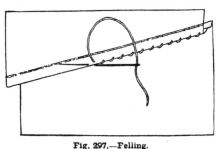

Fig. 297.—Felling.

Button-holes.

Fig. 298 shows how
to take the proper stitch.
Be careful in cutting
button-holes to make the
slit even to a thread and cut the outer corner rounded ; bar
the inner corner by taking two stitches across it, and overcast

the button-hole around three or four threads deep from the edge, or if the material is not inclined to ravel run it with

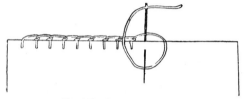

Fig. 298.—Button-hole Stitch.

thread, either double or single, drawing it a trifle tight ; then begin at the left-hand corner to work the button-hole, leaving one thread between each stitch ; keep the stitches exactly the same depth and the loop or pearl of the button-hole on the upper edge.

HERRING-BONE OR CAT'S-TOOTH STITCH

is used to keep the seams in flannel spread open and fastened neatly down. Fig. 299 shows how to take the stitch ; make the stitches all even and of the same size.

We have now given all the stitches which properly belong to plain sewing, and our next step will be

Darning and Mend-ing.

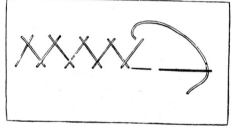

Fig. 299.—Herring-bone Stitch.

" A stitch in time saves nine ; " this much most of us know from experience, and it is wise to devote a little time on a certain day each week to look-ing over the wardrobe and making any repairs that may be needed ; the little care and time thus bestowed will prove a true economy, and it is a real comfort to have all one's cloth-ing in perfect order.

TO DARN A JERSEY OR A STOCKING.

With a needle and thread carefully draw out the uneven ravelled edges of the hole, in order to diminish its size as much as possible, and bring the loops and ends back in their proper places ; then place under it a wooden egg or anything that will answer the purpose, and using thread of the same texture and shade of color as the garment to be mended, run back and forth across the hole as far as the material is worn thin, leaving a

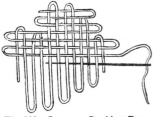

Fig. 300.—Jersey or Stocking Darn.

loop at the end of each turn. In crossing the threads, take up every other thread alternately each way (Fig. 300), and make the darn of an irregular shape, as one of an even outline does not wear well ; when the weaving or darning is finished the loops can be cut off.

TO DARN A TEAR.

Carefully bring the ragged edges together and baste the tear as nearly as possible in its original position ; then, if it is

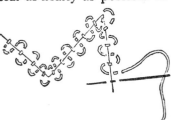

Fig. 301.—Tear Darn.

delicate muslin or dress material to be mended, use ravellings of the same instead of thread to darn with, and weave it in and out across the edges of the rent, as in Fig. 301 ; if the darn needs strengthening, baste a piece of the same material under the rent before darning, and catch down the edges of the piece on the under side of the goods. In mending broadcloth or like material, darn it on the wrong side, and when the darn is finished, ruff up the nap with the point of the needle at the edges of the tear on the right side to cover the stitches; then dampen the darn, and after laying a thin clean cloth over it, press with a moderately hot flat-iron; this should make the darn almost, if not quite, imperceptible.

How to Patch.

If possible cut the piece intended as a patch of the same goods as the garment to be mended, and if there is a pattern be careful to so cut and place the patch that it will match exactly; baste and hem down the patch on the right side of the worn part of the garment; then cut out the old material on the wrong side, leaving enough edge to form a firm hem; sew this to the patch, taking care that the stitches do not show on the right side.

How to Sew on a Button.

Should much strain come on the button, as in little children's clothes, first hem down a small double piece of muslin, on the wrong side of the garment, at the exact spot where the button is to be placed, and with strong thread take a stitch on the right side; then sew the button through about four times, being careful not to let the stitches spread on the wrong side; wind the thread three times around the shank of the button formed by the stitches, drawing the thread a little tight, pass the needle through and fasten the thread neatly on the wrong side; the extra piece of muslin can be omitted when not needed.

To Mend a Kid Glove.

If the glove is merely ripped, and there is no strain on the portion to be mended, sew the two edges together over and over on the right side with fine thread or sewing-silk matching in color the glove to be mended ; if, however, there *is* liability of its tearing out again, strengthen the edges by first working a button-hole stitch on each ; then sew them together over and over, passing the needle in and out of the loops of the button-hole stitch, so forming a narrow net-work of thread between the two pieces of kid. Should the glove need a patch, carefully cut a piece of kid out of the best part of an old kid glove corresponding in color to the one needing repairs ; make the patch exactly the shape and size of the hole, and button-hole stitch all around the edge of the hole and the edge of the patch ; then sew in the patch over and over, catching together the

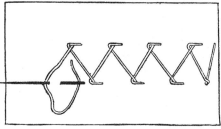

Fig. 302.—Feather Stitch.

loops of the button-hole stitches · this makes the mending firm, neat, and strong.

Fancy Stitches.

These are in many varieties of style ; one of the most useful is known as the

FEATHER STITCH.

Fig. 302 gives the position of the needle and the manner of taking the stitch. Remember to make all the stitches of an exact length and the same distance apart, first one on this side and then one on that, keeping them in a straight, even line.

CHAIN STITCH

sometimes takes the place of braiding ; it is the same stitch as that used in the old-fashioned tambouring (Fig. 303) ;

many Persian embroideries are made in silk with the chain-stitch.

A NEW IDEA IN OUTLINE STITCH.

The stitch (Fig. 304) is used for outline embroidery, and when made with fine black sewing-silk resembles pen-and-ink

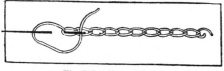

Fig. 303.—Chain Stitch.

work. We have seen figures outlined on linen with the drapery worked in colors, while the face, hands, and feet were simply in black and white ; being finely outlined, the effect was novel and artistic, for in this way the features were made as true as if drawn on paper with a pencil.

For filling in the solid colors take the common running stitch, but make the stitches long on the right side of the embroidery and very short on the wrong side, so as to give the appearance of the colored fabric copied.

Use filo-silk ; and English or French embroidery cottons, when

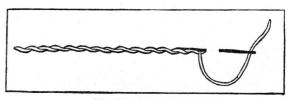

Fig. 304.—Outline Stitch.

colors are needed in the work. Always soak the silks and cottons in strong salt and water before using ; this sets the color and keeps it from running when washed.

HEM-STITCHING.

Decide upon the width of the hem and the width of the space for drawn threads ; carefully draw out the thread at one edge of the space, then the thread at the other edge; next all the intervening threads; this finished, fold and baste down the hem, allowing it to meet the edge of the drawn work, and taking five threads running lengthwise in the space, bind them together at the edge of the hem; at the same time stitch them to the hem, as in Fig. 305.

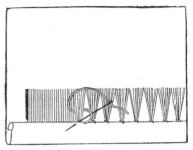

Fig. 305.—Hem-stitching.

Drawn Work

always looks well and is very serviceable when made of linen. Scarfs for buffets, bureaus, or tables, and tea-cloths, tidies, or chair-backs, can be made of crash, butchers' linen, and linen sheeting; it is better to have doylies of very fine linen.

In making drawn work, if the article is to be fringed, first draw out a few threads to measure the depth of the fringe, and at the opening thus made hem-stitch all around the edge of the material, leaving the ravelling out of the fringe until the drawn work is finished; proceed to draw the threads wherever spaces are desired, and before working the pattern always hem-stitch both edges of the spaces. In Fig. 306 the pattern marked B shows the stitch called fagotting, made by crossing every other group of threads back over the one preceding and drawing the linen thread through in such a way as to keep the groups twisted; the two lines marked A, in the Fig. 306, are intended

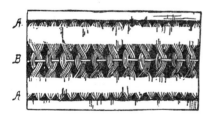

Fig. 306.—Fagotting Stitch.

more as a finish to some elaborate design than as a pattern in themselves; these are made by hem-stitching down a number of threads to each group. Fig. 307 gives a favorite pattern; for this count the threads, so that the spaces may be equal and regular; draw the threads in all the spaces running one way first; then draw the threads in the spaces crossing the first one and run linen threads diagonally across from the top of the

Fig. 307.—Drawn Work.

right-hand corner to the bottom of the left, dividing each linen square into two equal parts; cross these by threads also running diagonally across from the top of the left-hand corner to the bottom of the right, again dividing the linen squares, making four equal parts; then weave threads

 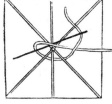

Fig. 308.—First Knot.   Fig. 309.—Second Knot.

through all the spaces running both horizontally and perpendicularly, using the fagotting stitch (Fig. 306), and when crossing the threads in the open spaces tie the centres of each in turn, as in Figs. 308, 309; finish the pattern by running a thread in and out several times around the knots in the centres of the wheels and fasten the ends by tying neatly. Another pattern is given in Fig. 310.

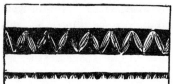

Fig. 310.—Border in Drawn Work.

Outline work is often combined with drawn work; fast colors, in either cotton, linen or silk, are used for the outline design. When the article worked is intended for daily use and must frequently be laundried, it is better to substitute in place of the fringe a wide hem-stitched hem edged with firm linen lace.

Very dainty fancy aprons are made of common scrim with spaces drawn and narrow ribbons of different colors simply woven in and out of the threads, running crosswise through the spaces.

Applique and Original Designs for Portières.

The pattern in this work is cut from one material and sewed on another.

Almost any kind of fabric can be used as either applique or foundation; velvet and plush are suitable for applique, but make poor groundwork, owing to the long nap; both materials in dark rich colors are handsome when used as a border on portières or table-covers. To applique a pattern of velvet or plush cut the design very exact and cover the wrong side with a slight coating of gum, being careful to have the gum thin on the edges so that it will not spread on the groundwork; then lay the velvet on the place it is to occupy, and after pressing it down very gently and lightly with your hand, allow it to dry; this accomplished, the edges of the pattern may be hemmed down neatly on the foundation. If a further finish is desired, outline the design by sewing all around the edge a small gold or silken cord.

Portières.

We give an original applique design for a portière in Fig. 311, representing Day. The foundation is of soft dark-blue momie-cloth, the sun a round piece of bright yellow or orange

satin, and the rays are of gold or heavy yellow silk thread
merely run in stitches of various lengths ; the cloud is of light
blue crape or crazy cloth, and the bird is one of those which
come prepared expressly for applique by the Japanese, and can
be purchased at almost any Japanese or fancy store ; if possible
a lark should be selected in preference to other birds. The
border is a band of old gold velvet. Our other design (Fig.

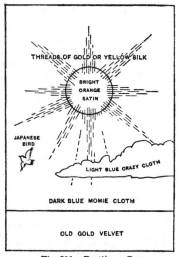

Fig. 311.—Portière. Day.

Fig. 312.—Portière. Night.

312) represents Night ; the foundation and band are the same as
those for the " Day " portière ; the star is of white silk, the
moon of very pale Nile green silk, and the cloud of dark pearl
gray crape or crazy cloth, much darker than the blue momie-
cloth.

The applique work must be done very carefully. First cut
out the designs, next turn in the raw edges evenly and smoothly,
and with a very fine thread and needle baste the edges down ;

then baste the designs carefully on the foundations, and, with a fine needle and sewing-silk matching in color the piece to be appliqued, hem each one down neatly, making the stitches almost invisible. The band of velvet can be sewed on the bottom edge of the momie-cloth, then turned up like a hem and hemmed down.

Lace.

Very beautiful lace is made by cutting out the heavy patterns which are still perfect, from old and worn laces and embroideries, and transferring the designs to new fine wash-net. After first basting them on, hem them down to the netting with a fine needle and thread ; in this way the embroideries last as long again and look as well as when new.

Ribbon Embroideries.

We can give a clearer idea of this work by means of an example, and we will take the common white daisy as an illustration.

Thread a long-eyed coarse needle with very narrow white ribbon, and beginning at the centre of the flower, pass the needle from the wrong side up through your material, drawing the ribbon out nearly its full length and leaving only a short piece on the wrong side to be fastened down ; now take a stitch straight out the length of a daisy petal and pass the needle through to the wrong side ; then, taking a very short stitch, draw the needle out through on the right side ; next take another long stitch back to the centre of the daisy, thus forming the second petal ; continue in the same manner, making the petals radiate out in a circle from the centre of the flower. Work the centres of the daisies with yellow silk and the stems in dark-green silk ; the leaves can be either worked or appliqued.

For half-blown daisies make only about a quarter of a circle of petals, and in place of the yellow centre, work a green calyx. Ox-eyed daisies can be made in the same way with soft, thin yellow ribbon, a little broader than the ribbon used for white daisies. The work is rapid and pleasing, and almost any flower can be imitated very perfectly with ribbon embroidery.

CHAPTER XXXV.

SCRAP-BOOK AND HOME-MADE BOOK-COVERS.

THE fashion of collecting pictured advertising cards, so much in vogue among the children a few years ago, seems to have run its course, and dying out, it has left on the young collectors' hands more cards than they know well what to do with. Many of the collections have been pasted in scrap-books, of which the children have long since tired. While examining one of these volumes with its row after row of cards, it occurred to me that these advertisements might be utilized in a new way by dividing and combining them. The experiment proved a success, and I will now try to show you how, with the aid of scissors and mucilage, the pictures which have become so familiar may be made to undergo changes that are indeed wonderful, and how from them may be formed a

Mother Goose Scrap-book.

The nursery scrap-books made of linen or paper cambric are, perhaps, familiar to most of our readers ; but for the benefit of those who may not yet have seen these durable little books, we will give the following directions for making one: Cut from a piece of strong linen, colored paper cambric, or white muslin, four squares twenty-four inches long by twelve inches wide. Button-hole-stitch the edges all around with some bright-colored worsted, then place the squares neatly together and stitch them directly through the centre with strong thread (Fig. 313). Fold them over, stitch again, as in Fig. 314, and your book is finished and ready for the pictures.

It is in the preparation of these pictures that you will find the novelty of the plan we propose. Instead of pasting in those cards which have become too familiar to awaken much interest, let the young book-makers design and form their own pictures by cutting special figures, or parts of figures, from different

Fig. 313.—Scrap-book Opened and Stitched through the Centre.

Fig. 314.—Scrap-book Folded and again Stitched.

cards, and then pasting them together so as to form new combinations.

Any subject which pleases the fancy can be illustrated in this way, and you will soon be deeply interested in the work and delighted at the strange and striking pictorial characters that can be produced by ingenious combinations.

Stories and little poems may be very nicely and aptly illustrated ; but the " Mother Goose Melodies " are, perhaps, the most suitable subjects with which to interest younger children, as they will be easily recognized by the little folk. Take, for instance, the "Three Wise Men of Gotham," who went to sea in a bowl. Will not Fig. 315 serve very well as an illustration of the subject? Yet these figures are cut from advertising cards, and no two from the same card. Fig. 316 shows the materials, Fig. 315 the result of combining them.

Again, the little man dancing so gayly (Fig. 317) is turned

Fig. 315.—"Three Wise Men of Gotham."   Fig. 318.—"Little Jack Horner."

Fig. 316.—Figures cut from Advertising Cards.

into "Little Jack Horner" eating his Christmas pie (Fig. 318), by merely cutting off his legs and substituting a dress-skirt and pair of feet clipped from another card. The Christmas pie in his lap is from still another card.

In making pictures of this kind, figures that were originally standing may be forced to sit; babies may be placed in arms which, on the cards they were stolen from, held only cakes of soap, perhaps, or boxes of blacking; heads may be ruthlessly torn from bodies to which they belong, and as ruthlessly clapped upon strange shoulders; and you will be surprised to see what amusing, and often excellent, illustrations

Fig. 317.—Figures cut from Christmas Cards.

present themselves as the result of a little ingenuity in clipping
and pasting.   Another kind, which we shall call the

Transformation Scrap-Book,

will be found exceedingly amusing on account of the various
and ever-changing pictures it presents.

Unlike any other, where the picture once pasted in must
remain ever the same, the transformation scrap-book alters

one picture many times.
To work these transfor-
mations a blank book is
the first article required ;
one eight inches long by
six and a half or seven
wide is a good size.

Cut the pages of this
book across, one-third of
the way down.   Fig. 319
shows how this should be

Fig. 319.—Transformation Scrap-book with Pages
cut.

done.   The three-cornered piece cut out near the binding allows
the pages to be turned without catching or tearing.   Leave the
first page uncut ; also the one in the middle of the book.

Cut from picture-cards, or old toy-books which have colored
illustrations, the odd and funny figures of men and women,
boys and girls, selecting those which will give a variety of costumes and attitudes.

Paste a figure of a woman or girl on the first page, placing
it so that when the lower part of the next page is turned, the
upper edge of it will come across the neck of the figure where it
is joined on to the shoulders.

Cut the heads from the rest of the pictured women, and
choosing a body as different as possible from the one just used,

Leaves from a Transformation Scrap-book.

paste it upon the lower part of the next page, directly under
the head belonging to the first body. Upon the upper part of

the same page paste any one of the other heads, being careful to place it so that it will fit the body. Continue in this way, pasting the heads upon the upper, and the bodies on the lower, part of the page, until the space allowed for the women is filled up ; then, commencing at the page left in the middle of the book, paste upon it the figure of a man, and continue in the same manner as with the woman, until the spaces are all used and the book is complete.

The combinations formed in this way are very funny. Old heads with young bodies ; young heads with old bodies ; then one head with a great variety of bodies, and so on.

The first picture may represent a man, tall and thin, dressed in a rowing costume, as shown in the illustration. Turn the lower part of the next page, and no longer is he thin and tall, but short and stout, the position of this body giving the expression of amazement, even to the face. The next page turned shows him to be neither tall nor short, thick nor thin, but a soldier, well-proportioned, who is looking over his shoulder in the most natural manner possible.

The figures in the illustration were cut from advertising cards, and the head belongs to none of the bodies.

A curious fact in arranging the pictures in this way is that the heads all look as though they might really belong to any of the various bodies given them.

Instead of having but one figure on a page, groups may be formed of both men and women, and in the different arrangement of the figures they can be made very ludicrous indeed.

A scrap-book for older girls, which might be termed more fitly

An Album,

can be made by mounting engravings, wood-cuts, photographs, and water-colors on pieces of thin card-board all of the same size.

If any one subject be chosen, and such pictures selected as tend in some way to illustrate that subject, the book will prove more interesting in the making, and will be quite valuable when finished.

There will be no difficulty in mounting the pictures; simply paste them on the card-board with good flour-paste, and press under a heavy weight, keeping them perfectly neat and free from smears of paste on the edges. When two or more are mounted at the same time, place clean pieces of blotting-paper between, pile one upon another, and put the heavy weight on top.

Such a scrap-book should be bound in a

Home-made Book-cover,

which is made in this way:

Take two pieces of heavy card-board a trifle larger than the book you wish to cover, make three holes near the edge of each (Fig. 320) and corresponding holes in the edges of the

 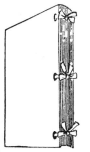 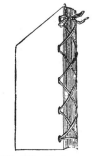

Fig. 320.—One Side of Book-cover with Holes cut near the Edge.

Fig. 321.—Book-cover Tied with Ribbons.

Fig. 322.—Book-cover Laced together with Silk Cord.

book, which must not be too thick—that is, contain too many leaves; pass narrow ribbons through these holes and tie in bow-knots, as in Fig. 321. If the leaves of the book are thin, more holes can be made in the back and the covers laced together with silk cord (Fig. 322).

These book-covers may be beautifully decorated by anyone who can paint in water-colors, and tinted card-board can also be used for them. They are pretty, and suitable as covers for manuscript poems or stories, or for a collection of autographs.

In making any kind of scrap-book it is very necessary that the paste used should be good. If the paste is poor, the pictures will peel off or the paste turn sour. The recipe given below we can recommend as an excellent one for

Flour-paste.

Mix one-half cup of flour with enough cold water to make a very thin batter, which must be smooth and free from lumps ; put the batter on top of the stove—not next to the fire—in a tin sauce-pan, and stir continually until it boils ; then remove from the stove, add three drops of oil of cloves, and pour the paste into a cup or tumbler. This will keep for a long time and will not become sour.

CHAPTER XXXVI.

A HEAP OF RUBBISH, AND WHAT TO DO
WITH IT.

IN almost every house there is an attic, and in almost every attic may be found a room where trunks are stored, where broken toys and disabled furniture are put out of sight, and where all articles not worth selling or giving away gradually accumulate until this attic room contains, literally, a heap of rubbish. Entering one of these lumber-rooms not long ago, and glancing over the medley which comprised so much, from a tin can to a piece of broken bric-à-brac, the thought occurred to me that something might be done with it, some use be made of at least a few of the articles consigned to the place as utterly useless.

That was rather a thrifty thought. Do you not think so, girls? Then let us make the most of it and together venture back into that mysterious and somewhat dusty chamber, and see if there really is anything there worth the making over.

In imagination we will stand in our attic lumber-room and begin to look about us with eyes and mind open to perceive possibilities.

On one side of the room, leaning against the wall, we see what was once a handsome old-fashioned mirror, quite large and of heavy plate-glass. It's poor dusty face, reflecting dimly its barren surroundings, is shattered in many pieces, and at first sight it seems hopeless to attempt to restore it to the plane of beauty or usefulness; but do not let us be hasty; we will examine it more closely. Yes, here is a piece of glass large enough to frame. Never mind its uneven shape and rough edges ; we will work out that problem later. Now we must put it carefully aside and continue our investigations.

Here is a large tin can, which can be made into a lantern to hang in the hall, and this baking-powder can may be of some use, so we will take it also.

The tops of three cheese-boxes ; something should be done with them. Perhaps they can be used for a table ; put them with the other chosen things.

A croquet-ball ! That will make a fine key-rack. This box of silks and ribbons we may need, and the large pasteboard-box will do for the foundation of our mirror frame.

We must have this piece of old brass chain this handful of large nails, the pasteboard roll which has been used for sending engravings through the mail, and that old broad-brimmed straw hat; also these three broomsticks and the piece of nice dark-gray hardware paper.

Now, seated in our own room, let us see what we can do with this rather unpromising array of objects spread around us. First we will try

The Mirror,

and must cast about us for the ways and means of framing it. The large pasteboard-box we have already decided will make a good foundation. After tearing off the sides, we will cut an even square from the bottom, which is smooth and unwarped.

Next laying the piece of mirror on the square of pasteboard we must cut, out of ordinary brown wrapping-paper, a square two inches larger all around than the pasteboard, make a hole in the centre as large as the shape of the mirror will allow, and

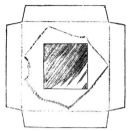

Fig. 323.—Brown Paper Pasted on Mirror and Pasteboard for Home-made Mirror-frame.

paste it down on the mirror and pasteboard (Fig. 323). Then, after clipping out the corners, we will turn the edges over on to the back of the pasteboard foundation and paste them down. Cutting four strips of the hardware paper, about two inches wide, we will fold them through the centre lengthwise and paste them around the glass, lapping them just a little over the edge of the other paper, the folded side being next to the glass (Fig. 324). This will form a bevel for our frame. From the same paper we will now cut a square, three inches larger on all sides than the foundation; then, exactly in the centre, mark a square half an inch larger all around than the square of mirror showing. In the centre of the square marked out we must insert our scissors, cut it like Fig. 325, and after clipping off the points, as indicated by the dotted lines L, M, O, N, turn back the four

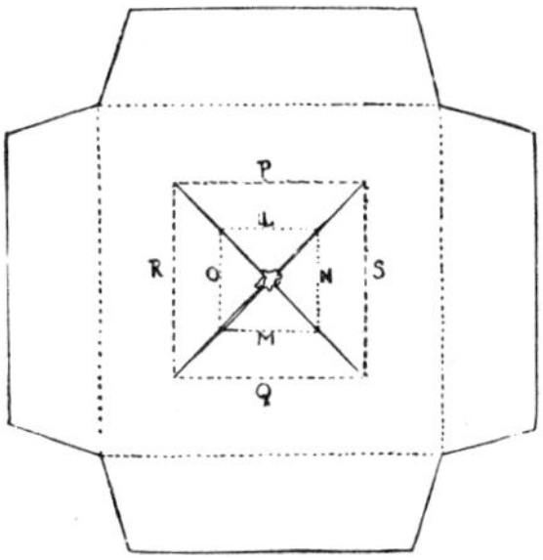

Fig. 325.—The Outside Covering for Mirror-frame.

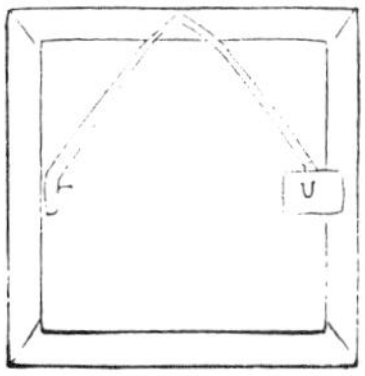

pieces at the dotted lines, P, Q, R, S, leaving an open square. Then placing it over the mirror so that the same width of bevelled edge shows on all sides of the mirror, we must paste it down. Clipping out the corners, as shown in diagram, we will bring the edges over and paste them down securely to the back of the frame. A piece of hardware paper, cut in a

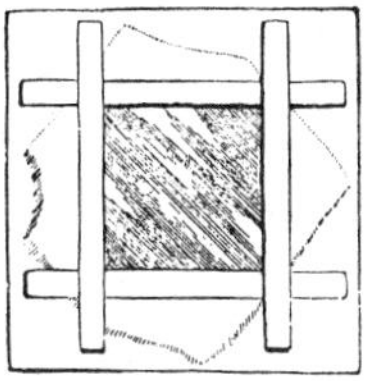

Fig. 324.—Bevel of Hardware Paper on Frame.

Fig. 326.—Back of Frame with Tape Attached.

square one inch smaller than the frame, we will paste on the back to finish it off and hide the edges of the paper where they have been turned over (Fig. 326).

Home-made Mirror-frame.

We must fasten on a piece of tape by which to hang the mirror, by pasting down the ends of the tape on the frame (letter T, Fig. 326), and pasting over each a strip of the hardware paper (letter U, Fig. 326). When the frame is quite dry we will paint a branch of dog-wood or some light-colored flower across it, and have as pretty a little mirror as anyone could wish for.

The next thing to commence will be

The Table,

which you can make yourselves by following these directions :

The three cheese-box lids will answer nicely as shelves for a work- or bric-à-brac table, and the broomsticks, which are all the same length, will do for the legs.

Upon each broomstick mark the distances for placing the shelves, allowing six inches from each end of the stick for the top and bottom, and the exact centre between these points for the middle shelf. With a pocket-knife cut narrow grooves

Fig. 327.--Narrow Grooves Cut around Broomstick for Table-leg.

Fig. 328.—Holes Bored in a Box-lid Used as a Table-shelf.

Fig. 329.—Manner of Fastening a Shelf to Table-leg.

Fig. 330.—Table-shelf and Leg Fastened securely together by Wire.

around each stick, one-half inch on either side of the points marked on them (Fig. 327). This will make six grooves on each stick. Now measure the box-lids to find their circumferences, and divide them into thirds, marking the distances on the rim to obtain the true position for the legs. At these points bore four holes with a gimlet, one inch apart, two above and two below (Fig. 328). Through one of the top holes pass a piece of pliable wire, place one of the broomsticks against the rim of the lid, pass the wire back through the other upper hole (Fig. 329), fit it into the upper groove of the stick, and draw it tight. Twice the wire must be put through the upper holes and around the stick in the top groove; then, bringing it down

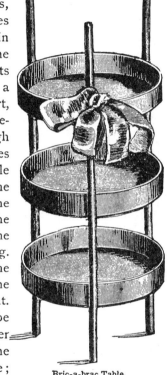

Bric-a-brac Table.

on the inside of the lid, you must put it twice through the lower holes and around the stick in the lower groove; then twist the ends and tuck them under the wire on the inside of the lid (Fig. 330). In this way each leg will have to be fastened to each shelf. When the table is all put together paint it black, and, as soon as it is dry, tie a bright ribbon on one of the sticks at the top, and a charming little bric-à-brac table will be the result of your labor.

You can make a very pretty

Lantern

of the old tin can ; but first you must have some tools to work with ; not many, only a piece of wood, rounded on one side to fit into the can, a hatchet or heavy hammer, and a few wrought iron nails. If the piece of wood is not large enough to fit the can, another stick can be put in to hold the first one firmly against the can. That being arranged, you must decide upon some kind of a pattern to be made by the holes, and indicate it on the can with a small paint-brush and paint or ink ; then, laying the can on its side, the rounded piece of wood being at the top, with one of the wrought iron nails puncture the holes where you have indicated the pattern. With the hammer drive the nail through the tin into the wood ; then draw it out, make another hole, and so on until all the holes you wish are driven through that part of the can held in place by the rounded piece of wood.

This wood, you see, keeps the can from bending when the nail is being driven through. In moving the wood as the work progresses, you must always keep it under that part of the can being punctured. To make the large hole, you will have to put a number of the small holes close together, and then drive the nail through the partitions, cutting them away. The pattern being completed, puncture three holes, close to the top of the can, at equal distances apart. These are for the chains to pass through, by which to suspend the lantern. In the cover of the baking-powder can make three holes at equal distances ; then divide the chain, which is about one yard and a quarter long, into three equal lengths, separating the pieces by prying open the links. Put an end of each piece through the holes made for

them at the top of the can, and fasten them by hooking the open links through the links of the chain a little farther up, and hammering them together again.

Now pass the ends of the chains through the holes made in the lid of the baking-powder can, and, bringing the ends together, fasten them by joining the links.

Fig. 331.　Fig. 332.
—Stand in Lantern, with Nails for Holding Candle.

Paint the lantern, chain and all, black, and while it is drying make a stand for the candle which is to furnish the light. A square piece of thin board, just large enough to fit into the can without touching the sides will do for the stand. Drive four small nails in the centre to hold the candle (Fig. 331).

Make handles for lifting the stand in and out of the lantern, by bending two pieces of wire like Fig. 331, and fastening them to the board with staple tacks (Fig. 332).

When the paint on the lantern is dry, paste red tissue-paper all around the inside to give a cheerful red glow to the light, which will shine through it. If you would like it to resemble a jewelled lantern, paste different colored papers over the large holes and leave the small ones open. An S hook passed through the loop

Lantern.

made by the three chains will serve to connect them to the chain which should suspend the lantern from the ceiling.

A Music-Roll

can be made of the pasteboard roll.

Cut a round piece of pasteboard just the size to fit into one end of the roll; then cut out another round piece, this time of paper, one inch larger than that made of pasteboard. Clip the

edges (Fig. 333) and paste it over the end of the roll which is filled in with the round of pasteboard (Fig. 334).

Among the scraps of silk and ribbons you will, perhaps, find a good-sized piece of dark-green or brown silk; use this for the case,

Fig. 333.—Paper Covering for End of Music-roll.

Fig. 334.—Paper Pasted over End of Music-roll.

which must cover the roll neatly. To make the case fit the end of the roll you have just filled up, mark on a piece of the silk a circle the size of that end of the roll. This can be done by standing the roll on the silk, and running a pencil around the edge. When cutting out the silk leave a margin of a quarter of an inch on the outside of the pencil-mark for the seam. Cut the silk for cover-ing the roll three inches longer than the roll, and wide enough to allow for a quarter of an inch seam.

Music-roll.

Sew up the long seam, and then sew the round of silk into the end of the case. Hem the other end of the case, and run in a narrow ribbon about an inch from the edge. This is for a draw-string.

When the roll is fitted snugly in its case, tie a ribbon,

matching it in color, around the roll, making a loop to form the handle. Fasten the ribbon by taking a few stitches under the bows, catching them on to the silk.

The old straw hat can be transformed into a dainty

Work-Basket.

It is stiff and harsh at present, but pour boiling water over it and the straw will become soft and pliable, and can be bent into any shape you like. When dry, it will be again stiff, and will retain the form you have given it. After scalding the hat bend the brim in toward the centre, in four different places, at equal distances apart. This will make a fluted basket. You

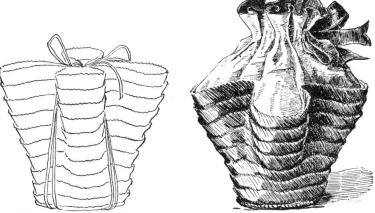

Fig. 335.—Straw Hat Tied in Shape for a
Work-basket.

Work-basket.

must tie it in shape (Fig. 335) and leave until perfectly dry; then bronze the basket, line it with silesia, and sew silk or satin around the top to form a bag. Run a draw-string of narrow ribbon near the top of the bag, and the pretty little work-basket is finished.

The croquet ball you can make into a

Key and Button-Hook Rack.

First you must gild it, and then around the middle of the ball, at regular intervals, insert small brass hooks. A yellow ribbon and bow, tacked on the top with small tacks, will serve to suspend it by, and completes the rack.

With the gilt left from gilding the ball, and a piece of bright ribbon you can make a

Paper-Weight

of six of the large nails. Gild each nail separately, let them dry, and then tie them securely together with a piece of ribbon.

Key Rack. Paper-weight.

All the articles brought from the attic have now been turned to some use, but there are many other things to be found there which we have not space to mention, and which with little trouble can be so transformed that no one would ever suppose they were taken originally from a heap of rubbish.

CHAPTER XXXVII.

HOW TO MAKE ATTRACTIVE BOOTHS AT A FAIR—A NEW KIND OF GRAB-BAG.

DECIDING to have our fair unlike those which have preceded it, we must do away with monotony and introduce not only variety, but originality as well. New ideas, something different from that which has served us heretofore, is what we strive for. Novelties are always attractive, let them be decorative also, and help to make the room or hall as inviting as possible.

The Tables

being the most important item, we will give them our first attention. Have each table or booth canopied in a style differing from all others, and make the canopy extend up as high as practicable, in order to avoid the flat, blank appearance so common in small fairs. If tables are arranged in this fashion, they will go far toward decorating the hall. Fig. 336 shows one style in which a framework for the roof or covering may be constructed. At the four corners of the table, where the top projects over the sides, fit in blocks of wood according to Fig. 337; the dotted lines represent the block. Nail the wood

The Fair.

fast to the table, so that the uprights may stand perfectly straight. Use laths or similar sticks for the four uprights, and screw or nail them at the corners of the table according to Fig. 336; then with small screws fasten a stick across the top of the laths at each side, and at the top of the sticks on the front of the table tie the two ends of a barrel-hoop to form the arch; also attach another hoop at the back to the other two uprights, and connect the top centre of each by a wire running across. The hoops are fastened to the laths by binding the ends of the hoops to the ends of the laths with strong twine, or wire, wound around in notches which have previously been cut

Fig. 336.—Framework for the Canopy of a Booth at a Fair.

Fig. 337. — Block of Wood Fastened on the side of Table.

in the ends of both sticks and hoops. Should the barrel-hoops be too short for the arch, take children's large-sized toy wooden hoops, and fasten them up in the same manner. Fig. 338 is another way to arrange the framework. The four upright sticks are attached to the table as described in Fig. 336; then in the top of each is driven a very large-sized tack, and a strong flexible wire is stretched from lath to lath and wound around each tack, thus connecting the four uprights together.* Flags, shawls, drapery curtains, sheets,

---

* If the uprights seem to need it, brace them with cross-sticks in place of wire.

and inexpensive cheese-cloth make good canopies ; undressed cambric and canton flannel in desirable colors drape nicely,

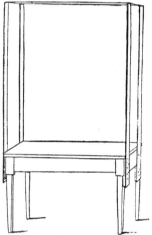

and can also be used for the purpose. Where you wish to produce light, airy effects, tarlatan, in one or more colors, will be found useful ; again, let some of the tables have only a suggestion of a roof, made by orna- menting the framework with flowers, or whatever is most suitable, accord- ing to the style of table and the place it is to occupy.

Try and have a variety of shapes and sizes in the booths, and avoid sombre dulness and monotony. Let the room fairly sparkle and shine with light and color.

Fig. 338.—Construction of Frame- work for the Canopy of a Table at a Fair.

To make a tent-like covering, firmly bind a large-sized Japanese umbrella to a pole, and fasten the pole in the centre of the table. To hold it securely, make a bench of two pieces of board, with a hole through the centre of each, and join them

together by a block of wood nailed in each end (Fig. 339). The bench can be made fast to the table by screws put through from the under side of the top of the table.

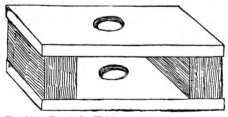

Fig. 339.—Bench for Holding a Pole as a Support for a Canopy of a Booth.

In erecting the can- opy place the end of the pole in the bench and it will be steady and firm. Attach pieces of string to several ribs on each side of the umbrella, stretch the strings down and fasten the ends securely to the table ; paste over the strings bright-colored tissue-paper fringe (Fig. 340). Cut the paper four or six thicknesses, and when pasted on turn the fringe part uppermost, so it will look fluffy and not hang down in a tame, fringe fashion. When a red umbrella is used, and the strings are covered with fringe of the same hue, it looks very pretty. Be extremely careful that no light comes dangerously near the tissue-paper, or any other inflammable material ; all the decorations must be arranged with a view to perfect safety from contact with gas, lamp, or candle.

In decorating the room remember to mass your color so the effect may be broad. If the colors are too much mingled the effect will be weakened, and in some cases lost entirely.

Paper-flowers and plants in great abundance will be needed, and if you can per-

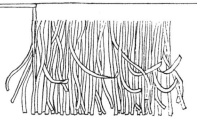

Fig. 340.—Tissue-paper Fringe.

suade all your friends, as well as those actively interested in the fair, to make paper-flowers or plants, they will prove very acceptable, and after the fair is over the floral decorations can be safely stored away to do service again on like occasion. Large, showy flowers, like peonies, dog-wood, and magnolias, as well as large-leaved plants, are best to use, though the smaller ones look well in a few places.

In making

Flowers for Decorations

we aim at general effect, with less regard to detail than if the blossoms were to be used in other ways. Fig. 341 is a pattern of the dog-wood. Cut the flowers of white writing paper and make them quite large. Use wire to fasten them to a

Fig. 341.—Dog-wood.

natural branch, and imitate nature as nearly as possible in the arrangement of the blossoms.

If you fold the paper a number of times and then place your pattern over it, you can cut out six or eight flowers at once, and save both time and labor.

Peonies are made of white, pink, or red tissue-paper, cut in squares of about eight inches each and pinked on the two opposite edges. Twelve squares are needed for one flower. With your fingers gather the squares up in the centre (Fig. 342); then fold over the pieces, as in Fig. 343; when all are ready string them on a wire and shape the bunch to resemble a peony; twist the wire up tight and fasten the petals together, leaving a length of wire for a stem.

Fig. 342.—Peony Petal Gathered through the Centre.

Make the cherry-blossoms (Fig. 344) in clusters of five or seven each, and attach green leaves (Fig. 345) cut in different sizes. Fig.

Fig. 343.—Peony Petal Folded over.

346 shows the method of giving the leaf a pretty, crimped appearance. By holding the point of the leaf firmly under the head of the pin with your left hand, and with the right hand pushing the leaf up toward the head of the pin, you can crimp the leaves very rapidly, and they look much more natural than when left plain.

All the materials necessary for the manufacture of flowers for fair decorations will be paper, wire, and paste. The buds of different flowers can be imitated by pinching together the petals of open blossoms. Figs. 347, 348, 349 are the petals of the magnolia ; the inside petals are five and one-half inches long, the others in proportion. Cut three of each size. No. 347 forms the innermost petals, No. 348 the next, and No. 349 the outermost ; these last should be double ; make the outside of pink tissue-paper and the inside white, all the other petals are white ; cut three, from Fig. 350, of green paper to form the calyx.

Fig. 344.— Fig. 345. —
Cherry   Green Leaf
Blossom.   of Cherry
            Tree.

Other ornamental flowers may be manu-

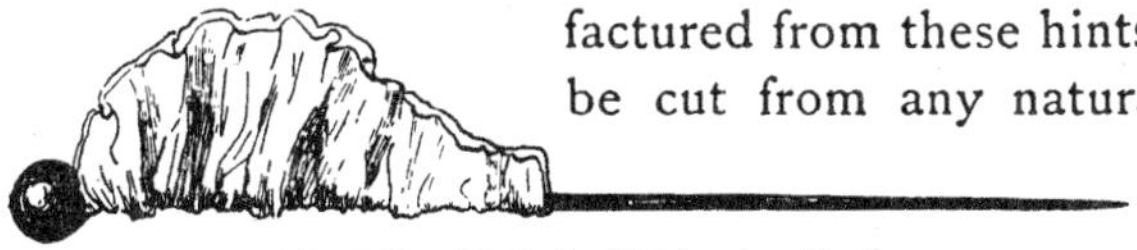

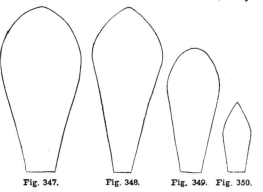

Fig. 346.—Method of Crimping Leaf.

factured from these hints. Patterns can be cut from any natural flowers, and they may be made without the aid of further directions. When natural blossoms can be obtained, they are far preferable, though the paper plants make splendid substitutes and at a little distance cannot be distinguished from the natural ones.

If the fair comes off in the season when the trees are leafless, bare

Fig. 347.   Fig. 348.   Fig. 349. Fig. 350.

branches with green paper leaves wired on will help very much where foliage is needed.

An excellent scheme in the arrangement of a fair is to divide

the tables into twelve separate booths and let each one represent
one month in the year. They should contain articles appropriate only to the month represented, and when planned in this
way each month should be of appropriate color. For example :

December

can be all white, with tufts of cotton scattered about for snow,
and mica or isinglass sprinkled around and over places to represent frost and ice. Icicles, varying in size, depending from
the arch or canopy, add to the effect. The icicles are made of
strips of paper first rolled up like paper-lighters, then completely covered with tallow from the dripping of a lighted
candle ; the tallow being allowed to harden on in raised places
makes the twisted paper resemble in form a real icicle ; the
tallow icicle is next covered with a wash of mucilage, and
powdered mica or isinglass is sprinkled all over it, so that it
sparkles and shines.

In place of the usual grab-bag at this booth, there should be
a Christmas-tree without lights and burdened with little gifts
tied up in colored tissue-paper. Santa Claus must have charge
of the tree.

July

calls for flags and decorations of red, white, and blue, as well as
flowers, fruits, and green foliage ; the table should be presided
over by Columbia.

May.

Deck this table in spring blossoms and make the canopy of
a slender May-pole. Pass the pole through the holes in the
bench (Fig. 339) and screw the bench tight on the centre of
the table ; fasten a wreath of flowers and the ends of a number
of ribbons at the top of the pole ; bring the ribbons down and

tack them to the sides of the table. Give the Queen of May care of the booth.

November

may be gay with late fall leaves and berries, and a very large pumpkin, which has been previously scraped out and lined with paper, can serve as a receptacle for odds and ends. A little Puritan maid should be in charge of the booth.

June

is all rose color, with the queen of flowers, the rose, holding the post of honor. This month is very suitable for the flower-table, and Flora, the Goddess of Flowers, may preside over it.

We have chosen these few months only as suggestions of the manner in which the idea can be carried out.

Those in charge of the different booths might wear as a badge a conspicuous sign of the zodiac appropriate to the month represented.

The Five·Senses

can be illustrated by five booths, each one bearing its proper symbol as a sign. To represent

HEARING,

make a large pasteboard ear-trumpet and cover it with silver paper ; fasten this on the highest point of the booth and place the word Hearing in large letters under the trumpet; have these signs in plain sight, where none can fail to see and read. The articles on the table should consist of everything pertaining to the sense of hearing, such as sheet-music, musical instruments, telephones, and suitable toys.

It would be a great addition if a phonograph could be

rented or borrowed for the occasion, and a certain sum charged to each one speaking in the instrument and hearing the echo of his own words and tones ground out to him again.

An oracle would be a capital thing at this table, each person consulting it paying so much a question.

SEEING

likewise must be labelled with a sign in the shape of a very large pair of spectacles cut out of stiff pasteboard and placed over the lettering.

The goods offered here for sale should pertain to the sense of sight; and could be such articles as pictures, decorated candles, kaleidoscopes, and common blue glasses. All things pleasing to look upon may find place at the Seeing Table. Any kind of a peep-show can be used, five cents being required from every curious person wishing for a peep behind the curtain.

FEELING

is more difficult to portray. Perhaps an ordinary riding-whip will answer the purpose, with the word Feeling in large type under it.

Sofa-cushions, quilts, mittens, canes, muffs, fancy toilet articles, and almost anything adding to our personal comfort, or pleasant to handle, are suitable for the Feeling booth.

TASTING.

As an emblem for this booth make a huge cornucopia for candy, with the sign "Tasting" beneath, and the booth can be the candy-table.

SMELLING

naturally suggests perfumes and sweet-scented flowers. This sense will most fitly be represented by an immense bouquet fastened up over the table. The booth, of course, must be the flower-table.

If you have only a few tables, make four booths of them, and let each booth represent a season. They should be decorated in keeping with the time represented, and the idea fully carried out in all the details.

When the booths stand for different nations there is a great field for variety and beautiful decoration. But in this, as in all cases where an attempt is made to carry out an idea, it must be faithfully adhered to, or the effect will not be that intended.

When it is necessary to decorate the

Walls

use flags, bright, soft draping cloth, and large palm leaves; also branches of leaves, showy flowers, and anything that can be arranged to look well. As rooms differ so much in size and style, it is impossible to give any but general directions, leaving it to the taste of the decorator to carry out the details.

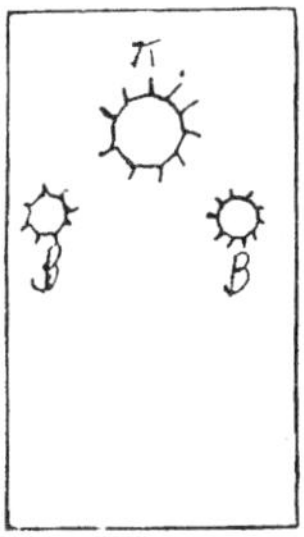

Fig. 351.—Grab-bag of a Sheet with Holes Cut for Face and Arms.

Grab-Bags.

On a narrow sheet hung up in a door-way, and fastened securely at the sides, or attached to a frame, cut a hole large enough to allow of a false face being fitted in (Fig. 351 A). The flaps of the cloth are left for pasting inside the face; now cut two more holes for the arms to pass through (Fig. 351 B). In these holes sew sleeves of the same material as the skirt, which is made of bright-colored cambric in the

Fig. 352.—Apron Skirt Sewed on Sheet.

Fig. 353.—Grab-bag.

form of an apron, and sewed on the sheet (Fig. 352). The sides of the skirt are basted down on the sheet. When pasting in the false face, first cover the flaps, left at the opening for the face with stiff paste ; then paste these flaps down into the inside of the false face, which will bring it up close against the sheet. If small openings are left, or the sheet puckers a little after the face is fastened on, never mind, as all defects can be covered by sewing on a thin white frill all around the face, to form a cap, and making a collar of the same material (Fig. 353).

Leave an opening, or pocket-hole, through the sheet at one side of the dress, so that the hand can be slipped through to get the packages, which are placed within reach at the back of the curtain. Fig. 354 shows the inside of the sheet, and C the opening for the hand. Someone must

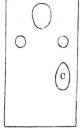

Fig. 354.—Inside of Sheet for Grab-bag.

stand or be seated behind this curtain, and slip her arms into the sleeves, then she can look out through the mask and see with whom she is talking. In one hand she may hold a package, while she receives the money with the other.

On the sheet print these words : " Five cents for what is in my pocket."

The Lady of the Lake.

You will need a tin bath-tub for the lake, the longest one you can find, and a toy boat which will not easily tip or turn over. Place tiny flags in the bow and stern, and in one end of the boat glue a doll dressed like the "Lady of the Lake" in Scott's poem. Attach a pulley to each end of the tub, and fasten the string to the boat, as it must be run back and forth by means of the pulleys. Fill the tub nearly full of water, then cover the edges with moss and vines. The bath-tub must be completely disguised, and surrounded by plants and foliage, with an opening left at one end for purchasers, and another small one near the other end for the boat to pass through to those stationed behind the shrubbery, who have charge of the boat, and where the parcels are kept. At the store-room end the screen of vines or leaves should be so arranged that those in charge can see all that is going on outside without being seen themselves.

The boat should be stationed at the farther end of the lake, and whoever wishes to make a purchase must give the doll five cents ; then the boat may immediately leave, sail across the lake, and disappear behind the screen, only to emerge again laden with a parcel in place of the money, and lightly skimming over the water arrive at her destination, when the purchaser can relieve the " Lady of the Lake " of her package.

The Bubble Range described on page 335 can be used in a fair with advantage. Unless the fair is very small, it is better to have two Bubble Ranges, to prevent the tiresome waiting for a turn, and give all who wish to try their skill the opportunity to enjoy the sport.

Fortune's Wheel.

Cut of stiff pasteboard a large circle (Fig. 355) with a point on the edge at the end of one of the spokes, for the circle must be painted to resemble a wheel. With a large round nail fasten the wheel through the centre to a board, which has previously had numbers painted on in a circle somewhat larger than the circumference of the wheel (Fig. 356); the wheel should turn around easily on

Fig. 355.—Circle for Fortune's Wheel.

the nail. Hang the board up flat against the wall. The gypsy in charge of the Fortune's Wheel should be stationed by its side, holding a basket filled with many envelopes numbered to correspond to the figures on the board, each envelope containing some appropriate fortune-telling lines; and when the people come to seek their fortunes the gypsy must allow each in turn to give the wheel a twirl, sending it around rapidly, and then hand to the fortune-seeker an envelope whose number corresponds with the figure at which the wheel pointed when it stopped turning.

Fig. 356.—Fortune's Wheel.

Rag-Balls.

Prepare a number of carpet-rag balls with a small gift in the centre of each one. These sell rapidly, and it is very amusing to see the buyers unwinding their balls to discover the contents, which may prove to be a thimble, a bundle of jackstraws, a grotesque Japanese toy, or any little comical conceit which can be hidden in the odd receptacle.

The same idea might be applied to the always pleasing pop-corn balls; then the knick-knacks must be first wrapped in soft paper to protect them from the candy used in making the balls.

Pleasant mysteries and surprises are always popular at fairs, and the more that can be invented the better.

Window Decorated with Imitation Stained Glass and Dutch Curtain.

CHAPTER XXXVIII.

WINDOW DECORATION.

OW, girls, we must have practicable ideas in regard to our decorations; they should consist of something which we *know* will be easy to make and at the same time look well; the materials employed must be within possible reach of all, and nothing expensive or difficult to obtain allowed to enter into their manufacture. What are commonly called Dutch curtains are very popular; they are short curtains of some thin, transparent fabric, fastened with rings to a slender rod of bamboo, and when drawn, cover the lower part of the window without intercepting the light. The curtains are very useful, but, while they do not obstruct the light, they do obstruct the vision.

We all know that the front window is just the place to sit when sewing or doing fancy-work, and although few ladies care to be seen by every passer-by, yet they all like to see what is going on outside, and while their deft fingers ply the needle their bright eyes take in the landscape out of doors and derive amusement and entertainment from the birds and flowers, if it be in the country, or the ever-moving throng, if in the city.

An ornamental screen, therefore, that will shield one and

yet not interfere with the view is desirable. What might be termed the

Oriental Window-Shade

not only comes up to the above requirements, but is inexpensive, and not difficult to construct.

Make a small lawn-tennis net, long enough to reach across the width of the window and about eight inches deep ; make loops of the rope on the ends for hanging the screen to knobs or hooks screwed in the framework of the window ; spread the net out and fasten it up on a door, between two chairs, or any convenient place ; then cut a number of pieces of fine twine, about four feet long, and attach them, a quarter of an inch apart, along the bottom rope (Fig. 357); A shows a loosened loop and B the tightened ones. The ends of the twine hang free. On each double strand string glass beads and slender pieces of bamboo, reeds, painted clay pipe-stems, or macaroni broken in pieces of equal length and used in their natural color, or painted with oil-paints to any desired tint. Have the reeds four inches long, and thread them on alternately with the beads (Fig. 358) ; or you can form a design by cutting the reeds into different lengths ; at the end of each strand fasten a large bead or glass button. A very simple

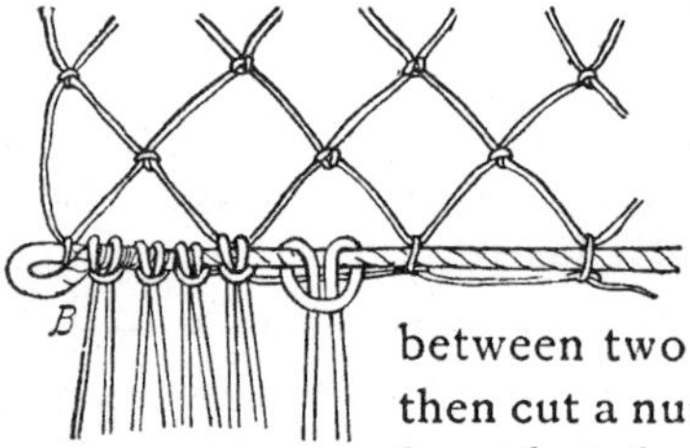

Fig. 357.—Manner of Making Fringe for Oriental Window-shade.

Ribbon-Curtain

is of red, blue, yellow, and black ribbons all cut the same length and sewed, a quarter of an inch

Fig. 358.—Fringe of Macaroni and Beads.

apart, on a narrow strip of black cloth long enough to reach across the window. The strip may be used as a band, or attached to a slender pole by means of small brass rings. The ribbons should be silk, and thin enough to admit of the light shining through ; they hang down fringe-like, with three glass beads fastened on the end of each ribbon (Fig. 359 or Fig. 360). If you

Fig. 359.

prefer to have the shade all one color make it yellow, which gives a pleasant, mellow light. Any pattern you choose can be made by taking short pieces of ribbon and joining them together with glass beads. In this way bits of ribbon could be utilized, but those used must be semi-transparent, showing the color when held up to the

Fig. 360.—
Beads on the
Ends of Rib-
bons.

light. Even smooth pieces of silk with their edges neatly hemmed might do service, only be very careful to join either ribbon or silk with the beads in such a manner as to prevent its twisting ; the beads must be heavy enough to keep the fringe straight.

Nearly all homes have their bags of silk and worsted pieces, and from these can be made a handsome

Drapery of Very Small Scraps.

Cut the pieces of silk or worsted into squares about an inch each way, using any and all colors ; then take a piece of twine of the length you desire your curtain, and with a large needle string the bright bits on the twine until the whole string is completely and closely covered ; next fasten the twine well to prevent its slipping, and with a large pair of scissors trim off the rough edges of the silken strand until the surface is rounded and even ; on one end attach a small brass curtain-ring, and on the other a heavy bead or button ; make as many strands as you will need to hang across the window and fasten them to a pole in which small hooks have been screwed.

This drapery resembles chenille; it is rich in color, will wear well, and is best adapted for full-length curtains.

As a substitute for stained glass we give directions for

Painting Window-Panes.

These are very pretty and satisfactory. If good designs are chosen the window will surpass in beauty your expectations.

The materials necessary are : some of Winsor & Newton's transparent colors, such as rose-madder, Prussian blue, raw and burnt umber, burnt sienna, ultramarine, gamboge, ivory-black, viridian green, and orient yellow. Any transparent color can be used. For purple, mix rose-madder with Prussian blue.

Prepare the paints to be used by mixing each color separately with a little oil and siccatif Courtray. Almost any brush will do to paint with, but one of medium size made for oil-colors is the best, and another smaller one is necessary for the outlining, which takes the place of leading in stained glass. The dabber is a ball of raw cotton tied in a piece of fine cotton-cloth, and the manner of tinting or grounding is exactly the same as in china-painting; lac-varnish will be needed as a wash after the painting has dried.

When you have an opportunity, carefully examine real stained-glass windows, and you will see that each window is one complete design. The corners and borders are usually in rich, dark colors, while the central portion is of lighter tints or clear glass.

Always make your corners and borders first, and if you desire a centre-piece, it should be placed in position next, and the space between it and the border filled in afterward. A Gothic window may be imitated by painting the corners black, thus making it arched at the top. Very often good patterns can be

Fig. 361.—Border Pattern.

found in the many art and fashion papers. One copy may serve for an entire border, if it be pasted at the four corners to one pane of glass, and, when that is outlined, removed and gummed to the next, and so on until the border is finished.

Fig. 361 is intended as a border. Fig. 362 is a very simple pattern of cracked glass, which you can readily make without any copy. Place a ruler across the woodwork of the window-pane, first one way, then another, and with its aid paint your straight lines, being careful

Fig. 362.—Cracked Glass.

not to have any two run parallel. A conventional design is always to be preferred. Should any mistakes occur during the progress of the work, remove the paint with a cloth dampened with turpentine and try again. The painting is not difficult, and the only delays are in waiting for the colors to dry.

First decide on your design, then trace it, making the outlines heavy and black; gum the pattern by the four corners to the outside of the window-pane, which it is essential to have perfectly clean and dry; close the window, and with a small brush dipped in black paint follow the outlines of your copy, keeping the lines of equal thickness throughout; when this is finished remove the pattern. In the same manner go over all the outlines you wish to make on the window, then leave the color to harden and dry, which will probably require hours. Begin again by laying on flat washes of paint to match the prevailing colors of the copy, and use the dabber in tinting each color as it is applied, so the surface may be even and uniform. While the decoration is drying it is best to protect it from dust by pinning up a newspaper or a large piece of cloth on the window-frame. When dry, the painting can be touched up if necessary.

After the last color has entirely dried apply a wash of white lac-varnish; when this is dry give the window another coat of lac-varnish and then it will be finished. Should your copies be in black and white, use your own taste in coloring the glass.

Another method of imitating stained glass is

Painting on Lawn,

batiste, or any kind of sheer white muslin. For this you will need the same paints that are used for painting on glass; these are mixed only with turpentine and the color put on as a stain.

Cut a piece of new thin white batiste large enough to cover a window-sash, with a margin left for turning in, and make an outline on it of the exact size of the sash; then select your pattern and place the lawn over it, when the outlines should show through ; trace these carefully with gum-arabic dissolved, but made *very* stiff, and when the entire design has been traced let the gum dry ; then go over it with ivory-black unmixed ; this latter makes the leading ; be careful to keep the lines even and of the same size. When the outlines have dried fill in the spaces with the stains made of paint and turpentine ; the gum prevents the colors from spreading. When the paint has dried you may add a few touches where they are needed, and the stained-glass design will be ready to place on the window. Use stiff mucilage or tiny tacks to keep it in place, having first turned in the margin left for the purpose.

An attractive window can be made with the upper sash of imitation stained glass, while the lower one is screened by a Dutch curtain, as in the illustration.

For the benefit of those who prefer sewing to painting we now tell how to

Imitate Stained Glass

with a piece of stiff white rice-net, such as is commonly used for bonnet-frames, and some pieces of thin batiste, or lawns, of the requisite colors. Cut the rice-net the proper size and lay it over your design ; then carefully trace off the pattern ; when all the outlines are finished cut the different-colored lawns of the shape and size to correspond to the different portions of the design ; baste these on in the places they must occupy ; then sew them on with the Automatic Sewing-machine, following with coarse black thread the outlines on the wrong side of the foundation, so that the chain-stitch will appear on the right side to form the leading ; or the stitching may be made by hand, or a very narrow black braid can be used as leading. When all the batiste is sewed on, cut out the net back of the design to allow the light to shine through.

We have seen such an imitation of stained glass, and when placed up against the window it was very good; but care must

Fig. 363.—Imitation of Ground Glass.

be taken to have the colored lawns thin and of the right shades; if too heavy they obstruct the light and the colors do not look bright.

For full-length window-drapery of inexpensive material there may be had at any of the leading dry-goods stores beautiful soft fabrics, in yellows and different colors, the designs of which equal those of much higher-priced goods. These draperies hang in graceful folds and come as low as ten cents a yard; some of them are also well adapted for the useful Dutch curtains.

Windows of Imitation Ground Glass

can be made of white tissue-paper, cut in simple patterns and fastened on the inside of the glass with white lac-varnish. The window must be perfectly clean and dry. If possible have the pieces of tissue-paper exactly the same size as

Fig. 364.—Folded Paper with Diamond Pattern for Imitation of Ground Glass.

the window-panes, fold and refold the paper lengthwise until it

Fig. 365.—Paper Marked with Design for Imitation of Ground Glass.

is an inch or so in width; then cut from stiff cardboard your pattern. If it be a diamond, as in Fig. 363, have it exact, and

cut it in halves; use one-half as a pattern, place this on the edge of the paper, as in Fig. 364, and with a lead pencil draw a line around it; remove the pattern and place it lower down about a quarter of an inch from the first tracing, and again mark around the edge. Continue in the same way until you have the pattern marked on the entire length of the tissue-paper. Make the same pattern on the other edge of the paper (Fig 365). Cut out the pattern, then unfold the paper and smooth it free of wrinkles; give the window-pane a thin coating of white lac-varnish, and apply the paper, being very careful to have it *perfectly* smooth when on the glass. Sometimes it is necessary to join two or more pieces of paper, but if you are careful to make the edges come *exactly* together, the joins will not be noticeable.

Lac-varnish dries very quickly, and it takes only a short time to decorate a window in this manner.

When all the panes of glass are covered with tissue-paper, finish by varnishing each one with the white lac-varnish; at a little distance it is difficult to distinguish a window so covered from one really formed of ground glass.

For bath-rooms, or where the window is rather out of the way and the outlook not agreeable, the imitation of ground glass is suitable and useful.

CHAPTER XXXIX.

FURNITURE OLD AND NEW.

 NLY the other day we were appealed to by a friend for suggestions on how to furnish a room prettily, and at the same time inexpensively, and we know that there are many girls like this friend who, loving to surround themselves with beauty and comfort, have not the means of doing so in the ordinary way ; but must depend largely upon their own skill and ingenuity for the gratification of this taste. After all, there is more real pleasure in planning and contriving the furnishing of one's room, even with only a small sum for outlays, than there is in ordering a set from the furnishers which is exactly like a hundred others. In the former case we make our room expressive of our individuality ; in the latter we walk in the beaten track of those who have little or no individuality to express.

So much for the sentiment of the idea. Now let us turn to the practical side, and find the best way of carrying it out, and putting our theories into practice.

In mentioning old furniture in the heading of this chapter, we do not allude to the antiques in such high favor just now ; they are unique and handsome enough in themselves, requiring no contriving to beautify them ; but there are few families who do not possess furniture that is out of date, old-fashioned without being antique ; furniture that time and hard usage has reduced to a state of shabbiness anything but beautiful, yet not worth sending to the cabinet-makers to be furbished up. It is the renovation of such furniture that will help much toward making a room pretty and attractive.

We need not attempt to restore the furniture to its original state, that would be impracticable. But we can work wonders in transforming it ; in turning a homely article into one that will be an adornment instead of a blemish.

Bookcase.

Take, for instance, an old bureau belonging to a cottage set. The mirror, perhaps, is broken, or if it is not it can be used to better advantage elsewhere. Removing that, there is left merely a chest of drawers, which we will proceed to convert into a bookcase by the addition of shelves placed on top. If you have a brother who is handy with his tools the matter is simple enough ; without him a carpenter may have to be employed to make the shelves, or, by taking the plan and measurements

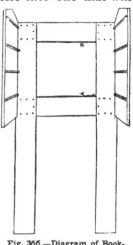

Fig. 366.—Diagram of Book-
shelves.

to a carpenter-shop the materials can be obtained ready for use, and all you will have to do will be to put them together. Although there is a saying that "a girl can never drive a nail straight," we have reason to believe the contrary, and feel sure that a little practice will enable most girls to do many bits of light carpentry work as well as the boys. Three feet is the height of a bureau belonging to an ordinary set of cottage furniture, so we will take that as our standard for measurement, and make our shelves according to it.

Fig. 366 is the diagram for the frame of the shelves. The side pieces are made of boards three feet four inches long and nine inches wide ; the top of each of these boards is sawed into a point as shown in diagram. Four cleats made of sticks eight inches long and one inch thick are nailed to the side of each board, the distance between being nine inches.

The frame at the back is composed of two boards five and one half feet long and seven inches wide, and two, three feet three inches long (the width of the bureau) and seven inches wide. One of these short boards is nailed across the top ends of the long boards, and the other twenty-four inches below. The side pieces are nailed to the back as shown in diagram, the nails being driven through the back board into the edge of the side piece.

When the frame is made it is placed on the bureau, the sides resting on the top and the long back boards reaching down behind where they are nailed or screwed to the bureau. The shelves are thirty-seven inches long and nine inches wide. They rest on the cleats and are not nailed to the frame.

Screws may in some places, answer better than nails.

When the shelves have been adjusted, the whole is painted a dark olive green.

If the knobs are removed from the drawers before the bureau is painted, and brass handles substituted afterward, it will add materially to its appearance.

The bookcase shown in our illustration is finished off with curtains, which hang by brass rings from a slender bamboo pole. The pole is slipped through brass hooks screwed into the side pieces near the top.

Curtains of canton-flannel, or any soft material, are suitable for this bookcase. The colors may be a combination of olive green with old blue, yellow, cherry, copper color, dark red, or light brown.

The Chair

in the same illustration is an ordinary rocking-chair painted olive green, with cushions at the back and in the seat stuffed

Bureau Transformed into a Bookcase.

with excelsior, covered with bright cretonne, and tied to the chair with ribbons.

Chairs of this kind look well painted almost any color ; one of yellow, with yellow cushions and ribbons, is exceedingly pretty.

If the chair to be remodelled is bottomless, reseat it in this way : Cut some strips of strong cotton cloth about one inch wide and sew them together, lapping one piece over another, as in Fig. 367 ; fasten an end on to the edge of the chair with a tack, and then pass the cloth back and forth across, each time putting it under and bringing it over the edge of the chair.

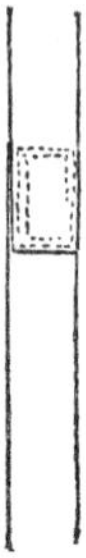

When the seat is filled up with the strips going one way, cut the cloth and tack the end to the chair ; then,

Fig. 367.

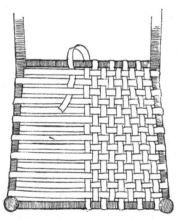

Fig. 368.—How to Reseat a Chair.

commencing at the side, cross these strips, passing the cloth in and out as if darning. Fig. 368 shows just how it is done. Be sure to draw the strip as tightly as you can every time it crosses the chair, for if too loose it will sag as soon as the chair is used. The edge of the chair may be covered with the cretonne, or a ruffle which is sewed around the cushion.

Fig. 369 is an old settee fitted up with cushions, and a sociable, comfortable seat it is. It offers plenty of room for two, and ensconced thereon the girls may rock and talk to their hearts' content.

These settees are not often seen in the city, but are to be found in many a farm-house and country town. The one from which our sketch is taken is painted black, but, like the chair, it would look well any color.

Fresh, dainty prettiness should be the principal feature of a young girl's room, and this can be obtained at very little expense, much less than most persons suppose.

Fig. 370 shows what can be done with the commonest

Fig. 369.—Come and Sit Here.

kind of furniture. This can be bought at the manufacturer's unpainted, and may be left its natural color and simply varnished, or, following the present fashion, it can be painted white, and decorated with slender bands or circles of gold.

As in the illustration,

The Bedstead

should have drapery suspended over it. This gives a soft, pretty effect, and takes away its stiffness. Dotted swiss or thin cottage drapery answers the purpose nicely.

Ten yards of material cut in two breadths of five yards each are required for these curtains. The breadths must be sewed together lengthwise and then passed through a small wooden hoop which has been gilded or painted white.

When the hoop is directly in the middle of the breadths, the material must be brought together close to the hoop and two of the edges sewed or basted together. This seam is to go at the back and keep the curtain from parting and hanging in two strips.

A ruffle of the same material, or lace, sewed on the edge and across the ends of the drapery gives it a soft, lacy effect. The ribbons which loop the curtains at either side should be of the prevailing colors of the room. If the furniture is white and gold, they should be yellow.

The hoop can hang from a brass chain fastened to a hook in the ceiling.

The bureau belonging to this style of furniture is too clumsy for our use, although without the mirror it will be convenient as a chest of drawers. Brass handles in place of knobs will improve it.

A Dressing-table

to take its place, like the one shown in Fig. 370, can be made of a small kitchen-table. The mirror suspended over it should have a broad flat frame of white pine, varnished or painted to match the furniture. Almost any cabinet-maker can frame a mirror in this way. Bracket candlesticks made of brass, which are very inexpensive, should be fastened to the frame on either side of the glass with brass nails or brass-headed tacks.

Fig. 370.—What can be done with Common Unpainted Furniture.

With a brass handle on the drawer, a pretty scarf of linen crash, ornamented with drawn work or outline, thrown over the table and hanging down at each end, and the addition of pin-cushion and toilet articles, this toilet-table looks very attrac-tive and readily chal-lenges admiration.

Fig. 371.—The Ordinary Unpainted Washstand in a New Light.

Washstand.

A piece of white mat-ting bound at top and bottom, with yellow cot-ton cloth for a splasher, as in Fig. 371, and a pretty scarf and toilet-set, presents this most ordinary washstand in a new light.

Three common kitch-en-chairs and one rocker, when painted white or varnished, as the case may be, and cushioned in pretty light-colored cretonne, completes this novel, pretty, and re-markably inexpensive set of furniture.

The curtains next to the windows should be of the same material as that used for the bed-drapery, with the inner one of cretonne like the chair-cushions.

White matting is suitable for the floor in summer, and dur-ing the cold weather it can be mostly covered with a pretty ingrain rug or art square, as it is called.

Instead of using gilt, the rings and bands on the furniture may be blue or red, in which case the trimmings of the room should correspond.

Fig. 372.—Hall Seat Made of a Common Wooden Bench,

A Hall Seat.

As another illustration of what can be done with the most ordinary piece of furniture, we have chosen a common wooden bench, and by painting it black and giving it a dark-red cushion with tassels at each corner, have transformed it into quite an elegant hall-seat. Fig. 372 gives the effect.

Fig. 373 – Window Seat and Book-shelves Combined, Made of Boxes.

Fig. 373 shows a

Window Seat and Book-shelves Combined,

made of boxes. Eight soap-boxes of the same size are required for the shelves, and a packing-box about two feet high, two

feet in width, and as long as the window is wide, for the
seat.

Remove the tops and two sides of the soap-boxes, and bore
holes with a red-hot poker in one corner of the bottoms of six
of the boxes, and in two of the tops which have been removed,
making the holes one inch from either edge (Fig. 374). In
the other two boxes bore in the same place, but not entirely
through, making the holes about half an inch deep.

Place these last two on the floor and pile the others on top
of them, three on each, nailing the
bottom of each box to the top edge
of the one beneath it. On the two
upper boxes nail the tops in which
the holes have been made.

Have ready two slender bamboo
rods about four feet long. Insert a
rod in the hole in the top of an
upper box and let it pass down,
slipping it through the holes in the

Fig. 374.—Hole in Corner of Box
for Book-shelves.

bottoms of the other boxes and fitting it in the cavity in the
lower box.

In like manner put the other rod in place through the other
pile of boxes.

If the packing-box has a cover, it should be fastened on
with hinges, so that it may be used for a shoe-box as well as a
seat; if it has not, turn it upside down, place the soap-boxes at
each end and nail them to it.

Paint the shelves black or the color of the wood-work in the
room, and upholster the seat and the boxes on either side of it
with cushions made of strong muslin stuffed with excelsior and
covered with cretonne.

Fasten the edges of the side cushions to the boxes with
gimp braid and tacks. Make a deep plaiting of the cretonne

and tack it across the front of the large box. When there is a
lid a narrow plaiting must be tacked across its front edge, which
will, when the box is closed, lap over the top of the deeper
plaiting.

That this combination of window-seat and shelves is both
comfortable and convenient, one may easily imagine, and that
it adds not a little to the furnishing of a room, we leave to
our illustration to show.

CHAPTER XL.

SOMETHING ABOUT MANTEL-PIECES AND FIRE-PLACES.

 HE spirit of hospitality and comfort presides over the ruddy blaze of an open fire ; yet, as we gather cosily around and bask in the delightful warmth and radiance, its cheerful influence is too often retarded by its very unattractive surroundings. This lovely household spirit should have a more fitting habitation than the one frequently accorded it. The fire-place should at least be pleasant to look upon, and not depend wholly upon the bright fire to make it inviting.

The ordinary marble and marbleized slate or iron mantel-pieces are the reverse of beautiful, but they may be very much improved at the expense of a small outlay of money, time, and trouble.

The examples we give here of the treatment of commonplace mantel-pieces are simple, and can easily be managed by the girls themselves, with but trifling aid from a carpenter.

In a room occupied at one time by a young friend of the writer, there was an old-fashioned white-pine mantel-piece. It was stiff and plain, with no attempt at ornamentation, and the border of white marble, about five inches wide around the fire-place, was apparently inserted to protect the wood from

Fig. 375.—Shelves over Mantel-Piece.

the heat of the fire, and not for beauty. A hint from the writer was sufficient to set this girl's brain and fingers to work. Soon the white-marble border was transformed into a row of blue and white tiles, which were not only pretty and appropriate, but were also the means of dispelling the impressions of coldness and hardness the marble gave.

The manner of effecting this transformation was simple enough. First the marble was divided into squares, the lines being painted black ; then conventional patterns were sketched with a pencil on the squares and painted in blue, oil-paints being used for the purpose.

How the mantel-piece was otherwise reformed, the writer never saw, but it might have been greatly improved and altered by the addition of shelves above, or a suitable lambrequin upon the mantel-shelf. However that may or might have been, the tiles were a successful bit of work, and the painting of them within the capabilities of almost anyone. Then why should we long in vain for a tiled mantel-piece, when we have it in our power to gratify the wish ?

On a plain white-marble mantel a border around the fireplace may be marked out, and a set of tiles painted, which will look just as pretty as any that can be bought.

If the rest of the marble is painted black or brown, the tiles will look as though they were set in, and the contrast will make them more effective.

Fig. 375 illustrates our suggestion of putting shelves over the mantel-piece. The braces can be bought at any hardware-store, and the shelves may be of black-walnut or pine boards, stained or painted to match the mantel-piece.

Fig. 376 shows the effect of a mantel-shelf covered with enamel-cloth made in imitation of leather. The color of the material used for the one from which our sketch is taken is dark red, and has a dull, soft finish like Russian leather. It is ornamented with small brass curtain-rings sewed on in points or pyramids; a strip of enamel-cloth is also put behind the shelf, and at the top edge a piece of narrow gilt moulding is tacked.

Fig. 376.—Mantel-Shelf covered with Enamel-Cloth ornamented with Brass Curtain-Rings.

A mantel-board of pine, two inches longer and two inches wider than the shelf, is always necessary when there is to be a lambrequin, for upon this the lambrequin is tacked.

First, the board must be neatly covered with the material, enamel-cloth or whatever is used, the edges of the cloth being brought over and tacked under the edge of the shelf; then the strip composing the lambrequin must be turned in at the top edge and tacked across the front and two ends of the board with brass-headed tacks. It looks better if the corners of the board are rounded as shown in illustration.

The piece at the back of the shelf should be about eighteen inches deep and must be tacked at top and bottom with small tacks, the edge at each end being turned in and tacked to the wall with brass-headed tacks.

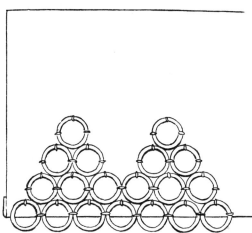

Fig. 377.—Enamel-Cloth ornamented with Brass Rings.

Fig. 377 is the diagram of enamel-cloth ornamented with brass rings, and shows a section of the pattern. The bottom row of rings should be sewed on first, and the edge of the cloth turned up as the rings are fastened on. The stitches which hold the rings catch the hem also. This first row of rings should extend half way below the edge of the cloth, as shown in Fig. 377. Strong yellow embroidery-silk or saddlers' silk is the best to sew them on with.

The gilt moulding can be bought by the foot and small headless nails are furnished to tack it with.

Another mantel is treated in very much the same manner as Fig. 376, the difference being that, instead of enamel-cloth, the covering for the shelf and the piece at the back are dark-red canton-flannel, and around the edge of the shelf is tacked a worsted fringe, about six inches deep, matching the canton-flannel in color. This has a warm, comfortable look and is quite

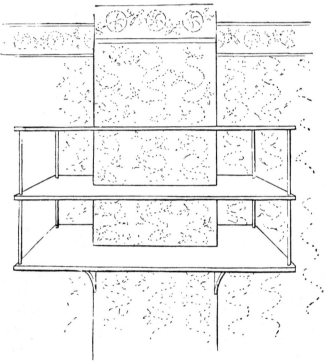

Fig. 378.—Shelves around Projecting Chimney.

appropriate for a bedroom, while the other should be used only in a library or dining-room.

The writer was once invited into a young girl's room which was very attractive in its daintiness. It was not pretty in shape, and an uncompromising chimney, in which there was no fire-place, projected into the room ; but taste had overcome these difficulties, and the effect produced was decidedly pleasing.

Pretty wall-paper and the arrangement of the furniture helped very much, but the greatest triumph was in subduing the awkwardness of that chimney by surrounding it with a set of shelves for holding pretty bits of bric-à-brac.

In case another girl may have the same difficulty to surmount in decorating her room, we give an outline drawing of the shelves (Fig. 378) that she may see and profit thereby.

CHAPTER XLI.

HOME-MADE CANDY.

 E have noticed that in none of the books we have seen, which were written especially for the amusement and entertainment of girls, has there been any directions or recipes for making candy. Knowing by experience that most girls consider candy-making one of their prime winter enjoyments, we consider the omission to be quite an important one, and we will in this chapter endeavor to supply the much-wished-for information.

Though cooking in general may not be regarded with much favor by the average school-girl, she is always anxious to learn how to make candy, and hails a new recipe as a boon.

The following recipes for peanut-candy, butter-scotch, and molasses-candy were obtained from a friend who makes the best home-made candy it has ever been our good-fortune to taste, and as she recommends them, we may rely upon their being excellent. We give them, with her comments, just as she wrote them.

Delicious Peanut-Candy.

Shell your peanuts and chop them fine ; measure them in a cup, and take just the same quantity of granulated sugar as you have peanuts. Put the sugar in a skillet, or spider, on the fire, and keep moving the skillet around until the sugar is dissolved ; then put in the peanuts and pour into buttered tins.

This is *delicious*, and *so* quickly made.

Butter-Scotch.

2 cups of brown sugar.

¼ cup of butter.

4 tablespoonfuls of molasses.

2 tablespoonfuls of water.

2 tablespoonfuls of vinegar.

Boil until it hardens when dropped into cold water, then pour into but·tered tins.

Molasses-Candy.

2 cups of brown sugar.

¼ cup of New Orleans molasses.

⅜ cup of vinegar and water mixed.

A piece of butter half the size of an egg.

When the candy hardens in cold water, pour into shallow buttered tins, and as soon as it is cool enough to handle, pull it until it is of a straw-color. *Splendid !*

Here are two recipes which another friend has kindly sent us :

Chocolate-Creams.

To the white of 1 egg add an equal quantity of cold water. Stir in 1 pound of confectioner's sugar. Flavor with vanilla. Stir until fine and smooth ; then mould into balls and drop into melted chocolate.

To melt the chocolate, scrape and put it in a tin-cup or small sauce-pan over a kettle where it will steam. Let the chocolate be melting while the cream is being prepared.

Walnut-Creams.

Make the cream as for chocolate-drops and mould into larger balls. Place the half of an English walnut on either side and press them into the cream.

The cream prepared in this way, we have found, can be used for various kinds of candy.

Small pieces of fruit of any kind and nuts can be enclosed in the cream, making a great variety. Chocolate may be mixed with it ; and if strong, clear coffee is used in place of the water, the candy will have the coffee flavor and color which some people like.

Walnut and Fruit Glacé.

Put 1 cup of sugar and ½ cup of water in a sauce-pan and stir until the sugar is all dissolved ; then place it over the fire and let it boil until it hardens and is quite crisp when dropped in cold water. Do not stir it after it is put on the fire.

When cooked sufficiently, dip out a spoonful at a time and drop in buttered tins, leaving a space of an inch or so between each spoonful. Place on each piece of candy the half of a walnut, or the fruit which has previously been prepared, and pour over them enough candy to cover them, always keeping each piece separate.

Any kind of fruit can be made into glacé. When using oranges, quarter them and remove the seeds. Strawberries, in their season, and peaches also make delicious glacé.

The remainder of our recipes have been taken from family recipe-books, and although we have not tested them ourselves, we think it may be safely said that they are good ones.

Marsh-mallow Paste.

Dissolve 1 pound of clean white gum-arabic in one quart of water ; strain, add 1 pound of refined sugar, and place over the fire. Stir continually until the syrup is dissolved and the mixture has become of the consistency of honey. Next add gradually the beaten whites of 8 eggs ; stir the mixture all the time until it loses its thickness and does not adhere to the finger. Flavor with vanilla or rose. Pour into a tin slightly dusted with powdered starch, and when cool divide into squares with a sharp knife.

Toasted Marsh-mallows.

Tie a string on the end of a cane or stick, fasten a bent pin on the end of the string, and stick the pin into a marsh-mallow-drop. Hold the marsh-mallow suspended over an open fire and let it gradually toast. When it begins to melt and run down it is done.

For a small party toasting marsh-mallows will be found quite a merry pastime, and a great many persons consider the candy much better for being thus cooked the second time.

Molasses Peanut-Candy.

2 cups of molasses.
1 cup of brown sugar.
1 tablespoonful of butter.
1 tablespoonful of vinegar.

While the candy is boiling remove the shells and brown skins from the peanuts, lay the nuts in buttered pans, and when the candy is done pour it over them. While it is still warm cut in blocks.

Chocolate-Caramels.

2 cups of sugar.
1 cup of molasses.
1 cup of milk.
1 tablespoonful of butter.
1 tablespoonful of flour.
½ pound of Baker's chocolate.

Grease your pot, put in sugar, molasses, and milk; boil fifteen minutes, and add butter and flour stirred to a cream. Let it boil five minutes, then add the chocolate, grated, and boil until quite thick. Grease shallow pans and pour in the candy half an inch thick, marking it in squares before it becomes hard.

Pop-Corn Balls.

6 quarts of popped corn.

1 pint of molasses.

Boil the molasses about fifteen minutes ; then put the corn into a large pan, pour the molasses over it, and stir briskly until thoroughly mixed. Then, with clean hands, make into balls of the desired size.

Saint Valentine.

CHAPTER XLII.

Saint Valentine's Day.

ID it never occur to any of you to wonder who Saint Valentine was, and why we should commemorate his day by sending cards or letters containing all sorts of nonsense, like true-lovers' knots, hearts pierced with arrows, etc. ?

It is easy enough to tell you about the saint, but what he had to do with the popular observances of the day dedicated to him is a matter for conjecture.

Saint Valentine, they say, was a grave and earnest bishop, who was put to death in Rome on the fourteenth day of February, about the year 270 A.D., for his too zealous efforts in converting the heathen. When he was canonized, the day of the month on which he died was dedicated to him.

The customs of Saint Valentine's Day are, no doubt, derived from those practised at some of the Pagan festivals, for they are of very ancient origin. In olden times, in England, it was kept as a great gala day, and all the houses were decked with evergreen in honor of it. Ben Jonson says:

> " Get some fresh hay, then, to lay under foot,
> Some holly and ivy to make fine the posts ;
> Is't not Saint Valentine's Day ? "

The principal feature of the ceremonies was always the choice of a valentine for the ensuing year. The cavalier was expected to wait upon his lady, execute all of her commands, and act as her escort at all social gatherings.

The choice of a valentine was generally left to chance, one of the methods being that the first unmarried member of the opposite sex a person saw on Saint Valentine's morning should be his or her valentine.

Of course you have all had some experience in sending and receiving valentines, and perhaps consider that the only way of celebrating the day; but don't you think it would be a good idea to invite some friends to your house and have a

Valentine-Party?

We will give several suggestions upon what to do at a valentine-party, that you may have some idea how the affair should be conducted.

In the first place, let each guest, upon his or her arrival, deposit a valentine in a large bag placed in the hall for that purpose. The valentines must be addressed to no particular person, but the girls should write on theirs, "To my cavalier," and the boys address the ones they send, "To my lady." On one corner of each valentine (not the envelope) the sender's name must be written.

When all the guests have assembled, someone disguised as Saint Valentine, in a skull-cap, long white beard, made of cotton or wool, and long cloak, should enter the parlor, carrying on his back the sack of valentines. He must stand in the centre of the room and auction off each valentine as he takes it from his pack.

All sorts of bids can be made, such as the promise of a dance, a necktie, her share of ice-cream at supper, by a girl. A compliment, the first favor asked of him, a paper of bonbons, by a boy. To make fun the bids should be as ridiculous as possible. Saint Valentine is to be at liberty to accept whatever bid he chooses. The payment of the debt must be rigidly exacted by the sender of a valentine, whose identity is revealed when the valentine is opened.

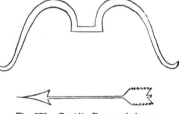

Fig. 379.—Cupid's Bow and Arrow.

If unable to comply immediately with the demand, the debtor must give the creditor a card or slip of paper on which is written "I O U a favor," or whatever it may be that is owed. This I O U entitles the creditor to claim payment of the debt at any time during the year.

Another feature of the party should be Cupid's bow and arrow, which must be suspended from the chandelier or placed in some prominent position. The device is to be used for delivering such valentines as may be addressed to particular persons. The valentine must be stuck onto the point of the arrow, and no one may remove it save the person to whom it is addressed. At any time during the evening the arrow may be found to bear a missive, and we would advise the hostess to provide a valentine, to be delivered in this way, for each of her guests, that none may feel neglected. The rest of the party can, to be sure, send as many valentines as they like.

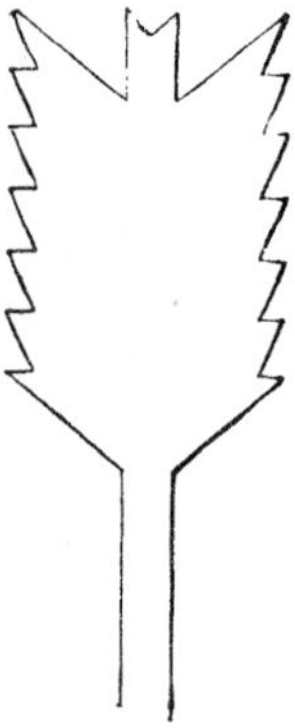

Make Cupid's bow and arrow of heavy pasteboard, like Fig. 379. Let the bow measure about

Fig. 380.—Notch in End of Feather. sixteen inches from tip to tip. Make the arrow twelve inches long, with a point or head three inches, and the feathers two inches, in length on the outside edge. Cut a notch in the feathered end, as shown in Fig. 380.

Strengthen the arrow by gluing a thin stick of wood along it to within one inch of the point. Gild both the bow and ar-

row, tie a silk cord to the tips of the bow, leaving it slack, and force the head of a worsted-needle into the point of the arrow (Fig. 381). Adjust the arrow by fitting the cord in the notch and pulling it back until the cord is taut; then fasten it to the bow by taking a few stitches with yellow silk through the bow and over the arrow. Fig. 382 shows how it should appear when in place.

To determine how the guests shall be paired off for supper, place the names of all the girls, written on slips of paper, in a bag; then let each boy in turn take out a slip, and the girl whose name it bears he shall escort to the supper-room and serve like a true cavalier.

Fig. 381.—Manner of fastening Needle in Arrow-head.

At a valentine-party the valentines should, if possible, all be original, or at least contain appropriate quotations. The more absurd the rhyme, the more fun it will create, and when one is unable to make a rhyme a bit of prose can be made to serve. As funny as you please let the valentines be, but remember to omit anything that is in the least rude, or calculated to hurt another's feelings.

With Saint Valentine's Day ends our vacation-calendar and with it we also bring this book to a close, for a whole year of

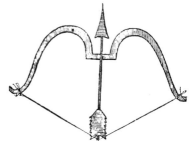

Fig. 382.—Cupid's Bow with Arrow in Position.

holidays, sports, and entertainments are now contained within its covers. If we may hope that our work has not been without profit, as well as entertainment, if we have been successful in opening any new avenues of enterprise and enjoyment for you, we are satisfied. If we have done more, and with any of our suggestions have prompted the thought of adding to the comfort and happiness of others, we have achieved a success, and the mission of the AMERICAN GIRL'S HANDY BOOK is accomplished.

INDEX.

A CATALOG OF SELECTED DOVER
BOOKS IN ALL FIELDS OF INTEREST

CONCERNING THE SPIRITUAL IN ART, Wassily Kandinsky. Pioneering work by father of abstract art. Thoughts on color theory, nature of art. Analysis of earlier masters. 12 illustrations. 80pp. of text. 5⅜ x 8½. 0-486-23411-8

CELTIC ART: The Methods of Construction, George Bain. Simple geometric techniques for making Celtic interlacements, spirals, Kells-type initials, animals, humans, etc. Over 500 illustrations. 160pp. 9 x 12. (Available in U.S. only.) 0-486-22923-8

AN ATLAS OF ANATOMY FOR ARTISTS, Fritz Schider. Most thorough reference work on art anatomy in the world. Hundreds of illustrations, including selections from works by Vesalius, Leonardo, Goya, Ingres, Michelangelo, others. 593 illustrations. 192pp. 7⅛ x 10¼. 0-486-20241-0

CELTIC HAND STROKE-BY-STROKE (Irish Half-Uncial from "The Book of Kells"): An Arthur Baker Calligraphy Manual, Arthur Baker. Complete guide to creating each letter of the alphabet in distinctive Celtic manner. Covers hand position, strokes, pens, inks, paper, more. Illustrated. 48pp. 8¼ x 11. 0-486-24336-2

EASY ORIGAMI, John Montroll. Charming collection of 32 projects (hat, cup, pelican, piano, swan, many more) specially designed for the novice origami hobbyist. Clearly illustrated easy-to-follow instructions insure that even beginning papercrafters will achieve successful results. 48pp. 8¼ x 11. 0-486-27298-2

BLOOMINGDALE'S ILLUSTRATED 1886 CATALOG: Fashions, Dry Goods and Housewares, Bloomingdale Brothers. Famed merchants' extremely rare catalog depicting about 1,700 products: clothing, housewares, firearms, dry goods, jewelry, more. Invaluable for dating, identifying vintage items. Also, copyright-free graphics for artists, designers. Co-published with Henry Ford Museum & Greenfield Village. 160pp. 8¼ x 11. 0-486-25780-0

THE ART OF WORLDLY WISDOM, Baltasar Gracian. "Think with the few and speak with the many," "Friends are a second existence," and "Be able to forget" are among this 1637 volume's 300 pithy maxims. A perfect source of mental and spiritual refreshment, it can be opened at random and appreciated either in brief or at length. 128pp. 5⅜ x 8½. 0-486-44034-6

JOHNSON'S DICTIONARY: A Modern Selection, Samuel Johnson (E. L. McAdam and George Milne, eds.). This modern version reduces the original 1755 edition's 2,300 pages of definitions and literary examples to a more manageable length, retaining the verbal pleasure and historical curiosity of the original. 480pp. 5³⁄₁₆ x 8¼. 0-486-44089-3

ADVENTURES OF HUCKLEBERRY FINN, Mark Twain, Illustrated by E. W. Kemble. A work of eternal richness and complexity, a source of ongoing critical debate, and a literary landmark, Twain's 1885 masterpiece about a barefoot boy's journey of self-discovery has enthralled readers around the world. This handsome clothbound reproduction of the first edition features all 174 of the original black-and-white illustrations. 368pp. 5⅜ x 8½. 0-486-44322-1

STICKLEY CRAFTSMAN FURNITURE CATALOGS, Gustav Stickley and L. & J. G. Stickley. Beautiful, functional furniture in two authentic catalogs from 1910. 594 illustrations, including 277 photos, show settles, rockers, armchairs, reclining chairs, bookcases, desks, tables. 183pp. 6½ x 9¼. 0-486-23838-5

AMERICAN LOCOMOTIVES IN HISTORIC PHOTOGRAPHS: 1858 to 1949, Ron Ziel (ed.). A rare collection of 126 meticulously detailed official photographs, called "builder portraits," of American locomotives that majestically chronicle the rise of steam locomotive power in America. Introduction. Detailed captions. xi+ 129pp. 9 x 12. 0-486-27393-8

AMERICA'S LIGHTHOUSES: An Illustrated History, Francis Ross Holland, Jr. Delightfully written, profusely illustrated fact-filled survey of over 200 American lighthouses since 1716. History, anecdotes, technological advances, more. 240pp. 8 x 10¾. 0-486-25576-X

TOWARDS A NEW ARCHITECTURE, Le Corbusier. Pioneering manifesto by founder of "International School." Technical and aesthetic theories, views of industry, economics, relation of form to function, "mass-production split" and much more. Profusely illustrated. 320pp. 6⅛ x 9¼. (Available in U.S. only.) 0-486-25023-7

HOW THE OTHER HALF LIVES, Jacob Riis. Famous journalistic record, exposing poverty and degradation of New York slums around 1900, by major social reformer. 100 striking and influential photographs. 233pp. 10 x 7⅞. 0-486-22012-5

FRUIT KEY AND TWIG KEY TO TREES AND SHRUBS, William M. Harlow. One of the handiest and most widely used identification aids. Fruit key covers 120 deciduous and evergreen species; twig key 160 deciduous species. Easily used. Over 300 photographs. 126pp. 5⅜ x 8½. 0-486-20511-8

COMMON BIRD SONGS, Dr. Donald J. Borror. Songs of 60 most common U.S. birds: robins, sparrows, cardinals, bluejays, finches, more—arranged in order of increasing complexity. Up to 9 variations of songs of each species.
Cassette and manual 0-486-99911-4

ORCHIDS AS HOUSE PLANTS, Rebecca Tyson Northen. Grow cattleyas and many other kinds of orchids–in a window, in a case, or under artificial light. 63 illustrations. 148pp. 5⅜ x 8½. 0-486-23261-1

MONSTER MAZES, Dave Phillips. Masterful mazes at four levels of difficulty. Avoid deadly perils and evil creatures to find magical treasures. Solutions for all 32 exciting illustrated puzzles. 48pp. 8¼ x 11. 0-486-26005-4

MOZART'S DON GIOVANNI (DOVER OPERA LIBRETTO SERIES), Wolfgang Amadeus Mozart. Introduced and translated by Ellen H. Bleiler. Standard Italian libretto, with complete English translation. Convenient and thoroughly portable–an ideal companion for reading along with a recording or the performance itself. Introduction. List of characters. Plot summary. 121pp. 5¼ x 8½. 0-486-24944-1

FRANK LLOYD WRIGHT'S DANA HOUSE, Donald Hoffmann. Pictorial essay of residential masterpiece with over 160 interior and exterior photos, plans, elevations, sketches and studies. 128pp. 9¼ x 10¾. 0-486-29120-0

FRENCH STORIES/CONTES FRANÇAIS: A Dual-Language Book, Wallace Fowlie. Ten stories by French masters, Voltaire to Camus: "Micromegas" by Voltaire; "The Atheist's Mass" by Balzac; "Minuet" by de Maupassant; "The Guest" by Camus, six more. Excellent English translations on facing pages. Also French-English vocabulary list, exercises, more. 352pp. 5⅜ x 8½.   0-486-26443-2

CHICAGO AT THE TURN OF THE CENTURY IN PHOTOGRAPHS: 122 Historic Views from the Collections of the Chicago Historical Society, Larry A. Viskochil. Rare large-format prints offer detailed views of City Hall, State Street, the Loop, Hull House, Union Station, many other landmarks, circa 1904-1913. Introduction. Captions. Maps. 144pp. 9⅜ x 12¼.   0-486-24656-6

OLD BROOKLYN IN EARLY PHOTOGRAPHS, 1865-1929, William Lee Younger. Luna Park, Gravesend race track, construction of Grand Army Plaza, moving of Hotel Brighton, etc. 157 previously unpublished photographs. 165pp. 8⅞ x 11¾.
0-486-23587-4

THE MYTHS OF THE NORTH AMERICAN INDIANS, Lewis Spence. Rich anthology of the myths and legends of the Algonquins, Iroquois, Pawnees and Sioux, prefaced by an extensive historical and ethnological commentary. 36 illustrations. 480pp. 5⅜ x 8½.   0-486-25967-6

AN ENCYCLOPEDIA OF BATTLES: Accounts of Over 1,560 Battles from 1479 B.C. to the Present, David Eggenberger. Essential details of every major battle in recorded history from the first battle of Megiddo in 1479 B.C. to Grenada in 1984. List of Battle Maps. New Appendix covering the years 1967-1984. Index. 99 illustrations. 544pp. 6½ x 9¼.   0-486-24913-1

SAILING ALONE AROUND THE WORLD, Captain Joshua Slocum. First man to sail around the world, alone, in small boat. One of the great feats of seamanship told in delightful manner. 67 illustrations. 294pp. 5⅜ x 8½.   0-486-20326-3

ANARCHISM AND OTHER ESSAYS, Emma Goldman. Powerful, penetrating, prophetic essays on direct action, role of minorities, prison reform, puritan hypocrisy, violence, etc. 271pp. 5⅜ x 8½.   0-486-22484-8

MYTHS OF THE HINDUS AND BUDDHISTS, Ananda K. Coomaraswamy and Sister Nivedita. Great stories of the epics; deeds of Krishna, Shiva, taken from puranas, Vedas, folk tales; etc. 32 illustrations. 400pp. 5⅜ x 8½.   0-486-21759-0

MY BONDAGE AND MY FREEDOM, Frederick Douglass. Born a slave, Douglass became outspoken force in antislavery movement. The best of Douglass' autobiographies. Graphic description of slave life. 464pp. 5⅜ x 8½.   0-486-22457-0

FOLLOWING THE EQUATOR: A Journey Around the World, Mark Twain. Fascinating humorous account of 1897 voyage to Hawaii, Australia, India, New Zealand, etc. Ironic, bemused reports on peoples, customs, climate, flora and fauna, politics, much more. 197 illustrations. 720pp. 5⅜ x 8½.   0-486-26113-1

GREAT SPEECHES BY AMERICAN WOMEN, edited by James Daley. Here are 21 legendary speeches from the country's most inspirational female voices, including Sojourner Truth, Susan B. Anthony, Eleanor Roosevelt, Hillary Rodham Clinton, Nancy Pelosi, and many others. 192pp. 5³⁄₁₆ x 8¼.   0-486-46141-6

THE MYTHS OF GREECE AND ROME, H. A. Guerber. A classic of mythology, generously illustrated, long prized for its simple, graphic, accurate retelling of the principal myths of Greece and Rome, and for its commentary on their origins and significance. With 64 illustrations by Michelangelo, Raphael, Titian, Rubens, Canova, Bernini and others. 480pp. 5⅜ x 8½.   0-486-27584-1

PSYCHOLOGY OF MUSIC, Carl E. Seashore. Classic work discusses music as a medium from psychological viewpoint. Clear treatment of physical acoustics, auditory apparatus, sound perception, development of musical skills, nature of musical feeling, host of other topics. 88 figures. 408pp. 5⅜ x 8½.   0-486-21851-1

LIFE IN ANCIENT EGYPT, Adolf Erman. Fullest, most thorough, detailed older account with much not in more recent books, domestic life, religion, magic, medicine, commerce, much more. Many illustrations reproduce tomb paintings, carvings, hieroglyphs, etc. 597pp. 5⅜ x 8½.   0-486-22632-8

SUNDIALS, Their Theory and Construction, Albert Waugh. Far and away the best, most thorough coverage of ideas, mathematics concerned, types, construction, adjusting anywhere. Simple, nontechnical treatment allows even children to build several of these dials. Over 100 illustrations. 230pp. 5⅜ x 8½.   0-486-22947-5

GREAT SPEECHES BY AFRICAN AMERICANS: Frederick Douglass, Sojourner Truth, Dr. Martin Luther King, Jr., Barack Obama, and Others, edited by James Daley. Tracing the struggle for freedom and civil rights across two centuries, this anthology comprises speeches by Martin Luther King, Jr., Marcus Garvey, Malcolm X, Barack Obama, and many other influential figures. 160pp. 5³⁄₁₆ x 8¼.
0-486-44761-8

OLD-TIME VIGNETTES IN FULL COLOR, Carol Belanger Grafton (ed.). Over 390 charming, often sentimental illustrations, selected from archives of Victorian graphics—pretty women posing, children playing, food, flowers, kittens and puppies, smiling cherubs, birds and butterflies, much more. All copyright-free. 48pp. 9¼ x 12¼.
0-486-27269-9

PERSPECTIVE FOR ARTISTS, Rex Vicat Cole. Depth, perspective of sky and sea, shadows, much more, not usually covered. 391 diagrams, 81 reproductions of drawings and paintings. 279pp. 5⅜ x 8½.   0-486-22487-2

DRAWING THE LIVING FIGURE, Joseph Sheppard. Innovative approach to artistic anatomy focuses on specifics of surface anatomy, rather than muscles and bones. Over 170 drawings of live models in front, back and side views, and in widely varying poses. Accompanying diagrams. 177 illustrations. Introduction. Index. 144pp. 8⅜ x11¼.   0-486-26723-7

GOTHIC AND OLD ENGLISH ALPHABETS: 100 Complete Fonts, Dan X. Solo. Add power, elegance to posters, signs, other graphics with 100 stunning copyright-free alphabets: Blackstone, Dolbey, Germania, 97 more—including many lower-case, numerals, punctuation marks. 104pp. 8⅛ x 11.   0-486-24695-7

THE BOOK OF WOOD CARVING, Charles Marshall Sayers. Finest book for beginners discusses fundamentals and offers 34 designs. "Absolutely first rate . . . well thought out and well executed."—E. J. Tangerman. 118pp. 7¾ x 10⅝. 0-486-23654-4

ILLUSTRATED CATALOG OF CIVIL WAR MILITARY GOODS: Union Army Weapons, Insignia, Uniform Accessories, and Other Equipment, Schuyler, Hartley, and Graham. Rare, profusely illustrated 1846 catalog includes Union Army uniform and dress regulations, arms and ammunition, coats, insignia, flags, swords, rifles, etc. 226 illustrations. 160pp. 9 x 12.   0-486-24939-5

WOMEN'S FASHIONS OF THE EARLY 1900s: An Unabridged Republication of "New York Fashions, 1909," National Cloak & Suit Co. Rare catalog of mail-order fashions documents women's and children's clothing styles shortly after the turn of the century. Captions offer full descriptions, prices. Invaluable resource for fashion, costume historians. Approximately 725 illustrations. 128pp. 8⅜ x 11¼.   0-486-27276-1

LIGHT AND SHADE: A Classic Approach to Three-Dimensional Drawing, Mrs. Mary P. Merrifield. Handy reference clearly demonstrates principles of light and shade by revealing effects of common daylight, sunshine, and candle or artificial light on geometrical solids. 13 plates. 64pp. 5⅜ x 8½. 0-486-44143-1

ASTROLOGY AND ASTRONOMY: A Pictorial Archive of Signs and Symbols, Ernst and Johanna Lehner. Treasure trove of stories, lore, and myth, accompanied by more than 300 rare illustrations of planets, the Milky Way, signs of the zodiac, comets, meteors, and other astronomical phenomena. 192pp. 8⅜ x 11. 0-486-43981-X

JEWELRY MAKING: Techniques for Metal, Tim McCreight. Easy-to-follow instructions and carefully executed illustrations describe tools and techniques, use of gems and enamels, wire inlay, casting, and other topics. 72 line illustrations and diagrams. 176pp. 8¼ x 10⅞. 0-486-44043-5

MAKING BIRDHOUSES: Easy and Advanced Projects, Gladstone Califf. Easy-to-follow instructions include diagrams for everything from a one-room house for bluebirds to a forty-two-room structure for purple martins. 56 plates; 4 figures. 80pp. 8¾ x 6⅜. 0-486-44183-0

LITTLE BOOK OF LOG CABINS: How to Build and Furnish Them, William S. Wicks. Handy how-to manual, with instructions and illustrations for building cabins in the Adirondack style, fireplaces, stairways, furniture, beamed ceilings, and more. 102 line drawings. 96pp. 8¾ x 6⅜. 0-486-44259-4

THE SEASONS OF AMERICA PAST, Eric Sloane. From "sugaring time" and strawberry picking to Indian summer and fall harvest, a whole year's activities described in charming prose and enhanced with 79 of the author's own illustrations. 160pp. 8¼ x 11. 0-486-44220-9

THE METROPOLIS OF TOMORROW, Hugh Ferriss. Generous, prophetic vision of the metropolis of the future, as perceived in 1929. Powerful illustrations of towering structures, wide avenues, and rooftop parks–all features in many of today's modern cities. 59 illustrations. 144pp. 8¼ x 11. 0-486-43727-2

THE PATH TO ROME, Hilaire Belloc. This 1902 memoir abounds in lively vignettes from a vanished time, recounting a pilgrimage on foot across the Alps and Apennines in order to "see all Europe which the Christian Faith has saved." 77 of the author's original line drawings complement his sparkling prose. 272pp. 5⅜ x 8½. 0-486-44001-X

THE HISTORY OF RASSELAS: Prince of Abissinia, Samuel Johnson. Distinguished English writer attacks eighteenth-century optimism and man's unrealistic estimates of what life has to offer. 112pp. 5⅜ x 8½. 0-486-44094-X

A VOYAGE TO ARCTURUS, David Lindsay. A brilliant flight of pure fancy, where wild creatures crowd the fantastic landscape and demented torturers dominate victims with their bizarre mental powers. 272pp. 5⅜ x 8½. 0-486-44198-9

Paperbound unless otherwise indicated. Available at your book dealer, online at **www.doverpublications.com**, or by writing to Dept. GI, Dover Publications, Inc., 31 East 2nd Street, Mineola, NY 11501. For current price information or for free catalogs (please indicate field of interest), write to Dover Publications or log on to **www.doverpublications.com** and see every Dover book in print. Dover publishes more than 400 books each year on science, elementary and advanced mathematics, biology, music, art, literary history, social sciences, and other areas.